AF531575

Cost and Management Accounting

Cost and Management Accounting

Samuel Moore

RANDOM PUBLICATIONS
NEW DELHI (INDIA)

Cost and Management Accounting

ISBN 978-93-5111-445-1

Published in 2014 in India by

RANDOM PUBLICATIONS

4376-A/4B, Gali Murari Lal, Ansari Road
New Delhi-110 002
Phone : +91-11-43580356, +91-11-23289044
e-mail: randomexports@gmail.com, sales@randompublications.com, info@randompublications.com

Reprinted 2019

Type Setting by: Friends Media, Delhi-110089
Digitally Printed at: Replika Press Pvt. Ltd.

Preface

Cost and Management accounting is a process of collecting, analyzing, summarizing and evaluating various alternative courses of action. Its goal is to advise the management on the most appropriate course of action based on the cost efficiency and capability. Cost accounting provides the detailed cost information that management needs to control current operations and plan for the future. Since managers are making decisions only for their own organization, there is no need for the information to be comparable to similar information from other organizations. Instead, information must be relevant for a particular environment. Cost accounting information is commonly used in financial accounting information, but first we are concentrating on its use by managers to make decisions. Unlike the accounting systems that help in the preparation of financial reports periodically, the cost accounting systems and reports are not subject to rules and standards like the Generally Accepted Accounting Principles. As a result, there is wide variety in the cost accounting systems of the different companies and sometimes even in different parts of the same company or organization. All types of businesses, whether service, manufacturing or trading, require cost accounting to track their activities. Cost accounting has long been used to help managers understand the costsof running a business. Modern cost accounting originated during the industrial revolution, when the complexities of running a large scale business led to the development of systems for recording and tracking costs to help business owners and managers make decisions.

In the early industrial age, most of the costs incurred by a business were what modern accountants call "variable costs" because they varied directly with the amount of production. Money was spent on labour, raw materials, power to run a factory, etc. in direct proportion to production. Managers could simply total the variable costs for a product and use this as a rough guide for decision-making processes.

Some costs tend to remain the same even during busy periods, unlike variable costs, which rise and fall with volume of work. Over time, these "fixed costs" have become more important to managers. Examples of fixed costs include the depreciation of plant and equipment, and the cost of departments such as maintenance, tooling, production control, purchasing, quality control, storage and handling, plant supervision and engineering. In the early nineteenth century, these costs were of little importance to most businesses. However, with the growth of railroads, steel and large scale manufacturing, by the late nineteenth century these costs were often more important than the variable cost of a product, and allocating them to a broad range of products lead to bad decision making. Managers must understand fixed costs in order to make decisions about products and pricing.

The chapters have been chosen to ensure that the reader gets a complete picture of this subject.

I thank all members of my team who have helped in the preparation of the book. My special thanks go to "Random Publications" who have published the book.

—Samuel Moore

Contents

1

Introduction

Cost accounting information is designed for managers. Since managers are taking decisions only for their own organization, there is no need for the information to be comparable to similar information from other organizations. Instead, the important criterion is that the information must be relevant for decisions that managers operating in a particular environment of business including strategy make. Cost accounting information is commonly used in financial accounting information, but first we are concentrating in its use by managers to take decisions. The accountants who handle the cost accounting information generate add value by providing good information to managers who are taking decisions. Among the better decisions, the better performance of your organization, regardless if it is a manufacturing company, a bank, a non-profit organization, a government agency, a school club or even a business school. The cost-accounting system is the result of decisions made by managers of an organization and the environment in which they make them.

The organizations and managers are most of the times interested in and worried for the costs. The control of the costs of the past, present and future is part of the job of all the managers in a company. In the companies that try to have profits, the control of costs affects directly to them. Knowing the costs of the products is essential for decision-making regarding price and mix assignation of products and services.

The cost accounting systems can be important sources of information for the managers of a company. For this reason, the managers understand the forces and weaknesses of the cost accounting systems, and participate in the evaluation and evolution of the cost measurement and administration systems. Unlike the accounting systems that help in the preparation of financial reports periodically, the cost accounting systems and reports are not subject to rules and standards like the Generally Accepted Accounting Principles. As a result, there is a wide variety in the cost accounting systems of the different companies and sometimes even in different parts of the same company or organization.

The following are different cost accounting approaches:

- standardized or standard cost accounting
- lean accounting
- activity-based costing
- resource consumption accounting
- throughput accounting
- marginal costing/cost-volume-profit analysis.

Classical cost elements are:

1. Raw materials
2. Labour
3. Indirect expenses/overhead.

Origins

Cost accounting has long been used to help managers understand the costs of running a business. Modern cost accounting originated during the industrial revolution, when the complexities of running a large scale business led to the development of systems for recording and tracking costs to help business owners and managers make decisions.

In the early industrial age, most of the costs incurred by a business were what modern accountants call "variable costs" because they varied directly with the amount of production. Money was spent on labour, raw materials, power to run a factory, etc. in direct proportion to production. Managers could simply total the variable costs for a product and use this as a rough guide for decision-making processes.

Some costs tend to remain the same even during busy periods, unlike variable costs, which rise and fall with volume of work. Over time, the importance of these "fixed costs" has become more important to managers. Examples of fixed costs include the depreciation of plant and equipment, and the cost of departments such as maintenance, tooling, production control, purchasing, quality control, storage and handling, plant supervision and engineering. In the early twentieth century, these costs were of little importance to most businesses. However, in the twenty-first century, these costs are often more important than the variable cost of a product, and allocating them to a broad range of products can lead to bad decision making. Managers must understand fixed costs in order to make decisions about products and pricing.

For example: A company produced railway coaches and had only one product. To make each coach, the company needed to purchase $60 of raw materials and components, and pay 6 labourers $40 each. Therefore, total variable cost for each coach was $300. Knowing that making a coach required spending $300, managers knew they couldn't sell below that price without losing money on each coach.

Any price above $300 became a contribution to the fixed costs of the company. If the fixed costs were, say, $1000 per month for rent, insurance and owner's salary, the company could therefore sell 5 coaches per month for a total of $3000 (priced at $600 each), or 10 coaches for a total of $4500 (priced at $450 each), and make a profit of $500 in both cases.

Elements of Cost

- Material (Material is a very important part of business)
  - Direct material
- Labour
  - Direct labour
- Overhead (Variable/Fixed)
  - Indirect material
  - Indirect labour
  - Maintenance & Repair
  - Supplies
  - Utilities
  - Other Variable Expenses
  - Salaries
  - Occupancy (Rent)
  - Depreciation
  - Other Fixed Expenses.

(In some companies, machine cost is segregated from overhead and reported as a separate element)

They are grouped further based on their functions as:

- Production or works overheads
- Administration overheads
- Selling overheads
- Distribution overheads
- Financial Expenses.

Classification of Costs

Classification of cost means, the grouping of costs according to their common characteristics. The important ways of classification of costs are:

- By nature or element: materials, labour, expenses
- By functions: production, selling, distribution, administration, R&D, development,
- By traceability: direct and indirect
- By variability: fixed, variable, semi-variable
- By controllability: controllable, uncontrollable
- By normality: normal, abnormal.

Standard Cost Accounting

In modern cost accounting, the concept of recording historical costs was taken further, by allocating the company's fixed costs over a given period of time to the items produced during that period, and recording the result as the total cost of production.

This allowed the *full cost* of products that were not sold in the period they were produced to be recorded in inventory using a variety of complex accounting methods, which was consistent with the principles of GAAP (Generally Accepted Accounting Principles). It also essentially enabled managers to ignore the fixed costs, and look at the results of each period in relation to the "standard cost" for any given product.

For example: if the railway coach company normally produced 40 coaches per month, and the fixed costs were still $1000/month, then each coach could be said to incur an overhead of $25 ($1000 / 40). Adding this to the variable costs of $300 per coach produced a full cost of $325 per coach.

This method tended to slightly distort the resulting unit cost, but in mass-production industries that made one product line, and where the fixed costs were relatively low, the distortion was very minor.

For example: if the railway coach company made 100 coaches one month, then the unit cost would become $310 per coach ($300 + ($1000 / 100)). If the next month the company made 50 coaches, then the unit cost = $320 per coach ($300 + ($1000 / 50)), a relatively minor difference.

An important part of standard cost accounting is a variance analysis, which breaks down the variation between actual cost and standard costs into various components (volume variation, material cost variation, labour cost variation, etc.) so managers can understand *why costs were different from what was planned* and take appropriate action to correct the situation.

The Development of Throughput Accounting

As business became more complex and began producing a greater variety of products, the use of cost accounting to make decisions to maximize profitability came under question. Management circles became increasingly aware of the Theory of Constraints in the 1980s, and began to understand that "every production process has a limiting factor" somewhere in the chain of production.

As business management learned to identify the constraints, they increasingly adopted throughput accounting to manage them and "maximize the *throughput dollars*" (or other currency) from each unit of constrained resource.

For example: The railway coach company was offered a contract to make 15 open-topped streetcars each month, using a design that included ornate brass foundry work, but very little of the metalwork needed to produce a covered rail coach. The buyer offered to pay $280 per streetcar. The company had a firm order for 40 rail coaches each month for $350 per unit.

The cost accountant determined that the cost of operating the foundry vs. the metalwork shop each month was as follows:

Overhead Cost by Department	*Total Cost*	*Hours Available per month*	*Cost per hour*
Foundry	$ 7,300.00	160	$45.63
Metal shop	$ 3,300.00	160	$20.63
Total	$10,600.00	320	$33.13

The company was at full capacity making 40 rail coaches each month. And since the foundry was expensive to operate, and purchasing brass as a raw material for the streetcars was expensive, the accountant determined that the company would lose money on any streetcars it built. He showed an analysis of the estimated product costs based on standard cost accounting and recommended that the company decline to build any streetcars.

Standard Cost Accounting Analysis	***Streetcars***	***Rail coach***
Monthly Demand	15	40
Price	$280	$350
Foundry Time (hrs)	3.0	2.0
Metalwork Time (hrs)	1.5	4.0
Total Time	4.5	6.0
Foundry Cost	$136.88	$ 91.25
Metalwork Cost	$ 30.94	$ 82.50
Raw Material Cost	$120.00	$ 60.00
Total Cost	$287.81	$233.75
Profit per Unit	$ (7.81)	$116.25

However, the company's operations manager knew that recent investment in automated foundry equipment had created idle time for workers in that department. The constraint on production of the railcoaches was the metalwork shop. She made an analysis of profit and loss if the company took the contract using throughput accounting to determine the profitability of products by calculating "throughput" (revenue less variable cost) in the metal shop.

Throughput Cost Accounting Analysis	***Decline Contract***	***Take Contract***
Coaches Produced	40	34
Streetcars Produced	0	15
Foundry Hours	80	113
Metal shop Hours	160	159
Coach Revenue	$14,000	$11,900
Streetcar Revenue	$ 0	$ 4,200
Coach Raw Material Cost	$(2,400)	$(2,040)
Streetcar Raw Material Cost	$ 0	$(1,800)
Throughput Value	$11,600	$12,260
Overhead Expense	$(10,600)	$(10,600)
Profit	$1,000	$1,660

After the presentations from the company accountant and the operations manager, the president understood that the metal shop capacity was limiting the company's profitability. The company could make only 40 rail coaches per month. But by taking the contract for the streetcars, the company could make nearly all the railway coaches ordered, and also meet all the demand for streetcars. The result would increase throughput in the metal shop from $6.25 to $10.38 per hour of available time, and increase profitability by 66 percent.

Activity-based Costing

Activity-based costing (ABC) is a system for assigning costs to products based on the activities they require. In this case, activities are those regular actions performed inside a company. "Talking with customer regarding invoice questions" is an example of an activity inside most companies.

Accountants assign 100% of each employee's time to the different activities performed inside a company (many will use surveys to have the workers themselves assign their time to the different activities). The accountant then can determine the total cost spent on each activity by summing up the percentage of each worker's salary spent on that activity.

A company can use the resulting activity cost data to determine where to focus their operational improvements. For example, a job-based manufacturer may find that a high percentage of its workers are spending their time trying to figure out a hastily written customer order. Via ABC, the accountants now have a currency amount pegged to the activity of "Researching Customer Work Order Specifications". Senior management can now decide how much focus or money to budget for resolving this process deficiency. Activity-based management includes (but is not restricted to) the use of activity-based costing to manage a business.

While ABC may be able to pinpoint the cost of each activity and resources into the ultimate product, the process could be tedious, costly and subject to errors.

As it is a tool for a more accurate way of allocating fixed costs into product, these fixed costs do not vary according to each month's production volume. For example, an elimination of one product would not eliminate the overhead or even direct labour cost assigned to it. ABC better identifies product costing in the long run, but may not be too helpful in day-to-day decision-making.

Lean Accounting

Lean accounting has developed in recent years to provide the accounting, control, and measurement methods supporting lean manufacturing and other applications of lean thinking such as healthcare, construction, insurance, banking, education, government, and other industries.

There are two main thrusts for Lean Accounting. The first is the application of lean methods to the company's accounting, control, and measurement processes. This is not different from applying lean methods to any other processes. The objective is to eliminate waste, free up capacity, speed up the process, eliminate errors & defects, and make the process clear and understandable.

The second (and more important) thrust of Lean Accounting is to fundamentally change the accounting, control, and measurement processes so they motivate lean change & improvement, provide information that is suitable for control and decision-making, provide an understanding of customer value, correctly assess the financial impact of lean improvement, and are themselves simple, visual, and low-waste. Lean Accounting does not require the traditional management accounting methods like standard costing, activity-based costing, variance reporting, cost-plus pricing, complex transactional control systems, and untimely & confusing financial reports. These are replaced by:

- lean-focused performance measurements
- simple summary direct costing of the value streams
- decision-making and reporting using a *box score*
- financial reports that are timely and presented in "plain English" that everyone can understand
- radical simplification and elimination of transactional control systems by eliminating the need for them
- driving lean changes from a deep understanding of the value created for the customers
- eliminating traditional budgeting through monthly sales, operations, and financial planning processes (SOFP)
- value-based pricing
- correct understanding of the financial impact of lean change.

As an organization becomes more mature with lean thinking and methods, they recognize that the combined methods of lean accounting in fact creates a lean management system (LMS) designed to provide the planning, the operational and financial reporting, and the motivation for change required to prosper the company's on-going lean transformation.

Marginal Costing

The cost-volume-profit analysis is the systematic examination of the relationship between selling prices, sales, production volumes, costs, expenses and profits. This analysis provides very useful information for decision-making in the management of a company. For example, the analysis can be used in establishing sales prices, in the product mix selection to sell, in the decision to choose marketing strategies, and in the analysis of the impact on profits by changes in costs. In the current environment of business, a business administration must act and take decisions in a fast and accurate manner. As a result, the importance of cost-volume-profit is still increasing as time passes.

Contribution Margin

A relationship between the cost, volume and profit is the contribution margin. The contribution margin is the revenue excess from sales over variable costs. The concept of contribution margin is particularly useful in the planning of business because it gives an insight into the potential profits that can generate a business. The following chart shows the income statement of a company X, which has been prepared to show its contribution margin:

Sales	\$1,000,000
(-) Variable Costs	\$600,000
Contribution Margin	\$400,000
(-) Fixed Costs	\$300,000
Income from Operations	\$100,000

Contribution Margin Ratio

The margin contribution can also be expressed as a percentage. The contribution margin ratio, which is sometimes called the profit-volume ratio, indicates the percentage of each sales dollar available to cover fixed costs and to provide operating revenue. For the company Fusion, Inc. the contribution margin ratio is 40%, which is computed as follows:

Contribution Margin Ratio = (Sales - Variable Costs) / Sales

The contribution margin ratio measures the effect on operating income of an increase or a decrease in sales volume. For example, assume that the management of Fusion, Inc. is studying the effect of adding \$80,000 in sales orders.

Multiplying the contribution margin ratio (40%) by the change in sales volume (\$80,000) indicates that operating income will increase

$32,000 if additional orders are obtained. To validate this analysis the table below shows the income statement of the company including additional orders:

Sales	$1,080,000
(-) Variable Costs	$648,000 (1,080,000 x 60%)
Contribution Margin	$432,000 (1,080,000 x 40%)
(-) Fixed Costs	$300,000
Income from Operations	$132,000

Variable costs as a percentage of sales are equal to 100% minus the contribution margin ratio. Thus, in the above income statement, the variable costs are 60% (100% - 40%) of sales, or $648,000 ($1'080,000 X 60%). The total contribution margin $432,000, can also be computed directly by multiplying the sales by the contribution margin ratio ($1'080,000 X 40%).

Accounting Systems

All accounting systems are designed to provide information to people who take decisions. Either way, it is desirable to classify accounting systems based in the primary user of the information. Investors (or potential investors), creditors, government agencies, tax authorities and others are outside the organization. Managers are within the organization. The classification of accounting systems in financial and cost (or managerial) systems capt this distinction between the people making decisions.

Financial Accounting

Information in financial accounting is designed for decision makers and who are not involved in the daily management of the company. These users are commonly outside the company. The information, at least for public companies, is public and typically available on the website of the companies. Managers at the company are seriously concerned at reports that generates the financial accounting, but anyway, the information is insufficient for making operational decisions of the company.

Individuals making decisions using information from the financial accounts are commonly interested in comparing other firms, for example, deciding whether to invest in the company Apple Computer or Microsoft. An important feature of financial accounting information is that it may be comparable between companies. This means that it is important that when an investor looks at, say, revenues from Apple

Computers, these represent the same thing for Microsoft. As a result, financial accounting systems are characterized by a series of rules that define how transactions should be treated.

Cost Accounting

Cost accounting information is designed for managers. Since managers are taking decisions only for their own organization, there is no need for the information to be comparable to similar information from other organizations. Instead, the important criterion is that the information must be relevant to decisions that managers operating in a particular environment of business including strategy make. Cost accounting information is commonly used in financial accounting information, but first we are concentrating in its use by managers to make decisions. The accountants who handle the cost accounting information and generate add value by providing good information to managers who are taking decisions. Among the better decisions, the better performance of your organization, regardless if it is a manufacturing company, a bank, a non-profit hospital, a government agency, a school club or even a business school. The cost-accounting system is the result of decisions made by managers of an organization and the environment in which they make them.

Cost Accounting and the Generally Accepted Accounting Principles

The main purpose of financial accounting is to provide investors (such as shareholders) or creditors (e.g. banks) information about the company and the performance of the administration. The financial information prepared for this purpose is governed by the Generally Accepted Accounting Principles (GAAP), which provide consistency in the accountancy data used for purposes of reporting from a company to another. This means that the information of cost accounting used to calculate the cost of goods sold, inventory valuation, accounting and other financial information used for external reports should be prepared in accordance with GAAP.

In contrast to the cost information for financial reporting to shareholders, the cost information for managerial use (that is, between the organization) need not to agree with the PGCA. The administration is free to set their own definitions for cost information. In fact, the accountancy data used for external reporting is most often inappropriate for making managerial decisions. For example, management decisions deal with the future, then the future estimated costs have more value in making decisions than historical cost or current that are reported externally. Unless otherwise provided contrary, we assume that the cost information is developed for internal use by managers and do not have to agree with the PGCA.

This does not mean that there is a "correct" or "incorrect" of accounting costs. This means that the best or correct accounting of costs is through the method that provides relevant information for decision makers so that he or she makes the best decision.

Clients of Cost Accounting

Of all the participants in a business to whom the administration must consider, the most important is *the customer*. Without customers, the organization loses its ability and reason to exist; customers provide the approach to the organization.

The cost information itself is a product with its own customers. Customers are managers. At the level of production, where products are assembled or services are performed, the information is needed to control and improve operations. This information is provided and is frequently used to monitor the efficiency of the activities performed. For example, if the average rate of defects is 1% in a manufacturing process and the information of cost accounting system indicates a default rate of 2% on the previous day, employees of production must use this information to identify what is causing the defect rate to increase and correct the problem.

In an average level of management, where managers supervise the work and decisions of operation, cost information is used to identify problems by seeing if some aspects of the operation are different from what was expected. At the executive level, the financial information is used to assess the overall performance of the company. This information is strategic in nature and is typically provided monthly, by quarter, or annually. The cost accountants must work with users (or clients) of the cost accounting information to provide the best possible information for management purposes.

The most serious problems with accounting systems occur when managers use accounting information that was developed for external reporting for decision-making. Decision-making requires information commonly different than that provided to shareholders in the financial statements. It is important that companies understand that the various uses of the accountancy data require different types of accounting information.

Cost Accounting and Ethics

The design of costing systems is ultimately about the allowance of costs to various activities, products, projects and corporate units, and people. The manner in which this is done affects prices, reimbursement and payment.

As some already know, based on events, the cost accounting systems design has the potential to be misused and fraud to customers, employees or shareholders. As user or preparer of the cost information, you need to be aware of what it implies how the information is used. And most important, you need to be aware of when the system has the potential to be abused.

Uses of Cost Data

The cost information is used for two purposes in most organizations: 1) the cost accounting systems provide information to evaluate the performance of an organizational unit or his manager, and 2) also provide the means for estimating the unit cost of products or services that the organization can manufacture or provide to others.

a. Performance measurement. This measurement can be done by comparing current costs with those who were expected - *or standard costs budgeted cost* - to the degree of knowing which of them have been controlled. Deviations of expected with the current - *variances* - can be identified, evaluated and discussed by managers.

b. Cost of goods and services. In manufacturing companies, the costs of goods must be measured to determine the cost of items transferred from work in process inventory to finished products. To meet the demands for information, a cost system should measure all the costs of manufacturing process and allocate a portion of those costs to each unit of output. The costs to obtain, maintain and manage the manufacturing plant or building should be added to the cost of material and productive work that requires each unit. The first are called indirect costs and the two last are called direct costs.

c. Profit analysis. Information in costs is essential to analyse the profits obtained from a product or product line. The information on the cost of a product enables managers to assess the contribution margin - *the difference between the price and variable costs* - and the gross margin - *the difference between the price and the total cost of the product.*

d. Product mix. For the companies that offer more than one product or service the cost information is key to handle the mix of products or services offered to customers. With information on cost-profit, a manager can lead the effort in sales and advertising for products that generate greater value. The products that do not create any profit can be removed, have a price reassignation, or tied up with products that have greater utility.

e. Price assignation. Regardless of where prices are determined by the forces of market demand, product differentiation and advertising offer to many managers some sort of idea to assign prices to products or services. The costs of products and trends commonly offer signals to managers that prices should be changed. An example could be the change in the cost of a material or critical component which can give a signal to reassess the price of a product or service.

f. Cost of service. Many products require the seller to provide additional services to customers. In such cases, the information about the cost of service is so important for managers as the cost of production. The same for companies that offer services only, unless the cost of service is measured, there is no way to know whether providing the service is profitable or not, or whether changes in prices or advertising are needed.

Looked from another angle, the uses that the administration of a company can give to the costs can be grouped into 4 categories, specified below:

Cost of getting costs	It provides reports on profits and valuates the inventory.
Cost of planning	Set goals and select roads economic-financial, leading the company to its achievement, from where you are.
Cost of controlling	Allows know if the targets set are being reached and in turn, serves as a basis for taking corrective actions.
Cost of decision making	It provides information to select the best alternative.

The Cost of Anything Depends on the Purpose to Determine the Cost.

Inventory Valuation

Inventories are considered by many companies as a very significant asset. The inventory accounting involves two major aspects: 1) the cost of inventory purchased or manufactured needs to be determined and 2) the cost is retained in the inventory accounts of the company until the product is sold.

Inventory Valuation Methods, Determine Cost of Sales

Specificidentification	Each item sold and each unit remaining in the inventory are individually identified
FIFO (First-in, first-out)	The actual physical flow is irrelevant, the important thing is that the flow of costs assumes that the first articlesin entering the inventory are the first to be sold (cost of sales) or consumed (cost of production). The final inventory is made up of the last articles that became part of inventories.
LIFO (Last-in, first-out)	The actual physical flow is irrelevant, the important thing is that the flow of costs assumes that the last articles that became part of the inventory are the first to be sold (cost of sales) or consumed (cost of production).The final inventory is comprised of the first articles that became part of inventories.
Weighted Average	This method requires calculating the average unit cost of the goods in the beggining inventory including the purchases made in the accounting period. Based on this average cost per unit is determined both the cost of sales (production) and the ending inventory of the period.

Examples of Inventory Valuation and Cost of Sales

METALS, INC.		COST FLOWS		
		FIFO	W. AVG.	LIFO
Brooches, Beggining Inventory 1-Jan-1999	29 @ $5.00	$145	$145	$145
Purchases, 1999		2,075	2,075	2,075
Goods available for sale, 1999		$2,220	$2,220	$2,220
Brooches, Ending Inventory 31-Dec-1999				
	50 @ $10.50 = $525 4 @ 9.00 = 36	$ 561		
	54 @ $7.96		$ 430	
	29 @ $5.00 = $145 25 @ 6.00 = 150			$ 295
Brooches, Cost of the Sales, 1999		$1,659	$1.790	$1,925

Cost Behavior

Knowing the behavior of costs is very useful in the management of a company for a variety of purposes. For example, know how costs behave, enables managers or administrators predict profits when sales volume and production changes. Knowing the behavior of costs is also useful for estimating costs. In turn, the estimated costs affect various decisions of the administration, like for example, if it should use machinery exceeded capacity to produce and sell a product at a reduced price. The behavior of a cost refers to the manner in which a cost changes at the time that a related activity changes. To understand the behavior of costs, the following two factors must be considered: First, the activities that is believed that cause the cost to be incurred mues be identified.

These activities are called *activity* bases (or *activity drivers*). Second, the activity range on which changes in the cost are of interest must be specified. This activity range is called *relevant rank*.

Variable Costs Behavior

When the activity level is measured in units produced, direct material and labour costs are generally classified as direct variable costs. The *variable costs* are costs that vary in proportion to the total change in the level of activity.

For example, assume that the company Sound, Inc. produces sound systems under the brand name "Loud". The parts for the sound system are purchased from external suppliers for $10 USD per unit and are assembled at the plant Sound, Inc. in San Benito, USA. The direct materials costs for the model Loud-10 in a relevant range are from 5000 to 30000 units of production are shown below:

Units produced (Loud Model-10)	*Direct Materials Cost per unit*	*Total Direct Material Cost*
5,000	$10	$50,000
10,000	10	100,000
15,000	10	150,000
20,000	10	200,000
25,000	10	250,000
30,000	10	300,000

The variable cost per unit is the same, while the total variable cost changes in proportion to changes in the basis of activity. For model Loud-10, for example, the cost of direct materials for 10,000 units ($100,000) is twice the cost of direct materials for 5,000 units ($50,000).

The total cost of materials varies in direct proportion to the number of units produced because the direct cost of materials per unit ($10) is the same for all levels of production.

Then, producing 20,000 additional units of product Loud-10 would increase the cost of direct materials by $200,000, to produce 25,000 additional units would increase the cost by $250000 and so on.

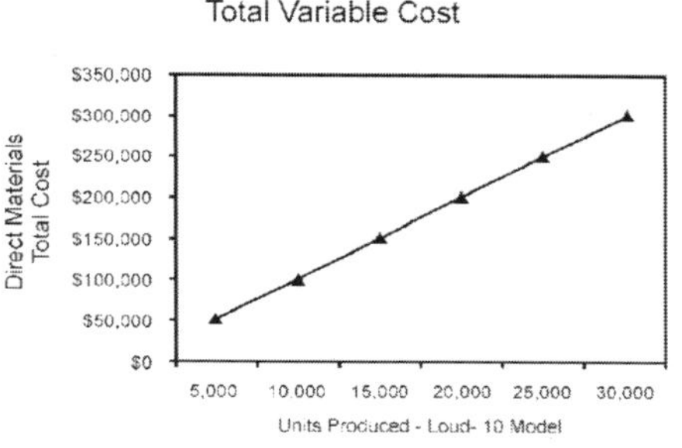

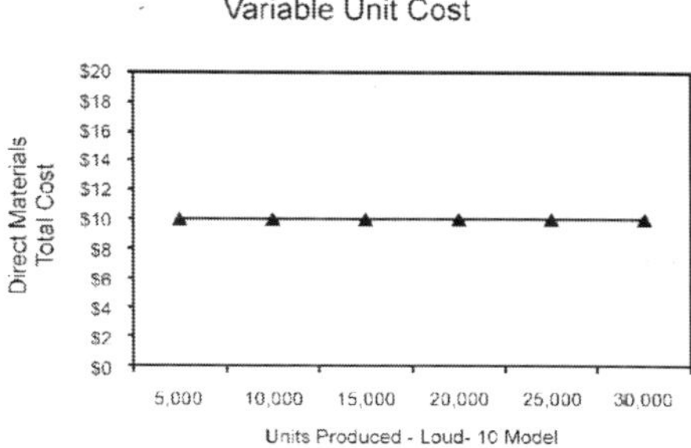

Fixed Costs Behavior

When units produced is a measure of activity, examples of fixed costs include the depreciation of equipment in a straight line of a factory, plant's machinery and equipment insurance, supervisors salaries, etcetera. The fixed costs are costs that continue the same in their total even if the level of activity changes.

As an example, assume that Hana Inc. produces and distributes cheese pies at its plant in Los Angeles, USA. The general production supervisor at the plant in Los Angeles is Vicente Fernandez, who is paid a salary of $ 75000 USD per year.

The relevant range of activity for a year is 50000 to 300000 cheese cakes. The salary of Vincent is a fixed cost that does not vary with the number of units produced. Regardless of the number of cakes produced between the range of 50000 to 300000, Vincent receives a salary of $ 75000.

Even if the fixed cost remains unchanged when the number of cakes produced changes, the fixed cost by cake changes. The more cakes are produced, total fixed costs are distributed among more cakes, and then lowers the cost per cake. This relationship can be seen in the wage example of $75,000 of Vicente Fernandez shown below:

Cakes Produced	*V. Fernandez Total Salary*	*Salary per cake produced*
50,000	$75,000	$1.500
100,000	75,000	0.750
150,000	75,000	0.500
200,000	75,000	0.375
250,000	75,000	0.300
300,000	75,000	0.250

Seen in graphics would be as follows:

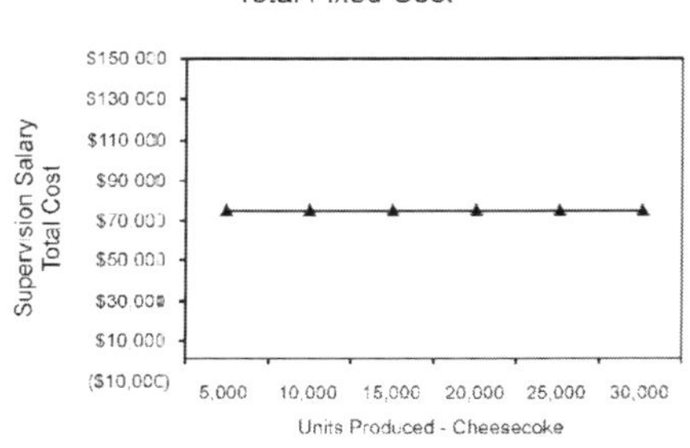

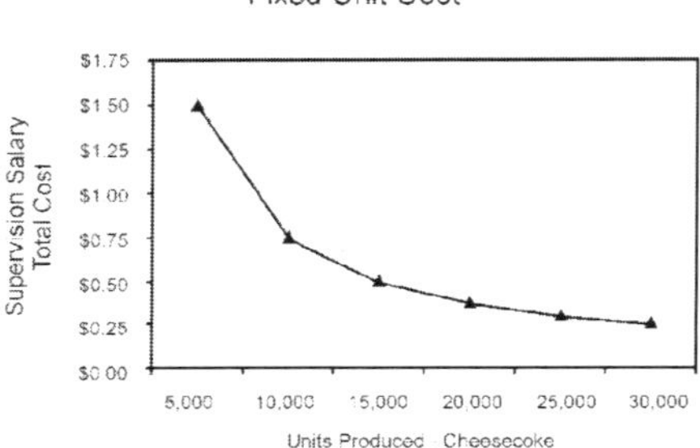

Cost Systems

The objective of a cost system or costing system is accumulate the costs of goods or services. The information on the cost of a product or service is used by managers to set the prices of the product, control operations, and develop financial statements. Also, the cost system improves control by providing information on the costs incurred by each department or manufacturing process.

Cost Systems Depending on how Costs of Production are Accumulated

Job Order Cost System

A job order cost system provides a separate record for the cost of each quantity of product passing through the factory. A quantity of each particular product is called *order*. A job order cost system fits better in the industries that develop products with that have different specifications most of the time or that have a wide variety of products in stock. Many service companies use this type of system for costing orders by accumulating the costs associated with providing services to their customers. Some characteristics of the job order cost systems are listed below:

- They accumulate in batches
- Production under specific orders
- Normally does not produces the same article
- Examples: Accounting firm, construction company, law practice, apparel manufacturing, movie studio.

Process Cost System

In a process cost system, costs are accumulated for each department or process in the factory. A process cost system fits more in companies manufacturing products which are not distinguishable with each other during a process of continuous production. Some characteristics of process cost systems are listed below:

- They accumulate costs by department
- Production continuous and homogeneous
- Examples: Oil Refinery, food processing, paper processing, soft drinks, medicines, buckets, toys, pants.

"When" should the cost of production be determined?

- Before we begin the process - Default costs (estimated or standard)
- After or at the same time of the process - Actual costs (current or historical).

Standard Costs and Variance Analysis

The standard costs are developed based on direct and indirect costs budgeted. The standard cost is a measure of how much should cost to produce or deliver a product or service. The standard cost of a product is made of the costs of the components required to produce that product. For example, the standard cost of a leather jacket includes:

- Cost of materials (leather, zipper, buttons, etc.)
- Direct labour cost (the time required to cut the design, sew it, etcetera, at the rate of production of employees who work in the process), and
- Indirect manufacturing costs related to the product (depreciation of the skin cutter machine, electricity, rent of the factory, etc.).

Once the standard cost is established, this provides the basis for decision-making, to analyse and control costs, and to measure the inventory and the cost of goods sold. The standard costs serve as a benchmark against which actual costs are compared. The differences between current costs and standard costs are called *variances. The* actual costs may differ from the standard costs due to differences in price, differences in quantity, errors, or other conditions.

To determine the reasons for the variances a corrective action may be suggested or demonstrate that the products are currently costing more or less than the anticipated.

Direct cost

The direct costs, such as materials and labour, are the costs that can be specifically assigned to a unit of products. The standard cost for the direct costs of a product involves two components: the price component and quantity component. The standard cost for one unit of production is calculated by multiplying the standard quantity to be used by the price per standard unit.

Example: Assume that our leather jacket contains an average of 2 meters of skin at a cost of $16.00 per meter, a zipper at a cost of $5.00 per meter and two buttons at a cost of $0.50 each. Based on a time study recently made by the administration, a jacket requires an average of 5 hours of time spent by an employee to be produced. The production workers are paid on average $10 per hour of work, including benefits. The standard cost for the direct costs (the one for indirect costs will be seen later in this section) shall be as follows:

Materials	*Quantity X Price*	*= Standard Cost*
Skin	2 meters X $ 16.00	$32.00
Zipper	1 Zipper X $ 5.00	$5.00
Buttons	2 X buttons $ 0.50	$1.00
Materials Total Cost		$38.00
Direct Labour Cost	5 hours X $10.00	$50.00
Total Direct Cost		$88.00

Throughout the year, our leather jacket company will buy leather, zippers and buttons, and also recruit and pay to production employees. But what hill happened 1) if the company found skin at a lower price with a new supplier, which it is offering a discount, 2) a new machine has been acquired by the company to minimize the amount of material required by each jacket reducing the material scrap; 3) due to a very special order, the company had to ask their workers to work overtime, which must be paid on time and a half the normal rate, i.e. 150%; 4) the new machine to improved productivity, and now are used only 4.8 hours to produce a jacket. These differences will lead to variations between actual cost and standard costs budgeted as follows:

Materials	***Quantity X Price = Standard Cost***	
Skin	1.5 meters X $12.00	$18.00
Zipper	1 Zipper X $5.00	$5.00
Buttons	2 botones X $0.50 2 X buttons $ 0.50	$1.00
Materials Total Cost		$24.00
Direct Labour Cost	4.6 hours X $ 15.00	$69.00
Total Direct Cost		$93.00

Now it's easy to see how jackets cost $5.00 more than what was budgeted. To understand a variance or variation, it must be analysed and broken into its component parts. The analysis of variance in material would be:

Materials	***Quantity X Price = Standard Cost***	
Skin:		
Budget	2 meters X $16.00	$32.00
Actual	1.5 meters X $12.00	$18.00
Material Variance		$14.00 Favorable
Price variance	($16.00 - $12.00) X 1.5 meters	$6.00 Favorable
Variance in quantity	(2.0 - 1.5) X $16.00	$8.00 Favorable
Material Variance		$14.00 Favorable

The analysis of variance in direct labour would be the following:

Direct Labour	***Quantity X Price = Standard Cost***	
DL:		
Budget	5 hours X $10.00	$50.00
Actual	4.6 meters X $15.00	$69.00
DL Variance		$ 19.00 Unfavorable
Price variance	($ 10.00 - $ 15.00) X 4.6 meters	$23.00 Unfavorable
Variance in quantity	(5.0 - 4.6) X $10.00	$4.00 Favorable
DL Variance		$19.00 Unfavorable

The variance is added as follows:

Standard Cost	$88.00
Actual Cost	$93.00
Total Variance	$5.00 Unfavorable
Material variance	$14.00 Favorable
DL Variance	$19.00 Unfavorable
Total Variance	$ 5.00 Unfavorable

The formulas to analyse variances can be expressed as follows:

Price Variance	(SP - AP) X AQ
Variance in quantity	(SQ - AQ) X SP
Total Variance	(SP X SQ) - (AP X AQ)
Where:	
SP = Standard Price	
AP = Current Price	
SQ = Standard Quantity	

Overhead or Indirect Costs

The direct costs vary in relation to the volume of units produced. Overhead or indirect costs or general expenses, however, are elements that vary directly with the volume (variable costs) and other elements that do not (fixed costs).

Overhead Budgets. One way to budget the overhead is ignoring the indirect effects of volume. This approach is called fixed *costs budget*. Under this approach, the administration determines the amount of overhead that should be taken based on a desired or normal level of production. The total expenditure becomes the overhead budget against which performance is measured, regardless of the level of production currently achieved. An example of this would be as follows:

Table : Overhead Permitted (in thousands)

Rent	$500
Machinery Depreciation	500
Supervision Salaries	1,000
Indirect Material	800
Electricity	800
Total	$3,600

The performance at the end of the year may be measured against the total $3'600,000. However, not taking into account the true nature of costs, may lead to a manager to take inaccurate conclusions about the performance. For example, lets assume that this budget is based on a "normal" level of production of leather jackets (160,000 units). Also assume that the costs of electricity, accounting in part for cutting machines and sewing, vary with the level of production. So, if 200,000 jackets are produced during the year, the cost of electricity will exceed $800,000, say that these were a total of $1'000,000. Comparing this with a fixed budget, the manager can say that the supervisor of the warehouse did his job poorly in terms of managing the costs of electricity, when in fact, excessive spending is due solely to 40,000 extra jackets that occurred.

The other approach for budgeting overhead is called *flexible budget.* A flexible budget specifies a cost permissible at each possible level of production. Once the period is completed and the volume of production known, the standard budget is determined by reference to flexible budget for the current level of production. This is a parallel method to the way used to determine the budget for direct materials and manpower. Example of a simplified flexible budget:

Amounts in Thousands

Utilization Capacity	40%	60%	70%	80% (Normal)	100%	
Direct Labor Cost (rate per piece)	$4,000	$6,000	$7,000	$8,000	$10,000	
Overhead Allowed						**Cost Behavior**
Rent	$500	$500	$500	$500	$500	No change or Fixed
Depreciation	500	500	500	500	500	No change or fixed
Supervision	500	1,000	1,000	1,000	1,500	Phased Cost
Indirect Material	400	600	700	800	1,000	Variable at 10% of Direct Labor
Electricity	600	700	750	800	900	Semivariable: $400 + 5% of DL
TOTAL	**$2,250**	**$3,300**	**$3,450**	**$3,600**	**$4,400**	

A flexible budget allows us to analyse in a more intelligent way the variable overhead.

Overhead absorption. Now that our flexible budget is established, we need to establish how we are going to allocate indirect costs to our products. The total cost of a product should include all indirect costs that were generated to bring the product to its complete form. So apart from the direct labour and materials, the standard cost of a product includes indirect costs as well. But, manpower and materials are easy to measure and allocate their products. It is much more difficult to determine how much rent, indirect material, or depreciation was consumed by a particular product.

The accountants solve this problem by using an overhead allowance method. This is called *overhead absorption.* First indirect costs are collected in *sets of costs.* A group can include all the rent, other all the costs associated with the inspection, other the costs of supervision, etc. Now the sets of costs are allocated to products using a *driver of cost*. For simplicity, in the rest of this note we will assume that all indirect costs are added in a single set of cost for assignment.

In companies that produce a single product, the overall costs can be allocated based on units, using the units produced in the period as a driver of cost.

The total budgeted indirect cost ($ 3.6 million using the example above) will be divided between the volume of production planned (assuming 200,000 jackets). Then for each jacket produced, $18.00 ($ 3.6 million between 200,000) shall apply as indirect costs. The standard cost per jacket under this method would be then:

Table 1: *Standard Cost*

Materials	$38.00
Manpower (Direct labour)	$50.00
Overhead (Indirect cost)	$18.00
Total Standard Cost	$106.00

In multi-product firms, it is necessary to use a different method or cost driver than the number of units produced, so a more fair distribution of indirect cost between products can be made. For example, if our company makes leather gloves in addition to jackets and gloves can be manufactured in a quarter of the time it takes to produce a jacket, it would be unfair to charge each pair of gloves the same indirect cost that is charged to each jacket. Some other method of utilization of capacity must be used, as the labour hours, the amount paid by workforce in currency (either dollars, pesos, quarters, etc.) or machine hours. The choice for a business in particular should be based on which variable is the one that best measures the level of utilization of capacity for that business. For example, the overall costs of machinery depreciation can be allocated based on the number of machine hours per product as a cost driver. The entire cost of supervision can be distributed using the direct labour hours as a cost driver.

Since our production process of jackets is just more intense in direct labour, we will use the monetary cost of labour as a method of allocation (in this example we will use as currency the U.S. dollars). Using the direct labour dollars, the standard cost of overhead for a jacket would be $0.45 for each dollar of direct labour ($3.6 million of budgeted indirect cost divided by the total $8.0 million of budgeted manpower). Then, for a jacket $22.50 would be applied by indirect cost ($50.00 dollars per jacket multiplied by the $0.45 rate of indirect cost per DL dollar). The total standard cost for a leather jacket would be as follows:

Table 2: *Standard Cost*

Materials	$38.00
Manpower (Direct labour)	$50.00
Overhead (Indirect Cost)	$22.50
Total Standard Cost	$110.50

This would be the amount to be accumulated as inventory by each jacket produced. However, differences between the planned and actual volume will make a *volume variance* to emerge. The volume variance can be explain as follows:

	Plan	***Actual***
Direct Labour / jacket	$50.00	$50.00
Overhead rate	x $0.45	x $0.45
Overhead cost / Jacket	$22.50	$22.50
Jackets produced	160,000	140,000
Total Overhead Absorption	$3,600,000	$3,150,000

If the plan was to produce 160,000 jackets and currently there were only 140,000, and if we assume that the $3.6 million in indirect costs are fixed and that at the end of the year we only have $3.15 million of absorption by finished product; if the actual costs were $3.6 million, that compared with the absorption have led to a volume variance of $450,000.

Cost-volume-profit Analysis

The *cost-volume-profit analysis* is the systematic examination of the relationship between selling prices, sales, production volumes, costs, expenses and profits. This analysis provides very useful information for decision-making in the management of a company. For example, the analysis can be used in establishing sales prices, in the product mix selection to sell, in the decision to choose marketing strategies, and in the analysis of the impact on profits by changes in costs. In the current environment of business, a business administration must act and take decisions in a fast and accurate manner. As a result, the importance of *cost-volume-profit* is still increasing as time passes.

Contribution Margin

A relationship between the cost, volume and profit is the *contribution margin.* El margen de contribucion es el exceso de ingresos por ventas sobre los costos variables. The contribution margin is the revenue excess from sales over variable costs. The concept of contribution margin is particularly useful in the planning of business because it gives an insight into the potential profits that can generate a business. The following chart includes the income statement of the company Fusion, Inc. which has been prepared to show its contribution margin:

Sales	$1,000,000
(-) Variable Costs	600,000
= Contribution margin	$400,000
(-) Fixed Costs	300,000
= Income from Operations	$ 100,000 $ 100.000

Contribution Margin Ratio

The margin contribution can also be expressed as a percentage. The *contribution margin ratio,* which is sometimes called the profit-volume ratio, indicates the percentage of each sales dollar available to cover fixed costs and to provide operating revenue. For the company Fusion, Inc. the contribution margin ratio is 40%, which is computed as follows:

Sales -
Variable Costs Contribution margin
ratio = ------------------------
Sales

Contribution margin ratio = ($1,000,000 - $600,000) / $1,000,000 = 40%

The contribution margin ratio measures the effect on operating income of an increase or a decrease in sales volume. For example, assume that the management of Fusion, Inc. is studying the effect of adding $80,000 in sales orders. Multiplying the contribution margin ratio (40%) by the change in sales volume ($80,000) indicates that operating income will increase $32,000 if additional orders are obtained. To validate this analysis the table below shows the income statement of the company including additional orders:

Sales	$1,080,000
(-) Variable Costs ($1,080,000 X 60%)	648,000
Contribution margin ($1,080,000 X 40%)	$432,000
(-) Fixed Costs	300,000
Income from Operations	$132,000

Variable costs as a percentage of sales are equal to 100% minus the contribution margin ratio. Thus, in the above income statement, the variable costs are 60% (100% - 40%) of sales, or $648,000 ($1'080,000 X 60%). The total contribution margin $432,000, can also be computed directly by multiplying the sales by the contribution margin ratio ($1'080,000 X 40%).

Unit Contribution Margin

The unit contribution margin is also useful to analize the profit potential of proposed projects. The *unit contribution margin* is the dollars from each unit of sales available to cover the fixed costs of operation and provide operating profits. For example, if Fusion, Inc.'sunit selling price is $20 and its unit variable cost is $12, the unit contribution margin is $8 ($20 - $12).

The *contribution margin percentage* is most useful when the increase or decrease in sales volume is measured in sales dollars. To illustrate, assume that the company Fusion, Inc. sold 50,000 units. Its operating income is $100,000, as shown in the following contribution margin income statement:

Sales (50.000 units X $20)	$1,000,000
(-) Variable Costs (50,000 X $12)	600,000
Contribution Margin (50,000 units X $8)	$ 400,000
(-) Fixed Costs	300,000
Income from operations	$100,000

If sales of the company Fusion, Inc. could be increased by 15,000 units from 50,000 to 65,000 units, its operating income would increased by $120,000 (15000 units X $8), as shown below:

Sales (65,000 units X $20)	$1,300,000
(-) Variable Costs (65,000 units X $12)	780,000
Contribution margin (65,000 X $8)	$520,000
(-) Fixed Costs	300,000
Income from operations	$220,000

Base Costing

Activity Based Costing (ABC) is a two-stage product costing method that assigns costs first to activities and then to the products based on each product's use of activities. An activity is any discrete task that an organization undertakes to make or deliver a product or service. Activity-based costing is based on the concept that products consume activities and activities consume resources.

Activity-based costing involves the following four steps:

1. Identify the activities -such as processing orders- that consume resources and assign costs to them.
2. Identify the cost driver(s) associated with each activity. A cost driver causes, or "drives" an activity's costs. For the order-processing activity, the cost driver could be the number of orders.
3. Compute a cost rate per cost driver unit or transaction. The cost driver rate could be the cost per order, for example.
4. Assign costs to products by multiplying the cost driver rate by the volume of cost driver units consumed by the product. For example, the cost per order multiplied by the number of orders processed for a particular song during the month of March measures the cost of the order processing activity for that song during March.

Identifying activities that use resources: Often the most interesting and challenging part of the exercise is identifying activities that use resources because doing so requires understanding all activities required to make a product. In fact, much of the value of activity-based costing comes from this exercise even without changing the way product costs are computed. When managers step back and analize the prccesses (activities) they follow to produce a good or service, they often uncover many nonvalue-added steps, which they can eliminate.

Choosing cost driver: The following table shows several examples of the types of cost drivers that companies use. Most are related either to the volume of production or to the complexity of the production or marketing process.

Machine-hours used	Computer time used
Labour-hours or labour cost incurred	Number pf items produced or sold
Pounds of material handled	Customers served
Pages typed	Flight hours completed
Machine setups	Surgeries performed
Purchased orders completed	Scrap/rework orders completed
Quality inspections performed	Hours of testing time spent
Number of parts installed in a product	Number of different customers served

Miles Driven

The best cost driver is one that is causally related to the cost being allocated. Finding an allocation base that is causally related to the cost is often not possible. With an ABC system, the selection of an allocation base, or cost driver, is often easier because we can use a measure of the activity volume. For example, a reasonable allocation base for machine set-up costs is machine set-up hours. Notice that many of the cost drivers in the previous table refer to an activity.

Computing a Cost Rate per Cost Driver. In general, predetermined rates for allocating indirect costs to products are computed as follows:

Predetermined rate = Estimated indirect cost / Estimated volume of allocation base

This formula applied to any indirect cost, wheter manufacturing overhead or administrative, distribution, selling, or any other indirect costs. Workers and machines perform activities on each product as it is produced. Costs are allocated to a product by multiplying each activity's predetermined rate by the volume of activity used in making it. In the two-stage cost system, the first stage consists of activities, not departments. Instead of a department rate, activity-based costing computes a cost driver rate for each activity center. This means that each activity has an associated cost pool.

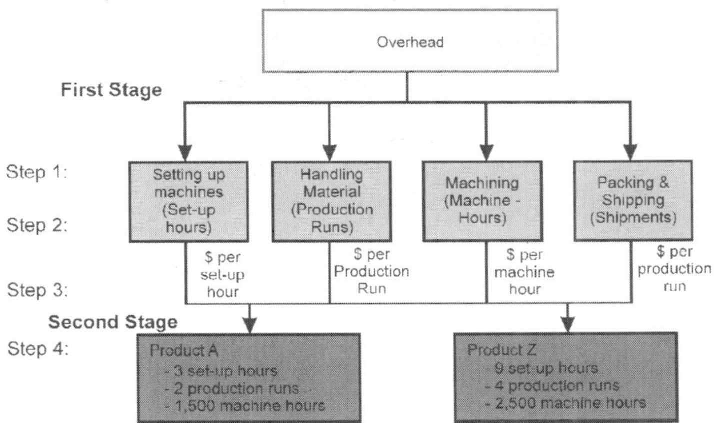

If the cost driver for material handling is the number of production runs, for example, the company must be able to estimate the costs of material handling before the period and, ideally, track the actual cost of material handling as it is incurred during the period. Assigning costs to products. The final step in the activity-based costing system is to assign the activity costs to products. We do this just as we have done for the other product costing systems we have considered. We multiply the cost driver rates by the number of units of the cost driver in each product. The following table shows a cost flow diagram with the four steps of developing activity-based costs graphically.

Cost Overrun

A cost overrun, also known as a cost increase or budget overrun, is an unexpected cost incurred in excess of a budgeted amount due to an under-estimation of the actual cost during budgeting. Cost overrun should be distinguished from cost escalation, which is used to express an *anticipated* growth in a budgeted cost due to factors such as inflation.

Cost overrun is common in infrastructure, building, and technology projects. A comprehensive study of cost overrun published in the Journal of the American Planning Association in 2002 found that 9 out of ten construction projects had underestimated costs. Overruns of 50 to one hundred percent were common. Cost underestimation was found in each of 20 nations and five continents covered by the study, and cost underestimation had not decreased in the 70 years for which data were available.[For IT projects, an industry study by the Standish Group found that the average cost overrun was 43 percent; 71 percent of projects were over budget, exceeded time estimates, and had estimated too narrow a scope; and total waste was estimated at $55 billion per year in the US alone.[

Many major construction projects have incurred cost overruns. The Suez Canal cost 20 times as much as the earliest estimates; even the cost estimate produced the year before construction began underestimated the project's actual costs by a factor of three. The Sydney Opera House cost 15 times more than was originally projected, and the Concorde supersonic aeroplane cost 12 times more than predicted.] When Boston's "Big Dig" tunnel construction project was completed, the project was 275 percent ($11 billion) over budget. The Channel Tunnel between the UK and France had a construction cost overrun of 80 percent, and a 140-percent financing cost overrun.

Causes

Three types of explanation for cost overrun exist: technical, psychological, and political-economic. Technical explanations account for cost overrun in terms of imperfect forecasting techniques, inadequate data, etc. Psychological explanations account for overrun in terms of optimism bias with forecasters. Scope creep, where the requirements or targets rises during the project, is common. Finally, political-economic explanations see overrun as the result of strategic misrepresentation of scope or budgets.

All three explanations can be considered forms of risk. A project's budgeted costs should always include cost contingency funds to cover risks (other than scope changes imposed on the project). As has been shown in cost engineering research, poor risk analysis and contingency estimating practices account for many project cost overruns. Numerous studies have found that the greatest cause of cost growth was poorly-defined scope at the time that the budget was established. The *cost growth*, or overrun of the budget before cost contingency is added, can be predicted by rating the extent of scope definition, even on complex projects with new technology.

Professor Bent Flyvbjerg of Oxford University and Martin Wachs of University of California, Los Angeles have shown that big public-works projects often have cost overruns due to strategic misrepresentation—"that is, lying", as Flyvbjerg defines the term.

Cost overrun is typically calculated in one of two ways: either as a percentage, namely actual cost minus budgeted cost, in percent of budgeted cost; or as a ratio of actual cost divided by budgeted cost. For example, if the budget for building a new bridge was $100 million, and the actual cost was $150 million, then the cost overrun may be expressed by the ratio 1.5, or as 50 percent.

2

Management Accounting

Theory is an explanation of what is observed in practice. The development of theory from practice is the result of a process of research. Practice informs theory, which in turn, via various forms of publication and education, can influence the spread of practice between organisations and countries. Otley argued that management accounting research 'has, in a number of respects, lost touch with management accounting practices' having concentrated too much on accounting and not enough on management.

Otley reinforced earlier arguments that management accounting had become 'irrelevant to contemporary organisations, but worse that it was often actually counterproductive to good management decision-making' and that we need to 'put the management back into management accounting'.

Hopper et al. argued that there have been few British scholars who have achieved innovation in practice, either because of 'the anti-intellectualism of British managers and accountants... or the marginal role of academics in British policy making'. Both issues are important, because an understanding of accounting tools and techniques without an understanding of theory has the same problems as theories divorced from business practice.

An understanding of the underlying assumptions of accounting and the limitations of the tools and techniques of accounting is essential. If we ignore those assumptions and limitations, we are likely to make decisions on the basis of numbers that do not adequately reflect any underlying business reality.

Theory has been integrated with practical examples in this book to reflect the importance of taking an interpretive and critical perspective on financial reports. Theory is not developed by academics in ivory towers divorced from practical business situations. It is developed from research, which typically takes one of two forms:

- a quantitative study of a large number of business organisations that yields a large database that can be analysed statistically in order to produce generalizations about accounting practice;
- a qualitative study of a single organisation or a small number of organisations through case studies comprising interviews, observation and documentary research that aims to explain accounting practice in the context in which it is situated.

Both methods are valuable in helping to understand accounting practice. Hopper et al. traced the development of accounting research through four approaches:

- conventional teaching emphasizing the needs of the professional accounting bodies;
- the application of economics and management science;
- history and public-sector accounting;
- behavioural and organisational approaches.

The first approach is that traditionally taken by students of accounting. The second approach relies heavily on econometric and mathematical models, which are outside the scope of this book. This book has taken the view that managers who use accounting information do not need as thorough an understanding of how to prepare accounting information, but rather that they should take a more interpretive and critical perspective.

This implies a concern with the behavioural and organisational approach, rooted in organisational history and the unique circumstance of each organisation. Power described his own experience of a professional accounting education and argued that 'the lived reality of accounting education shows that it does not serve the functional ends that are claimed for it'.

He described: the institutionalization of a form of discourse in which critical and reflective practices are regarded as 'waffle'... of a cynicism and irony among students towards the entire examination process... and the public game that they are required to play. Power concluded that this 'may be dysfunctional for the profession itself and for the goal of producing flexible and critical experts'. Research in management accounting tends to fall into two distinct categories:

- The normative view – what ought to happen – that there is one best way of doing accounting, that accounting information is economically rational and serves an instrumental purpose in making decisions in the pursuit of shareholder value.
- The interpretive and critical view – what does happen – the explanation of how accounting systems develop and are used in particular organisational settings.

This view recognizes that people do not necessarily make decisions based on economically rational reasons but have limited information, limited cognitive ability and are influenced by organisational structures and systems (including, but not limited to, accounting systems) and by organisational power and culture. The interpretive and critical view has been evident in the theories and case studies presented in the book.

This second – interpretive and critical – view is descriptive or qualitative rather than statistical or quantitative. This is a necessary approach to explain the practice of accounting in both its organisational setting and the wider social context in which it exists. This second view has tended to be developed through case study research.

For example, Kaplan argued for empirical studies of management accounting systems in their organisational contexts, by 'observing skilled practitioners in actual organisations'. Kaplan described empirical research methods, especially case or field studies that communicate the 'deep, rich slices of organisational life' and are 'the only mechanism by which management accounting can become a scientific field of inquiry'. Spicer argued that case study research is appropriate when 'why?' or 'how?' questions are asked about contemporary events. He classified two types of case study research: descriptive and/or exploratory and informing and/or explanatory, arguing that: the case method, when used for explanatory purposes, relies on analytical not statistical generalization. The objective of explanatory case research is not to draw inferences to some larger population based on sample evidence, but rather to generalize back to theory.

Hopper et al. emphasized the rise of behavioural and organisational accounting research from 1975. In the UK, a paradigm shift occurred that did not happen in the US (where agency theory remains the dominant research approach), as contingency theory and neo-human relations approaches were abandoned for more sociological and political approaches that drew from European social theory and were influenced by Scandinavian case-based research.

Under Thatcherism: accounting data and the consulting arms of accounting firms had been central to economic and policy debates, involving privatization, industrial restructuring, reform of the public sector and worries about de-industrialization... it appeared apparent that accounting had to be studied in its broader social, political and institutional context. Humphrey and Scapens argued for the capacity of explanatory case studies 'to move away from managerialist notions of accounting and to provide more challenging reflections on the nature of accounting knowledge and practice' and to its 'intricacies, complexities and inconsistencies'. One problem that has arisen in academic research is the variety of theories used to explain practice, which Humphrey and Scapens believe excessively dominate the analysis of case study evidence. Similarly, Hopper et al. argued that 'the research thrust may lie in attempting to integrate and consolidate the variety of theories and methodologies which have emerged in recent years, rather than seeking to add yet more'.

For example, case study researchers are: becoming aware of the need to study accounting change from the perspective of global competition... there is a need to re-incorporate economics into social theory and case study based research. This book has attempted to integrate both views, i.e. to understand the tools and techniques of accounting as though they were rational, while also introducing alternative ways of seeing accounting.

It is hoped that it may also encourage readers to undertake research into accounting, either in an academic environment or in their own business organisations, in order to challenge conventional wisdom and better understand the context in which accounting is practised and the consequences of the use of accounting information for decision-making. In their introduction to a special issue of Management Accounting Research devoted to management accounting change, Burns and Vaivio noted that many firms have experienced significant change in their organisational design (structures and processes), competitive environment and information technologies. There is a need for management accounting change, despite the relatively recent (in the last 20 years) introduction of activity-based costing and the Balanced Scorecard.

Information technology in particular is driving the routine financial accounting functions into centralized head offices or is being outsourced. However, management accounting is increasingly decentralized to business units, where it becomes the responsibility of functional and business unit managers. These operating managers are more and more responsible for setting and achieving budget targets. As the role of non-accounting managers is being extended to encompass (management) accounting functions, the role of the professional accountant is also changing to a business consultant, advisory or change management role, often with responsibilities outside the traditional accounting one. One of the reasons for this changed role for accountants is that they do understand the numbers, both financial and non-financial. The challenge for nonaccounting managers is to understand the numbers sufficiently well to be able to contribute to the formulation and implementation of business strategy. Those who do not understand, or who do not want to understand, the numbers are likely to be increasingly marginalized in their organisations.

Research in Management Control

Giglioni and Bedeian review the contribution of the general management and organisational theory literature for the period 1900–1972, drawing out several different strands to conclude that 'even though control theory has not achieved the level of sophistication of some other management functions, it has developed to a point that affords the executive ample opportunity to maintain the operations of his firm under check.'

Parker argues that accounting control developments lagged developments in the management literature and criticizes accounting models for offering only an imperfect reflection of management models of control. Hofstede offers an early survey of the behavioural approach to budgetary control. He explores how the role of budgets has been viewed in accounting theory, in motivation theory and from the perspective of systems theory. Finally, the brief overview of research into control in complex organisations by Merchant and Simons takes a broad view of what constitutes control. It differs, however, in also paying attention to agency theory literature and psychologist research both omitted from consideration here.

It will be argued that one of the unintended consequences of Anthony's seminal work is that management control has primarily been developed in an accounting-based framework which has been unnecessarily restrictive. Although radical theorists have studied control processes more extensively, their attention has been focused much more on the exercise of power and its consequences than on the role of control systems as a means of organisational survival. This is an important area, but one which is outside the remit set for this review which is in closer alignment with Mills who argued for the place of management control as a central management discipline. He suggested that it was a more appropriate integrating discipline for general management courses than the tradition of using business policy or corporate strategy courses. 'Control' is itself a highly ambiguous term as evidenced by the difficulty of translating it into many European languages and the list of '57 varieties' in its connotations given by Rathe. Given this diversity some attention will be paid to matters of definition and the establishment of appropriate boundaries for this review.

Anthony's classic definition of management control was 'the process by which managers assure that resources are obtained and used effectively and efficiently in the accomplishment of the organisation's objectives.'

He saw management control as being sandwiched between the processes of strategic planning and operational control; these processes being super-imposed upon an organisational hierarchy to indicate the respective managerial levels at which they operate. Strategic planning is concerned with setting goals and objectives for the whole organisation over the long term. By contrast, operational control is concerned with the activity of ensuring that immediate tasks are carried out. Management control is the process that links the two. Global goals are broken down into sub-goals for parts of the organisation; statements of future intent are given more substantive content; long-term goals are solidified into shorter term goals. The process of management control is designed to ensure that the day-to-day tasks performed by all participants in the organisation come together in a coordinated set of actions which lead to overall goal specification and attainment. This can be seen primarily as the planning and coordination function of management control. The other side of the management control coin is its monitoring and feedback function. Regular observations and reports on actual achievement are used to ensure that planned actions are indeed achieving desired results.

It may be argued that Anthony's approach is too restrictive in that it assumes away important problems. The first problem is concerned with problems of defining strategies, goals and objectives. Such procedures are typically complex and ill-defined, with strategies being produced as much by accident as by design. It is clear that Anthony was aware of the problems of ambiguity and uncertainty when he located these issues in the domain of strategy, but he then avoided their further consideration. The second problem concerns the methods used to control the production (or service delivery) processes, which are highly dependent upon the specific technology in use and which are widely divergent. Anthony conveniently relegates these issues to the realm of operational control. Finally, his textbooks concentrate upon planning and control through accounting rationales and contain little or no discussion of social-psychological or behavioural issues, despite his highlighting the importance of the latter. Anthony's approach can, thus, be seen as a preliminary ground-clearing exercise, whereby he limits the extent of the problem he sets out to study. In a complex field this was probably a very sensible first step, however, it greatly narrowed the scope of the topic.

A broader view of management control is suggested by Lowe in a more comprehensive definition:

> *'A system of organisational information seeking and gathering, accountability and feedback designed to ensure that the enterprise adapts to changes in its substantive environment and that the work behaviour of its employees is measured by reference to a set of operational sub-goals (which conform with overall objectives) so that the discrepancy between the two can be reconciled and corrected for.'*

This stresses the role of a management control system (MCS) as a broad set of control mechanisms designed to assist organisations to regulate themselves, whereas Anthony's definition is more specific and limited to a narrower sub-set of control activities. Machin continues this line of thought in his critical review of management control systems as a specialist subject of academic study. He explores each of the terms 'management', 'control' and 'system', defining a research focus:

> *'Those formal, systematically developed, organisation-wide, data-handling systems which are designed to facilitate management control which "is the process by which managers assure that resources are obtained and used effectively and efficiently in the accomplishment of the organisation's objectives." '*

Machin notes that such a definition has the merit of leaving scope for academics to disagree violently whilst still perceiving themselves to be studying the same thing! Further, Machin argues that research in MCSs, led, as it was, by qualified accountants, made the research questions 'virtually immune from philosophical analysis', a critique also reflected in Hofstede's criticism of the 'poverty of management control philosophy', – the narrow, accounting focus which had become so prevalent.

Such diverse opinions leave a number of issues to be clarified. First, is the meaning of the term 'control'. In this review we will include within the definition of control both the ideas of informational feedback and the implementation of corrective actions. Equally, we explicitly exclude the exercise of power for its own sake, restricting ourselves to those activities undertaken by managers which have the intention of furthering organisational objectives (at least, insofar as perceived by managers). We are, thus, primarily concerned with the exercise of legitimate authority rather than power. This is no doubt a controversial position, but gives the review a clear managerial focus.

There is also a distinction to be drawn between management control and financial control, which is of some importance given the accounting domination of the subject in recent years. Financial control is clearly concerned with the management of the finance function within organisations. As such it is one business function amongst many and comprises but one facet of the wider practice of management control. On the other hand, management control can be defined as a general management function concerned with the achievement of overall organisational aims and objectives. Financial information is thus used in practice to serve two interrelated functions. First, it is clearly used in a financial control role, where its function is to monitor financial flows; that is, it is concerned with looking after the money. Second, it is also often used as a surrogate measure for other aspects of organisational performance. That is, management control is concerned with looking after the overall business with money being used as a convenient measure of a variety of other more complex dimensions, not as an end in itself.

Whilst well known, these roots cannot be ignored as their influence is reflected in work which continues today. There follows a review of the literature that has evolved over the last 20 years both as a continuation of and as a reaction against those roots, using a heuristic map provided by Scott. Finally, we will suggest possible themes for future development.

The Starting Points

The roots of management control issues lie in early managerial thought. The significance of the work of Weber, Durkheim and Pareto upon the development managerial thought is well rehearsed. Less well known, but providing an excellent example of the classical management theorists, is the contribution of Mary Parker Follett, described by Parker as providing almost all of the ideas of modern control theory. Follett saw that the manager controlled not single elements but complex interrelationships and argued that the basis for control lay in self-regulating, self-directing individuals and groups who recognized common interests and objectives.

It may be that Follett was an idealist in her search for unity in organisations for she sought a control that was 'fact control' not 'man control' and 'correlated control' rather than 'superimposed control'.

Further she saw coordination as the reciprocal relating of all factors in a setting that involved direct contact of all people concerned. The application of these 'fundamental principles of organisation' was the control activity itself, for the whole point of her principles was to ensure predictable performance for the organisation. Scientific management, another important root of management control, is frequently associated with the work of F. W. Taylor although there were earlier contributors to this movement. For example, Babbage was concerned with improving manufacture and systems and analysed operations, the skills involved, the expense of each process and suggested paths for improvement.

In 1874 Fink developed a cost accounting system that used information flows, classification of costs and statistical control devices; innovations which led directly to 20th century processes of management control.

What seems to characterize these theorists is an attention to real problems, a scientific approach which centred upon understanding and conceptual analysis and a wish to solve problems. Their contribution to management control lay in their attention to authority and accountability, an awareness of the need for analytical and budgetary models for control, forging the link between cost and operational activities and the separation of cost accounting from financial accounting, with the former being a precursor of management accounting and control.

However, these practical theorists may have pursued rationality of economic action and the search for universal solutions too far, although their ideas are still current and form the basis for much work in the field, many being echoed in the work of Robert Anthony. The ideas of the common purpose of social organisations along with a concern for the relationship between effectiveness and efficiency foreshadow the concept of autopoeis (the view that systems can have a 'life of their own') developed by cyberneticians.

Evolution of the Management Control Literature

As previously noted, Parker argued that developments in accounting control have followed and lagged developments in management theory. Developments in management control seem to have followed a similar pattern, so we use the schema suggested by Scott for categorizing developments in organisation theory as a framework for organising this part of our review. We would argue that systems thinking has had an important influence on the development of MCSs and Scott's schema is based on a systems approach, so it is to this we now turn.

Themes for Future Development

Here, we suggest some lines of enquiry which we believe it would be fruitful to pursue in developing research in management control. These are our own views and we acknowledge we come to these issues from our own particular history and perspectives, thus running the risk of being both biased and incomplete. However, we believe they cover a wide-ranging agenda of important issues from both a practical and theoretical perspective.

The Environment of Control

The development of earlier MCSs theory took place in the context of large, hierarchically structured organisations. It centred upon accounting controls and developed measures of divisional performance, such as return on investment and residual income. It considered the issues raised in utilizing accounting performance measures to control large, diversified companies, in particular the construction of quasi-independent responsibility centres using systems of cost allocation and transfer pricing.

The central theme was to produce measures of controllable performance against which managers could be held accountable, yet the empirical evidence suggests that the 'controllability principle' was more often honoured only in its breach. It can also be argued that changes in the business and social environment have led to the replacement of large integrated organisations by smaller and more focused organisational units, which require appropriate control mechanisms to be developed. Several features of the business environment seem to point towards a change in emphasis. A key trend is in the impact of uncertainty. It is a moot point whether uncertainty has increased, but it is true that the rate of change in both the commercial and governmental environment is rapid, requiring considerable adaptation on the part of organisations. Change appears to be affecting a much broader range of the population, whether it be technological, social or political change. The process of adaptation can no longer be left to a few senior managers who develop organisational strategies to be enacted by others; rather the process of change has become embedded in normal operating practices and involves a wider range of organisational participants.

One consequence of this rapid rate of change has been encapsulated in ideas of global competition and 'world class' companies. As the rate of change increases, organisations need to devote more of their resources to adaptation and correspondingly less to managing current operations efficiently. One method of adaptation is planning, but this requires the prediction of the consequences of change, which is becoming more difficult; an alternative response is to develop the flexibility to adapt to the consequences of change as they become apparent. The 'management of change' remains an important managerial skill, but it should no longer be seen as a discrete event bounded by periods of stability; rather we are concerned with management in a context of continual change. This requires continual adaptation, a note which is reflected in the current popular terminology of 'continuous improvement'.

A second feature has been a movement towards reducing the size of business units, certainly in terms of the number of people employed. In part, this has been driven by technological change, but there has also often been a strategic choice to encourage units to concentrate on their 'core' business and to avoid being distracted by irrelevant side issues. In turn, this has led to 'non-core' activities being outsourced, a process which can be most reliably undertaken in the context of long-term alliances. Such a trend is emphasized by just-in-time production and the processes of 'market testing' which have been imposed upon the public sector in the UK. The number of middle managers is being reduced and the range of responsibilities of those who remain is being increased. The split between strategic planning, management control and operational control, which was always tendentious has now become untenable and a much closer integration between those functions has developed. The boundaries of the organisation and the boundaries of the control function are not necessarily co-terminus. Within the organisation, ideas of 'business process re-engineering' have reinforced the need to devise control mechanisms that are horizontal (i.e. which follow the product or service through its production process until its delivery to the customer) rather than solely vertical (i.e. which follow the organisational hierarchy within organisational functions). As production processes are increasingly spread across legal boundaries (and often across national boundaries) new processes for the control of such embedded operations are needed. That is, control systems need to be devised which coordinate the total production and delivery process regardless of whether these processes are contained within a single (vertically integrated) organisation or spread across a considerable number of (quasi-independent) organisations.

Traditional approaches to management control have been valuable in defining an important topic of study, but they have been predicated on a model of organisational functioning which has become increasingly outdated. This has resulted in the study of control systems becoming over narrow by remaining focused primarily upon accounting control mechanisms which are vertical rather than horizontal in their orientation. Contemporary organisations display flexibility, adaptation and continuous learning, both within and across organisational boundaries, but such characteristics are not encouraged by traditional systems. There is considerable anecdotal evidence to suggest that organisational practices are beginning to reflect these needs, so a key task for MCSs researchers is to observe and codify these developments.

In this type of changing environment the logic of systems theory could be argued to be of some importance in emphasizing issues such as the importance of environment and the holism of the organisation. Although MCSs theory often makes references to the concepts of cybernetics and sometimes to those of general systems theory, such approaches rarely inform empirical research work. Perhaps the most important contribution these disciplines can make is to broaden the horizons of management control researchers to include an appreciation of the overall context within which their work is located. The issues of the appropriate level of analysis, the definition of systems boundaries and the nature of systems goals deserve much more thorough attention. Even more importantly, the idea of control in an open system facing a complex and uncertain environment is also central for the design of effective systems to assist organisations to survive.

Managerial Accounting Research

Managerial accounting research, which has adapted organisational or sociological theories to examine the development, maintenance and change in managerial accounting practices, explicitly recognizes the centrality of issues of social control and coordination in organisations, thus providing intellectual approaches from which to study managerial accounting as problematic aspects of the organisational and social context.

In our effort to provide a sweeping critique of organisational and sociological perspectives, rather than a detailed and nuanced treatment of this stream of management accounting research from these theoretical perspectives, there are points of omission, under-representation and compression of the multitude of views within these theoretical traditions. And yet, it is precisely through such a broad treatment that we hope to reveal the distinctiveness of these organisational and sociological research traditions which exhibit a cluster of tendencies that distinguish it from the more familiar research traditions which draw on neoclassical economics and contemporary social and organisational psychology.

Contingency theory represents a rich blend of organisational theory – i.e., it has roots in the organisational decision-making perspectives of the 1950s – and sociological functionalist perspectives of organisations – i.e., it has roots in the sociological concerns about organisational structure of the 1960s. Contingency theory took the insights on such critical organisational processes as decision-making and control as depicted in the literature on organisational decision-making and combined these with sociological functionalist concerns regarding the impact of such structural factors as environment, size, technology, etc., on organisational behaviour. Important to both the decision-making perspective of organisations and the sociological concerns for organisational structure are issues of organisational control and coordination. This explicit concern for issues of coordination and control, in turn, has provided important contributions to managerial accounting research in our understanding of such issues as the design of information and control systems, budgeting and strategic planning.

The various organisational and sociological theories which concern themselves with the social construction and spread of rationality and, in turn, the manner in which this rationality impacts the power and politics in organisational functioning. These organisational and sociological theories – often referred to as interpretive perspectives – also draw from the organisational decision-making perspective, thus sharing intellectual heritage with contingency theory. We also see, however, the influence of more interpretive sociological traditions beginning with the work of Weber and his concerns for the "politics of rationality," as well as the work of Berger and Luckmann and their work on the social construction (the development of cognitive processes) and the manner which subjective meaning becomes objective facts. Specifically, we examine the relevance of interpretive perspectives by considering a number of organisational and social theories including institutional theory, resource dependency theories, political perspectives and the sociology of professions.

Perhaps the most important attribute of critical perspectives is its attention to issues of conflict, domination and power – an attention motivated by a theoretical backdrop of capitalist social relations and premised upon an irreducible conflict between capital and labour which ensures perpetual antagonistic relations between the classes.

Despite theoretical differences within critical perspectives regarding the manner and form in which to conceptualize power, a common attribute is that they eschew a consensus view of society.

These critical perspectives argue that functionalist and interpretive views of power stipulate that individual interests mesh into a harmony at the societal level which contrasts with the critical perspectives' focus on presumed perpetual antagonistic relations between the classes.

More specifically, whether through general equilibrium in economics (e.g., the functionalist concern for market value) or the public good in politics (the interpretive concerns for the negotiation and bargaining), the social interest is assumed to emerge from the interaction of individual interests.

In sharp contrast, critical perspectives deal explicitly with the role that accounting plays in relation to issues of conflict, domination and power as defined by the presumed irreducible conflict between capital and labour.

Here we will confine our attention to two major research strands of the many critical perspectives that have illuminated our understanding of managerial accounting: labour process theory which is concerned with the extraction of surplus from labourers and the Foucaultian perspective which is concerned with the methods by which the actions of individuals are made visible and susceptible to discipline and control, thereby rendering the individual to be governed.

Contingency Theory

Contingency theory has provided considerable inspiration to managerial accounting researchers through an elaboration of the basic theme that "tight" control systems should be used in centralized organisations faced with simple technology and stable task environments; "loose" control systems should be used in decentralized organisations, presumably faced with dynamic, complex task environments. Furthermore, a given means of control such as embedded inmanagerial accounting information can only be understood through reference to other control approaches used in organisations as well as their organisational/task environment context. For example, budgets may take on important meaning both for planning and control purposes for work processes or product lines which are more routine, standardized and predictable. However, in situations where the processes or product lines are less routine, less standardized and less predictable, the budgets may be generated but are subject to much revision and are of little use as a control benchmark. Contingency theory is essentially a theoretical perspective of organisational behaviour that emphasizes how contingent factors such as technology and the task environment affected the design and functioning of organisations.

For example, Thompson's Organisations in Action attempted to link task environment and technological contingencies to various organisational arrangements, focusing particularly on the different mechanisms of coordination which were appropriate for more complex, dynamic technologies and task environmental conditions. Perrow's theory of technology focused on the congruence between different types of technologies and organisational arrangements, emphasizing that more flexible, loosely-structured arrangements were more appropriate for organisations with non-routine technologies, while just the opposite type of organisational arrangements were more likely to fit routine technologies. Lawrence and Lorsch's Organisations and Environment developed, in a related manner the fit between organisational arrangements, including mechanisms of social control and coordination and environments of organisations.

The sociological tradition embedded in contingency theory developed during the 1960s through various "structural" approaches to organisational studies. These studies suggested that organisations' structures are contingent upon contextual factors which have been variously defined to include technology dimensions of task environment and organisational size. These contextual factors are hypothesized to influence dimensions of structure including the degree of formalization, specialization, differentiation and bureaucratization. Discussions of social control and coordination were sometimes elicited to explain some of the observed relationships among structural properties, but, by and large, were not of a central importance.

Not all functionalist theories of organisations developed during this period presented such static images of organisations. Contingency frameworks, for example, drew directly from these sociological functionalist theories of organisation structure, while also using March and Simon's organisational decision-making perspective. March and Simon developed a complex macro-perspective of organisations that viewed them as flexible, loosely-coupled systems in which human choice and voluntarism and hence unpredictability, were major characteristics.

The very essence of this decision-making perspective held that decision-makers in organisations are unlikely in most circumstances to have the information they need and want and therefore, that many if not most decisions are made under conditions of uncertainty. In short, the primary concern of the organisational decision-making perspective is for the treatment of the problematic "boundedly rational" person which, in turn, is the core legacy passed onto contingency theory as it seeks to provide insight as to this boundedly rational decision-maker in relation to the various contingent contextual factors (technology, environment, etc.) as suggested by the sociological structural perspectives.

March and Simon's depiction of the organisational decision-maker under such conditions of uncertainty was influenced by an earlier organisational theory tradition: the "human relations" approach to organisational analysis as developed in the work of Mayo and more concretely articulated by Barnard's seminal work, The Functions of the Executive. Perhaps the fundamental insight of this human relations approach in terms of its contribution to the organisational decision-making of March and Simon and eventually the contingency theory perspective, was that social and psychological attitudes were significant factors to be considered in the design of production processes and its related control systems. The human relations approach, in turn, extended the early scientific management work of Frederick W. Taylor was concerned with the rationalization of work in order to maximize efficiency and productivity and, hence, profits. Scientific management ushered in the monitoring of the individual worker, but ultimately contributed to the monitoring of work units within organisations as well.

The fascinating issue which the human relations perspective brought forth (as compared to earlier scientific management work) and pervades through contingency theory was the depiction of corporations existing in a tentative equilibrium which is inherently fragile, short lived and ever subject to a complex of personal, social, physical and biological destructive forces. As Miller and O'Leary argued, it was axiomatic for the human relations perspective that all organisations are founded on self-interest and a contractual principle; this is the core reason that they are so fragile. This characterization of the organisations founded on self-interest and contractual principles becomes a major thrust of the organisational decision-making perspective as articulated in the work of March and Simon but also in the related work of Simon and the later work of Cyert and March and March and Olsen.

In summary, March and Simon and the organisational decision-making perspective started with an image of human behaviour and individual decisionmaking that was considerably more complex than the human relations perspective that had preceded them, but nonetheless, reflected a common concern for the managing of the organisation. In turn, contingency theory blended the insights on human behaviour and individual decision-making as depicted in March and Simon's organisational decision-making perspective with the sociological functionalist concerns regarding the impact of such structural factors as environment, size, technology, etc., on organisational behaviour. Important in this lineage of work were issues of organisational control and coordination which are so germane to managerial accounting research. Traditional management accounting research which has been based in the contingency literature (as well as its predecessors – organisational decisionmaking, human relations and scientific management) suggests that managerial accounting information should reflect and promote rationality in decision-making. Accordingly, management accounting information used by managers serves as a quantitative expressions of organisational goals and are used to support rational decision-making.

The prescriptive character of managerial accounting information espoused by this traditional school of thought is essentially internal and downward and also prescriptive in character thus reflecting the strong scientific management heritage, albeit later becoming more complex when sociological and psychological as well as structural factors are brought in. Among the earliest managerial accounting research which adopted a contingency perspective was Hofstede's classic field work which found that economic, technological and sociological considerations have a significant impact on the way budgeting systems function, concluding that managers used budgetary information in difficult economic environments to pressure workers; but in more lucrative environments, the budget was used more in a problem solving mode. Golembiewski was also among the earliest to explicitly examine various aspects of organisational structure in relationship to the use of budgets.

In this tradition, Hayes investigated the appropriateness of management accounting systems for measuring the effectiveness of different departments in large industrial organisations, finding that contingency factors proved to be the major predictors of effectiveness for production departments. Extending this theme, Hirst examined external control factors such as environmental uncertainty and their impact on the reliance on accounting measures of performance. In applying contingency theories to control systems design, some researchers have sought to uncover direct relationships between these contextual factors and organisations' accounting and information systems.

Technology also was specifically introduced as a major explanatory variable of an effective accounting information system by Daft and MacIntosh. Others have articulated more subtle relationships between contextual factors, structural characteristics and control system design. For example, Gordon and Miller hypothesized that accounting information systems could be designed to cope with environmental uncertainty by incorporating more nonfinancial data, increasing reporting frequency and tailoring systems to local needs. Dent's focus was on the design of formal control systems in complex organisations, being concerned with the question of appropriate contingency principles underlying the design of such systems.

More recently, accounting researchers have sought to extend contingency arguments to embrace relationships between firms' strategies and the design of their control systems. For example, Kaplan reasoned that managerial accounting has served business inadequately; it has become overly simplistic, structured and misdirected. He urged a close scrutiny of organisational activity of successful organisations so that the managerial accounting systems adopted accurately reflect the complex conditions confronting contemporary organisations.

Merchant found contingent relationships between corporate context (size, product diversity and extent of decentralization) and the uses of budgeting information. Govindarajan found environmental uncertainty to be a major explanatory variable regarding the appropriateness of accounting data in evaluating the performance of business units. Govindarajan and Gupta extended the concern for contingency relationships between organisational control mechanisms and variables such as technology, environment and size, by exploring the utility of relating these contingency relationships to strategy, where the utility of a particular incentive bonus system is contingent upon the strategy of the focal strategic bonus unit. The work of Shank and Simons also are important research efforts which mobilized contingency principles in the examination of the use of managerial accounting systems and information in a strategic manner.

Reflecting concerns for the role of managerial accounting information in contemporary organisations, the work of McNair and Mosconi and McNair et al. also reflects an implicit contingency tradition, finding that changes in technologies are accompanied by changes in performance management systems. Furthermore, McNair's group found that actual costs have begun to replace standards in JIT environments because of the ability to trace costs more easily and because of the more simplified manufacturing process. On this point, Foster and Gupta provided a cross sectional comparison of manufacturing plants in an electronics firm, arguing that contingency variables (size and complexity of cost drivers) affect manufacturing overhead.

Patell's longitudinal study of JIT implementation and changes in cost accounting procedures also highlighted the importance of contingency structural factors in the coordination problems of many new manufacturing operations with regards to information for control and evaluation. The impact of structural factors is also apparent in the work of Banker et al. who found that firms that have implemented JIT or other teamwork programmes are more likely to provide manufacturing performance information to shop-floor workers.

A contingency theme underlies Young's work which raises the intriguing issue that power shifting can occur within the organisation as a result of the implementation of JIT. Here it is argued that workers are given much more power under JIT than management may realize (i.e., a workers' strike could cripple them) because of the tight coupling that takes place. Finally, Selto et al. provided a rather comprehensive contingency perspective of the adaptation of JIT manufacturing and a total quality control system (JIT/TQC system) when they considered JIT in relationship to classical contingency theory constructs, organisational structure, context and control to get some sense of the fit of these organisational variables and the JIT system. Drawing from Drazin and Van de Ven's review of the extensive contingency literature, Selto et al. found contingency theory to have intuitive appeal in understanding broad issues of management controls, but also argued that the extensive interaction of variables as well as continuous changes in organisations would make it difficult to apply contingency theory.

The influence of contingency theory and its precursor theoretical traditions on managerial accounting research, however, have been criticized for presenting a deterministic, ahistorical view of organisations which provides limited insight as to the mediating processes of organisations. Among the earlier critiques of the application of contingency theory in managerial accounting, Otley observed that reliance tended to be placed on a relatively few number of very general variables, task environment and structure, which, in turn, were used to explain organisation structure and design of managerial accounting systems.

He argued that these variables tended to be ill-defined and measured and were not comparable across earlier accounting studies, thus yielding fragmented results. Further, the proposal that the link between accounting systems design and organisational effectiveness was far from proven, Otley concluded that there remained a need to imbed accounting systems in the overall package of organisational control approaches, to develop more nuanced expressions of organisational effectiveness and in general to move to a more complex expression of the contingency framework. Also, he observed that many of the issues relating to the development of accounting systems and the relationships with the organisation's differentiated environment, were political as opposed to technical in nature and urged the application of a field study approach to examine these issues.

Interpretive Perspectives

By focusing on the management of complex relational networks and the exercise of coordination and control, contingency theory has adhered to the strong influence of the classical sociological functionalist perspectives at the cost of neglecting alternative sociological theories such as expressed in the work of Weber whose primary concern was with the source of formal structure: the legitimacy of rationalized formal structures. In contingency theory, legitimacy is given; assertions about bureaucratization such as the role of managerial accounting practices and information systems rest on the assumptions of norms of rationality.

When such norms do play causal roles in theories of bureaucratization, it is because they are thought to be built into modern societies and organisations as very general values, which are thought to facilitate formal organisation. But norms of rationality are not simply general values. They exist in much more specific and powerful ways in the rules, understandings and meanings attached to institutionalized social structures.

The causal importance of such institutions has been neglected. According to Meyer and Rowan: Formal structures are not only the result of their relational network in the social organisation... [t]he elements of rationalized formal structure are also deeply ingrained in and reflect, widespread understandings of social reality.... Such elements of formal structure are manifestations of powerful institutional rules which function as highly rationalized myths that are binding on particular organisations. Strands of this Weberian sociological tradition are embedded in March and

Simon's organisational decision-making model which provides a key contribution in its focus on the routine, taken-for-granted aspects of organisational life. Traces of a cognitive orientation in Weber's theory of bureaucracy – his emphasis on the role of calculable rules in reducing uncertainty and rationalizing power relations – are apparent in the richness of March and Simon's decisionmaking model where they urged a focus on understanding the initiation and preservation of power relationships on two fronts: (1) the power to set premises and define the norms and standards that shape and channel behaviour; and (2) the power to delimit appropriate models of bureaucratic structure and policy that go unquestioned for years. Weber's concern was to understand the dominance of organisations and their forms of rationality upon society's technical, economic and political forms of life. Weber reasoned that rationalization is concerned not only with the long-term process of social structure transformation, but simultaneously and more importantly, the perpetuation of existing power relations concealed in the advancement of rational imperatives. Thus, the critical issue is the politics of rationality itself.

This concern for the power and politics of rationality is inherent in other interpretive sociological work such as Berger and Luckmann's. The Social Construction of Reality, in which they reasoned that the central question for sociological theory is: How is it possible that subjective meanings become objective facts? Berger and Luckmann's argument is that social order is based fundamentally on a shared social reality which, in turn, is a human construction, being created in social interaction. The process by which actions become repeated over time and are assigned similar meanings by self and others is defined as institutionalization.

Further, Berger and Luckmann emphasized the importance of employing an historical approach, arguing that it is impossible to understand an institution adequately without an understanding of the historical processes in which it was produced. The result is the paradox "that man is capable of producing a world that he then experiences as something other than a human product".

Similarly, Garfinkel developed an approach to social investigation, ethnomethodology, which shifted the image of cognition from a rational, discursive, quasiscientific process to one that operates largely beneath the level of consciousness, a routine and conventional practical reason governed by rules that are recognized only when they are breached.

To this he added a perspective on interaction that casts doubts on the importance of normative or cognitive consensus. Here Garfinkel argued that action is largely scripted and justified, after the fact, by reference to a stock of culturally available legitimating accounts.

Critical Perspectives

Since the early 1980s an increasing number of researchers have begun to adopt diverse critical perspectives to explore and investigate the roles of accounting practices in society. These critical perspectives in accounting research are marked by a great deal of intellectual ferment evident in the different theoretical approaches and methodologies deployed and the wide range of topics and issues addressed. Accordingly, in the light of such heterogeneity and the constraints of space, our intent is to provide a flavour of these alternative accounting research agendas without claiming to be exhaustive.

Classifying these heterogeneous theoretical stances as "critical perspectives," in contrast to the functionalist and interpretative traditions explored above, can be justified by their singular attention to the interrelation between accounting and issues of conflict, domination and power. Despite the theoretical differences within the different strands of the critical perspectives regarding the manner and form in which to conceptualize power, they all avoid a consensus view of society that is the hallmark of both the functional and interpretive perspectives.

It may be argued that power, in both the functional and interpretive perspectives, is formulated as if it were a possession belonging to someone which he or she exercises for individual gain and further, that this power is diffused over society in a manner as to preclude the sustained and systematic negation of any individuals' preferences.

In sharp contrast, this individualist basis of power and ultimately consensus view of society is eschewed by the critical perspectives which attempt to deal explicitly with conflict, domination and power. For example, rather than treating various managerial accounting practices as a response to transaction costs considerations as in Johnson and Kaplan or agency cost considerations as in Christensen, they are treated as modes by which the extraction of labour from labourers is made possible and as methods by which the actions of individuals are made visible and susceptible to greater discipline and control. Accordingly, class conflict, the hegemony of elites and the power of experts and professionals are some of the elements that the critical perspectives systematically foreground (not all such analyses incorporate all of these emphases) in their attempt to understand accounting practices.

Despite the theoretical richness within the critical perspectives, we will confine our attention to two major research strands that have illuminated our understanding of managerial accounting. First, we will consider the labour process perspective which draws from the Marxist tradition and then we will examine the Foucaultian perspective which, as the name suggests, draws from the work of Michel Foucault. While both of these alternatives are critical in orientation, there are significant differences in the kinds of insights they offer and consequently, we will first describe their relevant theoretical infrastructure and then, tease out from extant accounting studies their implications for our understanding of managerial accounting.

The Foucaultian Perspective

Michel Foucault was both a philosopher and historian who used history to raise philosophical questions.6 A central motif that runs through his work and onewhich has also been productive for accounting scholarship is perhaps best described in his ownwords: "... the goal of my work during the last twenty years... has been to create a history of the different modes by which, in our culture, human beings are made subjects". To begin to unpack this seemingly innocuous statement let us consider the key word here – "subject" – in both the meanings that it admits: "subject to someone else by control and dependence and tied to his own identity by a conscience or self-knowledge.

Both meanings suggest a form of power which subjugates and makes subject to". While the first meaning is a relatively familiar one (hierarchical employment relations, prisoner-guard, parent-child etc.), the second hints at the radical and innovative nature of Foucault's thought. What is equally significant regarding the exercise of this power, is the interrelation between power and knowledge which Foucault signifies by the slash in the term "Power/ Knowledge."

Foucault argued that to properly grasp the conditions for the emergence of the "human sciences" – all those "sciences" that are concerned with describing, explaining, understanding, predicting and controlling human behaviour – one must understand its complicity with the historically unprecedented presence of a widespread and general control of human beings. Foucault argued that the "birth of the sciences of man" probably lies in the various written techniques (of notation, registration, columnar and tabular presentation, of measurement, classification etc.) by which individuals are turned into a "case." Transforming a human being into a "case" (patient, student, prisoner,worker) simultaneously homogenizes (by classifying as one within a series) and individualizes (by measuring the individual differences).

Implicit in such classification and measurement is the presence of normalizing judgments wherein the measurement of individual differences are made in regard to deviations from a norm (for example, students grades, standard cost, time and motion studies, budgets, benchmarks). According to Foucault, it was only by the late eighteenth century that this manner of describing, or more precisely, writing up individuals as cases became widespread and general.

It furthermore represented a reversal of historic proportions, as stated by Foucault: For a long time ordinary individuality – the everyday individuality of everybody – remained below the threshold of description. To be looked at, observed, described in detail, followed from day to day by an uninterrupted writing was a privilege.... The disciplinary methods reversed this relation, lowered the threshold of describable individuality and made of this description a means of control and a method of domination. Power, in this light, is not negative or repressive but rather positive and productive, because "it produces reality; it produces domains of objects and rituals of truth.

The individual and the knowledge gained of him belongs to this production". Accordingly, for Foucault power and knowledge are constitutive of, but not identical, to each other, since "between techniques of knowledge and strategies of power, there is no exteriority, even if they have specific roles and are linked together on the basis of their difference."

The scientific disciplines which generate our knowledge of human beings is thus also complicit in their disciplining, or as Foucault suggested, "The 'Enlightenment,' which discovered the liberties, also invented the disciplines." Foucault's work has, as already been stated, sparked much attention in the critical accounting tradition.

In a recent paper, Walsh and Stewart explored the history of managerial accounting practices from a rigourously Foucaultian perspective. In comparing "two assemblages of people making things," one from the 1700s and the other from the 1800s, they find support for one of Foucault's most provocative theses. By asserting that "the individual" was the result of disciplinary mechanisms, Foucault also is implying that prior to the late eighteenth century individuals could not be known and therefore controlled since they lay below the threshold of description.

Accordingly, what we consider axiomatic in managerial accounting – namely the linking of accounting calculations and measures to the work of individuals and groups – must not have been prevalent prior to the late eighteenth century. Indeed, this is precisely what Walsh and Stewart find when they compare the New Mills Woolen Manufactory with the New Lanark Cotton Factory.

Some features which characterized the manufactory of the late seventeenth century include: master-servant relationships between the managers and workers; customary rather than market driven rates of profit, calculations of selling prices and wages; use of the pillory and the prison as threats of retribution to workers for pilferage or shortages in piece work; bookkeeping as a "physical memory of the real proceedings of each day and each week to be certified by the masters".

While Walsh and Stewart focused on the early days of the factory system to provide some solid evidence and support for Foucault's thesis, Miller and O'Leary studied another time period to examine the rising popularity of standard costing and budgetary practices in the U.S. during the turn of the century. Again, using a Foucaultian perspective, they illuminated dimensions of that much studied period that have hitherto escaped attention.

Miller and O'Leary argued that such accounting practices as standard costing and budgeting should be understood "as a technology of government," where the latter is understood as "the ensemble of rationalities and technologies" by which "authorities attempt to act on the conduct of others, to shape their beliefs and behaviour in directions deemed desirable." Accordingly, the widespread emergence of standard costing and budgetary techniques by the 1930s in both the U.K. and the U.S. are seen as indicative of a new modality in the governance of economic life.

This emergence was linked not only to the scientific management movement associated with Taylor and the spread of industrial psychology but also to the concern with national efficiency in the U.K. and the "efficiency craze" in the U.S. The term efficiency was deployed in a wide range of contexts from individual performance on the factory floor to articulation the social responsibilities of the state in correcting the ills of society and subsumed under itself a host of financial and nonfinancial techniques. Linkages were also forged between the scientific management of industrial enterprises and the rational and orderly planning of society as a whole.

A host of such social sciences as public administration, engineering and sociology as well as a slew of such experts as accountants, urban planners and economists sought to "normalize and govern populations of individuals". It is this new modality of governing economic life that forms a context that is both constitutive of and constituted by the standard costing and budgetary practices of the early twentieth century.

To date, within accounting as well as organisational theory, a majority of work applying what has been termed Foucault's archeological and genealogical perspectives have had an historical perspective. However, the application of Foucault's insights into the functioning of modern societies is not limited to forays into the past. More pertinently, his work proves to be of continuing value as it is being profitably used to illuminate certain aspects of the contemporary uses and redefinitions of accounting.

For example, Preston studied the relative emergence of Diagnostic Related Groups (DRGs) as an "accounting technology based upon principles of cost control rather than cost reimbursement." Using a longitudinal study Preston showed how this practice of reimbursement cannot be exclusively related to a "a logic of economic incentives and rational economic behaviour."

Rather, a shifting complex of events, including Medicare and Medicaid, the private structure of American health care, the power of professional associations, changing public attitudes towards health care, is seen as being part of this transformation of accounting practices.

Accordingly, Preston, following Foucault, revealed the emergence of DRGs as being implicated in a wider and more general transformation in the "politics of health" which involves not only economic factors but more decisively, social and cultural ones as well.

On this same issue of contemporary application of Foucault's work, Rose argued for an interrelation between the mode of liberal democratic governance and the technology of quantification, numeracy and statistics.

Rose stated that "numbers have an unmistakable power in modern political culture" evident from opinion pools to the federal budget and the national income statistics. The role of accounting in this Foucaultian view, is that accounting, along with other various calculations, form the basis for democratic politics whose singular characteristic is "arms-length" management from a distance.

Consistent with the underpinnings of critical perspectives, the Foucaultian view situates management accounting in a wider political and social context. Specifically, in the Foucaultian approach, management accounting is considered as part of a larger historical trend through which people at large were subjected to a variety of disciplinary techniques.

Whereas in labour-process theory, management accounting appears within the context of a class-divided society to aid economic expropriation, the Foucaultian tradition reveals management accounting as an element of a general historical process by which people are made calculable and governable.

The Foucaultian view also considers management accounting as a social practice rather than a technique by examining the intricacies and richness in such social relations that are embedded in social patterns of interaction as language, discipline and intimacy, all cultural norms and forces which potentially impinge on the roles and nature of management accounting.

3

Cost Leadership Strategies

For years management scholars have debated whether firms can simultaneously pursue cost leadership and product differentiation. Students often ask the same question. One question that usually arises in discussions of product differentiation is: When a store advertises its low prices like Wal-Mart does, is that evidence of a cost leadership strategy or is that evidence of a product differentiation strategy? The answer is: Yes.

Most firms' strategies contain elements of both cost leadership and product differentiation. But, in the vast majority of firms one is clearly emphasized over the other. The relatively few firms that can effectively pursue both strategies are in an enviable position indeed. Anecdotal evidence suggests that firms that are able to simultaneously pursue both strategies started out with a sharp focus on one and in time were able to pursue the other as well. Conversely, anecdotal evidence also suggests that some firms that have tried to do both and failed weren't really achieving one before they started to pursue the other. Here are some quick examples from the discount retail market and the auto industry:

Wal-Mart started out with a sharp focus on cost leadership. This strategy allowed them to gain market share and become very profitable. In time, the firm could afford to advertise heavily to convince customers that they had the low price. Always. This heavy advertising is indicative of a product differentiation strategy. It is also interesting to note that local store managers, although obligated to follow fairly strict guidelines, are able to carry items of local interest that are not part of the national buying program.

Toyota developed a manufacturing system that drove costs to a minimum. Toyota recognized that they could achieve low manufacturing costs and very high quality simultaneously with their system. Most American consumers initially viewed Toyota as a low cost alternative to higher priced American cars. In time, Toyota began to differentiate its products on quality. Its Lexus line is very much a differentiated product that is manufactured at a very competitive cost among luxury car makers.

Mercedes developed a strong reputation for high quality cars. For many years, cost was not a critical issue for Mercedes. The introduction of car lines like the Lexus and the rising popularity of SUVs has forced Mercedes to focus more on cost. In other words, Mercedes is being forced to be concerned about cost. It remains to be seen if Mercedes will become competitive on cost or if Mercedes will further differentiate its cars on quality. Some industry analysts worry that Mercedes may hurt its reputation for quality if it tries to focus on cost too much.

Ford very successfully introduced the Taurus as described above. However, in 1996 Ford tried to move the Taurus up market. Other car makers had imitated many of the Taurus' most distinguishing features. Ford tried to differentiate the Taurus with even more 'rounding' of the body. The sticker price was raised about $2,500. This attempt to differentiate the Taurus was a failure. Many customers turned to the Toyota Camry and the Honda Accord. By 1996 the Taurus wasn't a cost leader and it wasn't highly differentiated. It seems to have become stuck in the middle.

K-Mart tried to differentiate itself by moving upscale in the mid-1990s. Having realized it couldn't compete with Wal-Mart on price, K-Mart seems to have decided to adopt a level of differentiation. Celebrities such as Kathy Ireland and Martha Stewart were used to try to generate more sales in clothing and household goods, respectively. Stores were remodeled.

Many were converted to "Big K" stores. Several years of financial performance, including a bankruptcy, suggest that this attempt at differentiation did not work. K-Mart seems to have tried to abandon cost leadership in favour of differentiation. In the end, it seems to have become stuck in the middle.

International Implementation of Product Differentiation

When a firm contemplates entering an international market, one of the main questions to be answered is: How much must the products and/or services of the focal firm be modified for the foreign market?

The answer to this question depends primarily on two issues. First, the degree of necessary modification depends on whether the product or service in question lends itself to standardization across national boundaries. Second, the degree of modification depends on how similar the tastes and preferences of the foreign customers are to the tastes and preferences of customers in the firm's domestic market.

If a global standard exists for a product or service, then local tastes and preferences are not a major concern. This is often the case with electronics and high technology products. Such a situation calls for what is known as a global international expansion strategy. Firms using this strategy rely on centralized decision making and strive for efficiencies from being able to produce at global volumes. The business functions remain centralized at headquarters. In many ways, the logic of the global strategy is similar to the cost leadership strategy. Historically, Japanese companies like Sony and Hitachi have been successful with global strategies.

On the other hand, if a product does not have a global standard and there are significant differences in local tastes and preferences from country to country, then what is known as a multi-domestic strategy is used. This strategy consists of replicating business functions in multiple countries as needed. For example, a firm using this strategy might establish marketing and finance organizations in each country where it operates. The implementation of this strategy is similar to the implementation of a product differentiation strategy in that managers and employees are given great latitude in responding to local tastes and preferences. Historically, European companies like Phillips, Siemens, and Unilever have been successful using the multi-domestic strategy. A hybrid of these two approaches, known as the transnational strategy, has been suggested as a way to exploit the benefits of both the global and multi-domestic strategies. The basic idea behind this strategy is that the local knowledge gleaned from *multi-domestic* operations can be transferred around the world through a *global* network of coordinated reporting relationships.

Non-price Competition

Non-price competition is a marketing strategy "in which one firm tries to distinguish its product or service from competing products on the basis of attributes like design and workmanship" (McConnell-Brue, 2002, p. 437-438). The firm can also distinguish its product offering through quality of service, extensive distribution, customer focus, or any other sustainable competitive advantage other than price. It can be contrasted with price competition, which is where a company tries to distinguish its product or service from competing products on the basis of low price. Non-price competition typically involves promotional expenditures, (such as advertising, selling staff, sales promotions, coupons, special orders, or free gifts), marketing research, new product development, and brand management costs. Firms will engage in non-price competition, in spite of the additional costs involved, because it is usually more profitable than selling for a lower price, and avoids the risk of a price war. Although any company can use a non-price competition strategy, it is most common among oligopolies and monopolistic competition, because firms can be extremely competitive.

Marketing

Marketing is the process associated with promoting for sale goods or services. It is considered a "social and managerial process by which individuals and groups obtain what they need and want through creating and exchanging products and values with others." It is an integrated process through which companies create value for customers and build strong customer relationships in order to capture value from customers in return. Marketing is used to create the customer, to keep the customer and to satisfy the customer. With the customer as the focus of its activities, it can be concluded that *marketing management* is one of the major components of business management. The evolution of marketing was caused due to mature markets and overcapacities in the last decades. Companies then shifted the focus from production more to the customer in order to stay profitable. The term *marketing concept* holds that achieving organisational goals depends on knowing the needs and wants of target markets and delivering the desired satisfactions. It proposes that in order to satisfy its organizational objectives, an organization should anticipate the needs and wants of consumers and satisfy these more effectively than competitors.

Organizational Orientation

In this sense, a firm's marketing department is often seen as of prime importance within the functional level of an organization. Information from an organization's marketing department would be used to guide the actions of other departments within the firm. As an example, a marketing department could ascertain (via marketing research) that consumers desired a new type of product, or a new usage for an existing product. With this in mind, the marketing department would inform the R&D department to create a prototype of a product/service based on consumers' new desires. The production department would then start to manufacture the product, while the marketing department would focus on the promotion, distribution, pricing, etc. of the product. Additionally, a firm's finance department would be consulted, with respect to securing appropriate funding for the development, production and promotion of the product.

Inter-departmental conflicts may occur, should a firm adhere to the marketing orientation. Production may oppose the installation, support and servicing of new capital stock, which may be needed to manufacture a new product. Finance may oppose the required capital expenditure, since it could undermine a healthy cash flow for the organization.

Mutually Beneficial Exchange

A further marketing orientation is the focus on a *mutually beneficial exchange*. In a transaction in the market economy, a firm gains revenue, which thus leads to more profits/market share/sales. A consumer on the other hand gains the satisfaction of a need/want, utility, reliability and value for money from the purchase of a product or service. As no one has to buy goods from any one supplier in the market economy, firms must entice consumers to buy goods with contemporary marketing ideals.

Herd Behaviour

Herd behaviour in marketing is used to explain the dependencies of customers' mutual behaviour. *The Economist* reported a recent conference in Rome on the subject of the simulation of adaptive human behaviour. It shared mechanisms to increase impulse buying and get people "to buy more by playing on the herd instinct."

The basic idea is that people will buy more of products that are seen to be popular, and several feedback mechanisms to get product popularity information to consumers are mentioned, including smart card technology and the use of Radio Frequency Identification Tag technology.

A "swarm-moves" model was introduced by a Florida Institute of Technology researcher, which is appealing to supermarkets because it can "increase sales without the need to give people discounts." Other recent studies on the "power of social influence" include an "artificial music market in which some 14,000 people downloaded previously unknown songs" (Columbia University, New York); a Japanese chain of convenience stores which orders its products based on "sales data from department stores and research companies;" a Massachusetts company exploiting knowledge of social networking to improve sales; and online retailers who are increasingly informing consumers about "which products are popular with like-minded consumers" (e.g., Amazon, eBay).

Further Orientations

- An emerging area of study and practice concerns *internal marketing*, or how employees are trained and managed to deliver the brand in a way that positively impacts the acquisition and retention of customers, see also *employer branding.*
- *Diffusion of innovations* research explores how and why people adopt new products, services and ideas.
- With consumers' eroding attention span and willingness to give time to advertising messages, marketers are turning to forms of *permission marketing* such as *branded content, custom media* and *reality marketing.*

Marketing Research

Marketing research involves conducting research to support marketing activities, and the statistical interpretation of data into information. This information is then used by managers to plan marketing activities, gauge the nature of a firm's marketing environment, attain information from suppliers, etc.

Marketing researchers use statistical methods (such as quantitative research, qualitative research, hypothesis tests, Chi-squared tests, linear regression, correlation co-efficients, frequency distributions, Poisson and Binomial distributions, etc.) to interpret their findings and convert data into information. The marketing research process spans a number of stages including the definition of a problem, development of a research plan, collecting and interpretation of data and disseminating information formally in form of a report.

A distinction should be made between *marketing research* and *market research.* Market research pertains to research in a given market. As an example, a firm may conduct research in a target market, after selecting a suitable market segment. In contrast, marketing research relates to all research conducted within marketing. Thus, market research is a subset of marketing research.

Marketing Environment

The term *marketing environment* relates to all of the factors (whether internal, external, direct or indirect) that affect a firm's marketing decision-making or planning and is subject of the marketing research. A firm's marketing environment consists of two main areas, which are:

Macro Environment

On the macro environment a firm holds only little control. It consists of a variety of external factors that manifest on a large (or macro) scale. These are typically economic, social, political or technological phenomena. A common method of assessing a firm's macro-environment is via a PESTLE (Political, Economic, Social, Technological, Legal, Ecological) analysis. Within a PESTLE analysis, a firm would analyse national political issues, culture and climate, key macroeconomic conditions, health and indicators (such as economic growth, inflation, unemployment, etc.), social trends/attitudes, and the nature of technology's impact on its society and the business processes within the society.

Marketing Communications

Marketing communications is defined by actions a firm takes to communicate with end-users, consumers and external parties. A simple definition of marketing communication is *"the means by which a supplier of goods, services, values and/or ideas represent themselves to their target audience with the goal of stimulating dialog leading to better commercial or other relationships". Marcoms* is a frequently used short-form for marketing communications. Marketing communications can be seen as a part of the promotional mix, as the exact nature of how to apply marketing communications depends on the nature of the product in question.

Accordingly, a given product would require a unique communications mix, in order to convey successfully information to consumers. Some products may require a stronger emphasis on personal sales, while others may need more focus on advertising. The process in which the differing modes of marketing communications are complemented and synthesised is called *integrated marketing communications (IMC).* It is used in order to create a single and coherent marketing communications process. As an example, a firm can advertise the existence of a sales promotion, via a newspaper, magazine, TV, radio, etc. The same promotion can also be communicated via direct marketing, or personal selling. The aim of IMC is to lessen confusion among a product's target market, and to lessen cost for the firm. Several different subsets of marketing communications can be distinguished.

Personal Selling

Oral presentation given by a salesperson who approaches individuals or a group of potential customers. Personal selling is often used in business to business (,i.e. "B2B") settings, in addition to business to consumer (,i.e. "B2C") scenarios in which a personal and face to face medium is required for the communication of the product. In B2B situations, personal selling is preferred if the product is technical in nature. Personal selling can compose of the use of presentations, in order to convey the benefits of a firm's good/service. In B2C settings, personal selling is utilised if the product requires to be tailored to the unique needs of an individual. Examples of this include car (and other vehicle) sales, financial services (such as insurance or investment), etc. Personal selling involves the following points:

- Live, interactive relationship
- Personal interest
- Attention and response
- Interesting presentation
- Clear and thorough.

Sales Promotion

Short-term incentives to encourage buying of products.

- Instant appeal
- Anxiety to sell.

An example is coupons or a sale. People are given an incentive to buy, but this does not build customer loyalty or encourage future repeat buys. A major drawback of sales promotion is that it is easily copied by competition. It cannot be used as a sustainable source of differentiation. Sales promotions are typically used to heighten sales/ revenue, especially if a firm holds dead/excess stock, or if the market for a product has matured.

Public Relations

Public Relations (or PR, as an acronym) is the use of media tools by a firm in order to promote goodwill from an organization to a target market segment, or other consumers of a firm's good/service. PR stems from the fact that a firm cannot seek to antagonize or inflame its market base, due to incurring a lessened demand for its good/ service. Organizations undertake PR in order to assure consumers, and to forestall negative perceptions towards it. PR can span:

- Interviews
- Speeches/Presentations
- Corporate literature, such as financial statements, brochures, etc.

Publicity

Publicity involves attaining space in media, without having to pay directly for such coverage. As an example, an organization may have the launch of a new product covered by a newspaper or TV news segment. This benefits the firm in question since it is making consumers aware of its product, without necessarily paying a newspaper or television station to cover the event.

Advertising

Advertising occurs when a firm directly pays a media channel to publicize its product. Common examples of this include TV and radio adverts, billboards, branding, sponsorship, etc.

Direct Marketing

Direct marketing is a process where a firm uses communication channels to attain and retain consumers for its product. It is a comparatively new mode of marketing communications (when compared with forms such as advertising, sales promotions, personal selling, etc.) Direct marketing involves carefully seeking out persons within a target market, and communicating to them about the nature of a product. This process is signified by brochures sent via the mail, e-mails from companies, etc. It can also constitute the use of telemarketing, in order to communicate with a target market.

International Marketing

International marketing can be defined as the application of marketing strategies, planning and activities to external or foreign markets. International marketing is of consequence to firms which operate in countries and territories other than their home country or the country in which they are registered in and have their head office. The factors influencing international marketing are culture, political and legal factors, a country's level of economic development and the mode of involvement in foreign markets. The reasons why a firm would engage in international markets are numerous, including:

- Maturity within domestic markets
- To increase general market share, sales or revenue.

Culture

Social norms, attitudes towards buying foreign goods, and the working practices of foreign markets are all cultural factors when opting to invest in foreign markets. Social norms affect business practices, since social norms are one factor in the demand for a product. A company marketing pork would experience less sales in an Islamic country, than it would in China (which is the world's largest consumer of pork). In Western societies, sexuality and sexual topics are often used in marketing communications (such as advertising, for instance). However, in a comparatively more conservative society (such as India for instance) social attitudes may shun the use of sexual topics to advertise products.

Political and Legal Factors

The following political/legal factors are of bearing in international marketing:

- Government attitude to business
- The level of governmental regulations, red-tape and bureaucracy
- Monetary regulations
- Political stability.

Not all governments are as open to foreign investment as others, nor are all governments equally favourable to business. Typically, a firm may opt to invest in an economy in which the government is more inclined to support business activity in a country. In other words, the "business-friendliness" of a foreign government is paramount in this instance.

Additionally, some economies are more "liberal" and less regulated, by comparison to other economies. Excessive regulations can be a hindrance on a firm, since they contribute to additional costs to a firm. Conversely, regulations can aid in assisting firms, by easing the path of doing business. A firm seeking to invest in foreign markets must gauge the regulatory arrangement of the economy it is looking to invest in. Monetary regulations, akin to the above points, can hinder the ability to do business. A high level of monetary regulations can hamper foreign investment within an economy. Lastly, the political stability of a country is also a key factor in foreign investment decisions. Nation-states experiencing continual coup-d'etat can appear unattractive to invest in, since the continual changes in political system can compound the inherent risk in investing.

Typically, a firm would opt to invest in a country which had a stable mode of government, in which handovers of power were peaceful and non-violent. Even if a country is not a liberal democracy, the level of political stability within a country may supersede the political system (or, more accurately, the perceived immorality of a government's policies/constitutional structure) of a given nation-state.

Level of Economic Development

The level of economic development of an economy can affect foreign investment decisions. Within the field of developmental economics, differing modes of economic development can be identified. These are:

- Developing economy
- Newly-Industrialised country
- Industrialised country (also known as a developed country, advanced economy or first world economy).

A developing economy has a comparatively low general living standard (as defined by material lifestyle/level of material possession). Moreover, a developing economy may also be at subsistence level, or possess a large share of its Gross Domestic Product in primary industries. Accordingly, a developing country would not be a profitable market for high-end consumer goods, or fast-moving consumer goods commonly found in developed/advanced economies. Exports of machinery (related to the extraction and processing of raw materials) may be viable for a developing economy, due to primary industries possessing a large share of national income.

A newly-industrialised economy is an economy which has experienced high recent economic growth, and thus has experienced a rise in general living standards. Coupled with the rapid economic growth, the emergence of a middle class leads to the development of a consumerist culture in the society. A newly-industrialised economy would consequently possess a small general demand for high-end consumer goods, but not to the extent of an advanced economy. A newly-industralised economy may export manufactured goods to other countries, and often possess secondary sector industries as a high percentage of its economic output. An industrialised economy is typically identified via a high Gross Domestic Product per capita, a high United Nations Human Development Index rating and a high level of tertiary/quaternary/quinary sector industries in the context of its national income. Thus, the high general living standard denotes the highest generalised demand for goods and services within all modes of economic development. Commonly, developed/advanced economies are high exporters of high-tech manufactured goods, as well as service sector products (such as financial services, for instance).

Green Marketing

Green marketing can be defined as the marketing of products which are environmentally sound. The notion of green marketing is a comparatively new one within general marketing thought, as it has chiefly grown in acceptance since the 1990s. Nonetheless, as a contemporary branch of marketing thought, it can be seen as one of the fastest growing areas of marketing principles.

The rationale for the devising and emergence of green marketing is thus:

- A higher quantity of persons willing and able to buy green products.
- Heightened awareness among consumers, concerning the potentially negative aspects of global climate change.

Green marketers thus target persons who are more environmentally conscious. The segmentation and market research processes of numerous firms denote that the target market for green products has grown widely in numerous years. Accordingly, green marketers are willing to supply what persons are willing and able to buy. It can also be stated that green products are often more expensive than "non-green" products, due perhaps to higher production costs. Nevertheless, green consumers are typically willing to pay higher prices, as a means of doing their part to safeguard the environment of the planet Earth.

Some drawbacks of green marketing are thus:

- The ideal of "green washing"
- Disputes and contention surrounding the exact meaning of a green product

Green washing pertains to when a firm misleadingly produces a product, with ostensible green characteristics, which is not actually environmentally sound. In addition to evident ethical issues concerning deceit, such conduct can undermine an organisation's drive to be deemed a "green" company. Accordingly, a firm must be sincere in its efforts to be environmentally sound, regarding its environmental practices and policies. Moreover, the extent and nature of a green product can be a moot point. To some, a product must be wholly green to be viewed as green. To others, a product may only possess a reduction in environmentally harmful inputs to be worthy of being labelled green. Nonetheless, a firm can enhance its green marketing efforts if it persuades consumers that the purchase of green products can enhance environmental protection.

Buying Behaviour

A marketing firm, in the course of its operations, must ascertain the nature of buying behaviour, if it is to market properly its product. In order to entice and persuade a consumer to buy a product, the psychological/behavioural process of how a given product is purchased. Buying behaviour consists of two prime strands, namely being consumer (B2C) behaviour and organisational/industrial behaviour (B2B).

B2C Buying Behaviour

This mode of behaviour concerns consumers, in the purchase of a given product. The B2C buying process is as thus:

- Need/want recognition
- Information search
- Search for alternatives (to satisfy need/want)
- Purchase decision
- Post-purchase evaluation.

As an example, if one pictures a pair of sneakers, the desire for a pair of sneakers would be followed by an information search on available types/brands. This may include perusing media outlets, but most commonly consists of information gathered from family and friends. If the information search is insufficient, the consumer may search for alternative means to satisfy the need/want. In this case, this may be buying leather shoes, sandals, etc. The purchase decision is then made, in which the consumer actually buys the product.

Following this stage, a post-purchase evaluation is often conducted, comprising an appraisal of the value/utility brought by the purchase of the sneakers. If the value/utility is high, then a repeat purchase may be bought. This could then develop into consumer loyalty, for the firm producing the pair of sneakers.

B2B buying Behaviour

B2B buying behaviour relates to organisational/industrial buying behaviour. B2C and B2B behaviour are not exact, as similarities and differences exist. Some of the key differences are listed below:

- Consumer behaviour
- Low in monetary value
- Low in volume/mass
- Swift purchase
- Transaction marketing-based
- Single buying instances
- Number of consumer is higher
- Individual/market-based demand
- Organisational behaviour
- High in monetary value
- High in volume/mass
- Lengthy purchase process
- Relationship marketing-based
- Multiple buying instances
- Number of consumers is lesser
- Demand is consumer derived (in that firms purchase goods to ultimately meet consumer demand) .

The organisational buying process is thush:

- Problem recognition
- Need description
- Product specification
- Supplier search
- Proposal solicitation
- Supplier selection
- Order routine specification
- Supplier performance review.

In a straight rebuy, the fourth, fifth and sixth stages are omitted. In a modified rebuy scenario, the fifth and sixth stages are precluded. In a new buy, all aforementioned stages are conducted.

The Decision Making Unit (DMU)

The DMU, in other terms, can be labelled as the Purchasing or Procurement departments of an organisation Accordingly, it is responsible for the purchasing of organisational items and assets. The persons comprising a DMU are as thus:

- Gatekeepers
- Users
- Buyers
- Decision Makers
- Influencers
- Initiators.

Areas of Marketing Specialization

- Agricultural marketing
- Article marketing
- Cause marketing
- Communal marketing
- Business marketing
- Database marketing
- Digital marketing
- Direct marketing
- Engagement marketing
- Ethical marketing
- Evangelism marketing
- Experiential marketing Global marketing
- Guerrilla marketing
- Integrated marketing
- International marketing
- Internet marketing
- Industrial marketing
- Macromarketing
- Mobile marketing
- Multichannel marketing
- Permission marketing
- Political marketing

- Product marketing
- Proximity marketing
- Public marketing
- Reality marketing
- Referral marketing
- Relationship marketing
- Reverse marketing
- Search engine marketing
- Shopper marketing
- Social media marketing
- Trade marketing
- Value-based marketing
- Wholesale marketing.

Market Segment

A market segment is a group of people or organizations sharing one or more characteristics that cause them to have similar product and/or service needs. A true market segment meets all of the following criteria: it is distinct from other segments (different segments have different needs), it is homogeneous within the segment (exhibits common needs); it responds similarly to a market stimulus, and it can be reached by a market intervention. The term is also used when consumers with identical product and/or service needs are divided up into groups so they can be charged different amounts. These can broadly be viewed as 'positive' and 'negative' applications of the same idea, splitting up the market into smaller groups.

"Positive" Market Segmentation

Market segmenting is dividing market into groups of individual with similar wants or needs that a company divides the market into distinct groups who have distinct needs, wants, behaviour or who might want different products & services.

Broadly, markets can be divided according to a number of general criteria, such as by industry or public versus private although industrial market segmentation is quite different from consumer market segmentation, both have similar objectives. All of these methods of segmentation are merely proxies for true segments, which don't always fit into convenient demographic boundaries. Consumer-based market segmentation can be performed on a *product specific* basis, to provide a close match between specific products and individuals.

However, a number of generic market segment systems also exist, e.g. the Nielsen Claritas PRIZM system provides a broad segmentation of the population of the United States based on the statistical analysis of household and geodemographic data. The process of segmentation is distinct from targeting (choosing which segments to address) and positioning (designing an appropriate marketing mix for each segment).

The overall intent is to identify groups of similar customers and potential customers; to prioritize the groups to address; to understand their behaviour; and to respond with appropriate marketing strategies that satisfy the different preferences of each chosen segment. Revenues are thus improved. Improved segmentation can lead to significantly improved marketing effectiveness. Distinct segments can have different industry structures and thus have higher or lower attractiveness (Michael Porter). With the right segmentation, the right lists can be purchased, advertising results can be improved and customer satisfaction can be increased leading to better reputation.

Positioning

Once a market segment has been identified (via segmentation), and targeted (in which the viability of servicing the market is determined), the segment is then subject to positioning. Positioning involves ascertaining how a product is perceived in the minds of consumers.

This part of the segmentation process consists of drawing up a perceptual map, which highlights rival goods within one's industry according to perceived quality and price. After the perceptual map has been devised, a firm would consider the marketing communications mix best suited to the product in question.

Top-Down and Bottom-Up

George S. Day (1980) describes model of segmentation as the top-down approach: *You start with the total population and divide it into segments.* He also identified an alternative model which he called the bottom-up approach. In this approach, you start with a single customer and build on that profile. This typically requires the use of customer relationship management software or a database of some kind. Profiles of existing customers are created and analysed. Various demographic, behavioural, and psychographic patterns are built up using techniques such as cluster analysis.

This process is sometimes called database marketing or micro-marketing. Its use is most appropriate in highly fragmented markets. McKenna (1988) claims that this approach treats every customer as a "micromajority". Pine (1993) used the bottom-up approach in what he called "segment of one marketing". Through this process mass customization is possible.

Creating a market segment will allow you to set yourself apart from other competitors.

Product Management

Product management is an organizational lifecycle function within a company dealing with the planning or marketing of a product or products at all stages of the product lifecycle.

Product management (inbound focused) and product marketing (outbound focused) are different yet complementary efforts with the objective of maximizing sales revenues, market share, and profit margins. The role of product management spans many activities from strategic to tactical and varies based on the organizational structure of the company.

Product management can be a function separate on its own or a member of marketing or engineering. While involved with the entire product lifecycle, product management's main focus is on driving new product development. According to the Product Development and Management Association (PDMA), superior and differentiated new products-ones that deliver unique benefits and superior value to the customer-is the number one driver of success and product profitability.

Aspects of Product Management

Depending on the company size and history, product management has a variety of functions and roles. Sometimes there is a product manager, and sometimes the role of product manager is held by others. Frequently there is Profit and Loss (P&L) responsibility as a key metric for evaluating product manager performance. In some companies, the product management function is the hub of many other activities around the product.

In others, it is one of many things that need to happen to bring a product to market. Product management often serves an inter-disciplinary role, bridging gaps within the company between teams of different expertise, most notably between engineering-oriented teams and business-oriented teams. For example product managers often translate business objectives set for a product by Marketing or Sales into engineering requirements. Conversely they may work to explain the capabilities and limitations of the finished product back to Marketing and Sales.

Brand

A brand is a name or trademark connected with a product or producer. Brands have become increasingly important components of culture and the economy, now being described as "cultural accessories and personal philosophies".

Concepts

Some people distinguish the psychological aspect of a brand from the experiential aspect. The experiential aspect consists of the sum of all points of contact with the brand and is known as the brand experience.

The psychological aspect, sometimes referred to as the brand image, is a symbolic construct created within the minds of people and consists of all the information and expectations associated with a product or service.

People engaged in branding seek to develop or align the expectations behind the brand experience, creating the impression that a brand associated with a product or service has certain qualities or characteristics that make it special or unique. A brand is therefore one of the most valuable elements in an advertising theme, as it demonstrates what the brand owner is able to offer in the marketplace. The art of creating and maintaining a brand is called brand management. Orientation of the whole organisation towards its brand is called integrated marketing.

Careful brand management, supported by a cleverly crafted advertising campaign, can be highly successful in convincing consumers to pay remarkably high prices for products which are inherently extremely cheap to make. This concept, known as creating value, essentially consists of manipulating the projected image of the product so that the consumer sees the product as being worth the amount that the advertiser wants him/her to see, rather than a more logical valuation that comprises an aggregate of the cost of raw materials, plus the cost of manufacture, plus the cost of distribution. Modern value-creation branding-and-advertising campaigns are highly successful at inducing consumers to pay, for example, 50 dollars for a T-shirt that cost a mere 50 cents to make, or 5 dollars for a box of breakfast cereal that contains a few cents' worth of wheat. Brands should be seen as more than the difference between the actual cost of a product and its selling price-they represent the sum of all valuable qualities of a product to the consumer. There are many intangibles involved in business, intangibles left wholly from the income statement and balance sheet which determine how a business is perceived.

The learned skill of a knowledge worker, the type of metal working, the type of stitch: all may be without an 'accounting cost' but for those who truly know the product, for it is these people the company should wish to find and keep, the difference is incomparable. Failing to recognize these assets that a business, any business, can create and maintain will set an enterprise at a serious disadvantage.

A brand which is widely known in the marketplace acquires brand recognition. When brand recognition builds up to a point where a brand enjoys a critical mass of positive sentiment in the marketplace, it is said to have achieved brand franchise. One goal in brand recognition is the identification of a brand without the name of the company present. For example, Disney has been successful at branding with their particular script font (originally created for Walt Disney's "signature" logo), which it used in the logo for go.com.

Consumers may look on branding as an important value added aspect of products or services, as it often serves to denote a certain attractive quality or characteristic. From the perspective of brand owners, branded products or services also command higher prices. Where two products resemble each other, but one of the products has no associated branding (such as a generic, store-branded product), people may often select the more expensive branded product on the basis of the quality of the brand or the reputation of the brand owner.

Brand Name

The brand name is quite often used interchangeably within "brand", although it is more correctly used to specifically denote written or spoken linguistic elements of any product. In this context a "brand name" constitutes a type of trademark, if the brand name exclusively identifies the brand owner as the commercial source of products or services. A brand owner may seek to protect proprietary rights in relation to a brand name through trademark registration. Advertising spokespersons have also become part of some brands, for example: Mr. Whipple of Charmin toilet tissue and Tony the Tiger of Kellogg's.

Brand names will fall into one of three spectrums of use- Descriptive, Associative or Freestanding.

Descriptive brand names assist in describing the distinguishable selling point(s) of the product to the customer (eg Snap, Crackle and Pop or Bitter Lemon). Associative brand names provide the customer with an associated word for what the product promises to do or be (e.g. Walkman, Sensodyne or Natrel). Finally, Freestanding brand names have no links or ties to either descriptions or associations of use. (eg Mars Bar or Pantene)

The act of associating a product or service with a brand has become part of pop culture. Most products have some kind of brand identity, from common table salt to designer jeans. A brandnomer is a brand name that has colloquially become a generic term for a product or service, such as Band-Aid or Kleenex, which are often used to describe any kind of adhesive bandage or any kind of facial tissue respectively.

Country of Origin

Country of origin (often abbreviated to COO), is the country of manufacture, production, or growth where an article or product comes from. There are differing rules of origin under various national laws and international treaties.

Country of Origin as a Marketing Strategy

From a marketing perspective, "country of origin" gives a way to differentiate the product from the competitors.

Research shows (Josiassen and Harzing, 2008, European Management Review) that the country of origin has an impact on the willingness to buy a product, and studies (Shimp and Sharma, 1987, Journal of International Business Studies) have shown that consumers may tend to have a relative preference to products from their own country or may tend to have a relative preference for or aversion to certain products that originate from certain countries. The effect of country of origin is however debated (Usunier, 2006, European Management Review) as studies (e.g. Chao, 2001, Journal of Advertising) have shown that the origin of design (for instance Apple computers or Nike shoes) can be more important than the country of origin.

Non-specific Country of Origin Labeling

While many products made within the European Union carry the country of origin label or marking "Made in EU" or "Made in EC", some non-EU manufacturers in Europe and some others outside the continent of Europe use vaguer markings, such as "Made in Europe" (made anywhere else in Europe, but not in the EU or EC; this may constitute any country geographically close to Europe or the EU that also wishes to be in) or "Made for Europe" (made anywhere else in the world, but not in Europe or the European Union).

These practices could lead to consumer deception, whereby a buyer not proficient in English may come to believe from looking at the label that the non-EU product he is interested in is made in the EU.

Country of Origin Contextual Importance for Consumer Choice

Consumers tend to utilize the country of origin more when they are less involved and less familiar (Josiassen et al., 2008, International Marketing Review). Consumers further tend to use country of origin more as a decision tool when they consider luxury products (Piron, 2000, Journal of Consumer Marketing).

Country of Origin in International Trade

When shipping products from one country to another, the products may have to be marked with country of origin, and the country of origin will generally be required to be indicated in the export/import documents and governmental submissions.

Country of origin will affect its admissibility, the rate of duty, its entitlement to special duty or trade preference programs, antidumping, and government procurement. Today, many products are an outcome of a large number of parts and pieces that come from many different countries, and that may then be assembled together in a third country. In these cases, it's hard to know exactly what is the country of origin, and different rules apply as to how to determine their "correct" country of origin.

Generally, articles only change their country of origin if the work or material added to an article in the second country constitutes a substantial transformation, or, the article changes its name, tariff code, character or use (for instance from wheel to car). Value added in the second country may also be an issue.

Country of Origin in Movie and Television Production

The International Federation of Film Archives defines the country of origin as the country of the principal offices of the production company or individual by whom the moving image work was made. No consistent reference or definition exists.

Sources include the item itself, accompanying material (e.g. scripts, shot lists, production records, publicity material, inventory lists, synopses etc.), the container (if not an integral part of the piece), or other sources (standard and special moving image reference tools). In law, definitions of "country of origin" and related terms are defined differently in different jurisdictions.

Europe, Canada, and the United States have different definitions for a variety of reasons, including tax treatment, advertising regulations, distribution; even within the European Union, different member states have different legislation. As a result, an individual work can have multiple countries as its "country of origin", and may even have different countries recognized as originating places for the purpose of different legal jurisdictions. Under copyright law in the United States and other signatories of the Berne Convention, "country of origin" is defined in an inclusive way to ensure the protection of intellectual rights of writers and creators.

Marketing Plan

A marketing plan is a written document that details the necessary actions to achieve one or more marketing objectives. It can be for a product or service, a brand, or a product line. Marketing plans cover between one and five years. A marketing plan may be part of an overall business plan. Solid marketing strategy is the foundation of a well-written marketing plan. While a marketing plan contains a list of actions, a marketing plan without a sound strategic foundation is of little use.

The Marketing Planning Process

The marketing process model based on the publications of Philip Kotler. It consists of 5 steps, beginning with the market & environment research. After fixing the targets and setting the strategies, they will be realised by the marketing mix in step 4. The last step in the process is the marketing controlling.

In most organizations, "strategic planning" is an annual process, typically covering just the year ahead. Occasionally, a few organizations may look at a practical plan which stretches three or more years ahead.

To be most effective, the plan has to be formalized, usually in written form, as a formal "marketing plan." The essence of the process is that it moves from the general to the specific; from the overall objectives of the organization down to the individual action plan for a part of one marketing program. It is also an interactive process, so that the draft output of each stage is checked to see what impact it has on the earlier stages-and is amended..

Marketing Planning Aims and Objectives

Behind the corporate objectives, which in themselves offer the main context for the marketing plan, will lay the "corporate mission"; which in turn provides the context for these corporate objectives. In a sales-oriented organization, marketing planning function designs incentive pay plans to not only motivate and reward frontline staff fairly but also to align marketing activities with corporate mission.

This "corporate mission" can be thought of as a definition of what the organization is; of what it does: "Our business is ...". This definition should not be too narrow, or it will constrict the development of the organization; a too rigorous concentration on the view that "We are in the business of making meat-scales," as IBM was during the early 1900s, might have limited its subsequent development into other areas. On the other hand, it should not be too wide or it will become meaningless; "We want to make a profit" is not too helpful in developing specific plans.

Abell suggested that the definition should cover three dimensions: "customer groups" to be served, "customer needs" to be served, and "technologies" to be utilized. Thus, the definition of IBM's "corporate mission" in the 1990s. might well have been: "We are in the business of handling accounting information for the larger US organizations [customer group] by means of punched cards [technology]."

Perhaps the most important factor in successful marketing is the "corporate vision." Surprisingly, it is largely neglected by marketing textbooks; although not by the popular exponents of corporate strategy-indeed, it was perhaps the main theme of the book by Peters and Waterman, in the form of their "Superordinate Goals." "In Search of Excellence" said: "Nothing drives progress like the imagination. The idea precedes the deed." If the organization in general, and its chief executive in particular, has a strong vision of where its future lies, then there is a good chance that the organization will achieve a strong position in its markets (and attain that future).

This will be not least because its strategies will be consistent; and will be supported by its staff at all levels. In this context, all of IBM's marketing activities were underpinned by its philosophy of "customer service"; a vision originally promoted by the charismatic Watson dynasty. The emphasis at this stage is on obtaining a complete and accurate picture.

A "traditional"-albeit product-based-format for a "brand reference book" (or, indeed, a "marketing facts book") was suggested by Godley more than three decades ago:

1. Financial data—Facts for this section will come from management accounting, costing and finance sections.
2. Product data—From production, research and development.
3. Sales and distribution data-Sales, packaging, distribution sections.
4. Advertising, sales promotion, merchandising data-Information from these departments.
5. Market data and miscellany-From market research, who would in most cases act as a source for this information. His sources of data, however, assume the resources of a very large organization. In most organizations they would be obtained from a much smaller set of people (and not a few of them would be generated by the marketing manager alone).

It is apparent that a marketing audit can be a complex process, but the aim is simple: *"it is only to identify those existing (external and internal) factors which will have a significant impact on the future plans of the company."* It is clear that the basic material to be input to the marketing audit should be comprehensive.

Accordingly, the best approach is to accumulate this material continuously, as and when it becomes available; since this avoids the otherwise heavy workload involved in collecting it as part of the regular, typically annual, planning process itself-when time is usually at a premium.

Even so, the first task of this *annual* process should be to check that the material held in the current *facts book* or *facts files* actually *is* comprehensive and accurate, and can form a sound basis for the marketing audit itself. The structure of the facts book will be designed to match the specific needs of the organization, but one simple format-suggested by Malcolm McDonald-may be applicable in many cases. This splits the material into three groups:

1. Review of the marketing environment. A study of the organization's markets, customers, competitors and the overall economic, political, cultural and technical environment; covering developing trends, as well as the current situation.

2. Review of the detailed marketing activity. A study of the company's marketing mix; in terms of the 7 Ps.
3. Review of the marketing system. A study of the marketing organization, marketing research systems and the current marketing objectives and strategies. The last of these is too frequently ignored. The marketing system itself needs to be regularly questioned, because the validity of the whole marketing plan is reliant upon the accuracy of the input from this system, and 'garbage in, garbage out' applies with a vengeance.
   - Portfolio planning. In addition, the coordinated planning of the individual products and services can contribute towards the balanced portfolio.
   - 80:20 rule. To achieve the maximum impact, the marketing plan must be clear, concise and simple. It needs to concentrate on the 20 percent of products or services, and on the 20 percent of customers, which will account for 80 percent of the volume and 80 percent of the profit.
   - 7 P's: Product, Place, Price and Promotion, Physical Environment, People, Process. The 7 P's can sometimes divert attention from the customer, but the framework they offer can be very useful in building the action plans.

It is only at this stage (of deciding the marketing objectives) that the active part of the marketing planning process begins'. This next stage in marketing planning is indeed the key to the whole marketing process. The "marketing objectives" state just where the company intends to be; at some specific time in the future. James Quinn succinctly defined objectives in general as: *Goals (or objectives) state what is to be achieved and when results are to be accomplished, but they do not state 'how' the results are to be achieved.* They typically relate to what products (or services) will be where in what markets (and must be realistically based on customer behaviour in those markets). They are essentially about the match between those "products" and "markets." Objectives for pricing, distribution, advertising and so on are at a lower level, and should not be confused with marketing objectives.

They are part of the marketing strategy needed to achieve marketing objectives. To be most effective, objectives should be capable of measurement and therefore "quantifiable." This measurement may be in terms of sales volume, money value, market share, percentage penetration of distribution outlets and so on. An example of such a measurable marketing objective might be "to enter the market with product Y and capture 10 percent of the market by value within one year." As it is quantified it can, within limits, be unequivocally monitored; and corrective action taken as necessary.

The marketing objectives must usually be based, above all, on the organization's financial objectives; converting these financial measurements into the related marketing measurements. He went on to explain his view of the role of "policies," with which strategy is most often confused: "Policies are rules or guidelines that express the 'limits' within which action should occur." Simplifying somewhat, marketing strategies can be seen as the means, or "game plan," by which marketing objectives will be achieved and, in the framework that we have chosen to use, are generally concerned with the 8 P's. Examples are:

1. Price-The amount of money needed to buy products
2. Product-The actual product
3. Promotion (advertising)-Getting the product known
4. Placement-Where the product is located
5. People-Represent the business
6. Physical environment-The ambiance, mood, or tone of the environment
7. Process-How do people obtain your product
8. Packaging-How the product will be protected.

(Note: At GCSE the 4 P's are Place, Promotion, Product and Price and the "secret" 5th P is Packaging, but which applies only to physical products, not services usually, and mostly those sold to individual consumers).

In principle, these strategies describe how the objectives will be achieved. The 7 P's are a useful framework for deciding how the company's resources will be manipulated (strategically) to achieve the objectives. It should be noted, however, that they are not the only framework, and may divert attention from the real issues. The focus of the strategies must be the objectives to be achieved-not the process of planning itself. Only if it fits the needs of these objectives should you choose, as we have done, to use the framework of the 7 P's. The strategy statement can take the form of a purely verbal description of the strategic options which have been chosen. Alternatively, and perhaps more positively, it might include a structured list of the major options chosen. One aspect of strategy which is often overlooked is that of "timing." Exactly when it is the best time for each element of the strategy to be implemented is often critical. Taking the right action at the wrong time can sometimes be almost as bad as taking the wrong action at the right time. Timing is, therefore, an essential part of any plan; and should normally appear as a schedule of planned activities. Having completed this crucial stage of the planning process, you will need to re-check the feasibility of your objectives and strategies in terms of the market share, sales, costs, profits and so on which these demand in practice. As in the rest of the marketing discipline, you will need to employ judgment, experience, market research or anything else which helps you to look at your conclusions from all possible angles.

Detailed Plans and Programs

At this stage, you will need to develop your overall marketing strategies into detailed plans and program. Although these detailed plans may cover each of the 7 P's, the focus will vary, depending upon your organization's specific strategies. A product-oriented company will focus its plans for the 7 P's around each of its products. A market or geographically oriented company will concentrate on each market or geographical area. Each will base its plans upon the detailed needs of its customers, and on the strategies chosen to satisfy these needs. Again, the most important element is, indeed, that of the detailed plans; which spell out exactly what programs and individual activities will take place over the period of the plan (usually over the next year). Without these specified-and preferably quantified-activities the plan cannot be monitored, even in terms of success in meeting its objectives. It is these programs and activities which will then constitute the "marketing" of the organization over the period. As a result, these detailed marketing programs are the most important, practical outcome of the whole planning process. These plans therefore be:

- Clear-They should be an unambiguous statement of 'exactly' what is to be done.
- Quantified-The predicted outcome of each activity should be, as far as possible, quantified; so that its performance can be monitored.
- Focused-The temptation to proliferate activities beyond the numbers which can be realistically controlled should be avoided. The 80:20 Rule applies in this context too.

- Realistic-They should be achievable.
- Agreed-Those who are to implement them should be committed to them, and agree that they are achievable. The resulting plans should become a working document which will guide the campaigns taking place throughout the organization over the period of the plan. If the marketing plan is to work, every exception to it (throughout the year) must be questioned; and the lessons learned, to be incorporated in the next year's planning.

Mass Customization

Mass customization, in marketing, manufacturing, call centres and management, is the use of flexible computer-aided manufacturing systems to produce custom output. Those systems combine the low unit costs of mass production processes with the flexibility of individual customization.

"Mass Customization" is the new frontier in business competition for both manufacturing and service industries. At its core is a tremendous increase in variety and customization without a corresponding increase in costs. At its limit, it is the mass production of individually customized goods and services. At its best, it provides strategic advantage and economic value.

Mass Customization is the method of "effectively postponing the task of differentiating a product for a specific customer until the latest possible point in the supply network." The concept of mass customization is attributed to Stan Davis in *Future Perfect* and was defined by Tseng & Jiao (2001, p. 685) as "producing goods and services to meet individual customer's needs with near mass production efficiency". Kaplan & Haenlein (2006) concurred, calling it "a strategy that creates value by some form of company-customer interaction at the fabrication and assembly stage of the operations level to create customized products with production cost and monetary price similar to those of mass-produced products".

Implementation

Many implementations of mass customization are operational today, such as software-based product configurators which make it possible to add and/or change functionalities of a core product or to build fully custom enclosures from scratch. This degree of mass customization has only seen limited adoption, however. If an enterprise's marketing department offers individual products (atomic market fragmentation) it doesn't often mean that a product is produced individually, but rather that similar variants of the same mass-produced item are available.

Companies which have succeeded with mass-customization business models tend to supply purely electronic products. However, these are not true "mass customizers" in the original sense, since they do not offer an alternative to mass production of material goods. Service industries are also waking up to the power of a mass customization orientation. Call centres are leveraging agent-assisted voice technology to build pre-programmed, pre-recorded call flows to handle customers' inquiries. The agent executes the process, varying it only as they need to because of something the customer says or needs, as opposed to varying everything, every time.

Variants

Pine II (1992) described four types of mass customization.

- Collaborative customization-firms talk to individual customers to determine the precise product offering that best serves the customer's needs. This information is then used to specify and manufacture a product that suits that specific customer. For example, some clothing companies will manufacture blue jeans to fit an individual customer.
- Adaptive customization-firms produce a standardized product, but this product is customizable in the hands of the end-user (the customers alter the product themselves)
- Transparent customization-firms provide individual customers with unique products, without explicitly telling them that the products are customized. In this case there is a need to accurately assess customer needs.
- Cosmetic customization-firms produce a standardized physical product, but market it to different customers in unique ways.

He suggested a business model, "the 8.5-figure-path", a process going from invention to mass production to continuous improvement to mass customization and back to invention.

Positioning (Marketing)

In marketing, positioning has come to mean the process by which marketers try to create an image or identity in the minds of their target market for its product, brand, or organization. It is the 'relative competitive comparison' their product occupies in a given market as perceived by the target market.

Re-positioning involves changing the identity of a product, relative to the identity of competing products, in the collective minds of the target market.

De-positioning involves attempting to change the identity of competing products, relative to the identity of your own product, in the collective minds of the target market.

The original work on Positioning was consumer marketing oriented, and was not as much focused on the question relative to competitive products as much as it was focused on cutting through the ambient "noise" and establishing a moment of real contact with the intended recipient. In the classic example of Avis claiming "No.2, We Try Harder", the point was to say something so shocking (it was by the standards of the day) that it cleared space in your brain and made you forget all about who was #1, and not to make some philosophical point about being "hungry" for business. The growth of high-tech marketing may have had much to do with the shift in definition towards competitive positioning.

Definitions

Although there are different definitions of Positioning, probably the most common is: "A product's position is how potential buyers see the product", and is expressed relative to the position of competitors. Positioning is a concept in marketing which was first popularized by Al Ries and Jack Trout in their bestseller book " Positioning-a battle for your mind".

This differs slightly from the context in which the term was first published in 1969 by Jack Trout in the paper *"Positioning" is a game people play in today's me-too market place"* in the publication *Industrial Marketing*, in which the case is made that the typical consumer is overwhelmed with unwanted advertising, and has a natural tendency to discard all information that does not immediately find a comfortable (and empty) slot in the consumers mind. It was then expanded into their ground-breaking first book, "*Positioning: The Battle for Your Mind*", in which they define Positioning as "an organized system for finding a window in the mind. It is based on the concept that communication can only take place at the right time and under the right circumstances." (p. 19 of 2001 paperback edition). What most will agree on is that Positioning is something (perception) that happens in the minds of the target market. It is the aggregate perception the market has of a particular company, product or service in relation to their perceptions of the competitors in the same category. It will happen whether or not a company's management is proactive, reactive or passive about the on-going process of evolving a position. But a company can positively influence the perceptions through enlightened strategic actions.

Product Positioning Process

Generally, the product positioning process involves.

1. Defining the market in which the product or brand will compete (who the relevant buyers are).
2. Identifying the attributes (also called dimensions) that define the product 'space'.
3. Collecting information from a sample of customers about their perceptions of each product on the relevant attributes.
4. Determine each product's share of mind.
5. Determine each product's current location in the product space.
6. Determine the target market's preferred combination of attributes (referred to as an *ideal vector*).
7. Examine the fit between.
   - The position of your product.
   - The position of the ideal vector.
8. Position.

The process is similar for positioning your company's services. Services, however, don't have the physical attributes of products-that is, we can't feel them or touch them or show nice product pictures.

So you need to ask first your customers and then yourself, what value do clients get from my services? How are they better off from doing business with me? Also ask: is there a characteristic that makes my services different? Write out the value customers derive and the attributes your services offer to create the first draft of your positioning. Test it on people who don't really know what you do or what you sell, watch their facial expressions and listen for their response. When they want to know more because you've piqued their interest and started a conversation, you'll know you're on the right track.

Positioning Concepts

More generally, there are three types of positioning concepts.

1. Functional positions.
   - Solve problems.
   - Provide benefits to customers.

- Get favourable perception by investors (stock profile) and lenders.

2. Symbolic positions.
   - Self-image enhancement.
   - Ego identification.
   - Belongingness and social meaningfulness.
   - Affective fulfilment.
3. Experiential positions.
   - Provide sensory stimulation.
   - Provide cognitive stimulation.

Measuring the Positioning

Positioning is facilitated by a graphical technique called perceptual mapping, various survey techniques, and statistical techniques like multi dimensional scaling, factor analysis, conjoint analysis, and logit analysis.

Repositioning a Company

In volatile markets, it can be necessary-even urgent-to reposition an entire company, rather than just a product line or brand. Take, for example, when Goldman Sachs and Morgan Stanley suddenly shifted from investment to commercial banks. The expectations of investors, employees, clients and regulators all need to shift, and each company will need to influence how these perceptions change. Doing so involves repositioning the entire firm. This is especially true of small and medium-sized firms, many of which often lack strong brands for individual product lines. In a prolonged recession, business approaches that were effective during healthy economies often become ineffective and it becomes necessary to change a firm's positioning. Upscale restaurants, for example, which previously flourished on expense account dinners and corporate events, may for the first time need to stress value as a sale tool. Repositioning a company involves more than a marketing challenge. It involves making hard decisions about how a market is shifting and how a firm's competitors will react. Often these decisions must be made without the benefit of sufficient information, simply because the definition of "volatility" is that change becomes difficult or impossible to predict.

Product Life Cycle Management

Product life cycle management is the succession of strategies used by management as a product goes through its product life cycle. The conditions in which a product is sold changes over time and must be managed as it moves through its succession of stages.

Product Life Cycle

The product life cycle goes through many phases, involves many professional disciplines, and requires many skills, tools and processes. Product life cycle (PLC) has to do with the life of a product in the market with respect to business/commercial costs and sales measures; whereas product life cycle management (PLM) has more to do with managing descriptions and properties of a product through its development and useful life, mainly from a business/engineering point of view. To say that a product has a life cycle is to assert four things:

- that products have a limited life.
- product sales pass through distinct stages, each posing different challenges, opportunities, and problems to the seller.
- profits rise and fall at different stages of product life cycle, and.
- products require different marketing, financial, manufacturing, purchasing, and human resource strategies in each life cycle stage.

Request for Deviation

In the process of building a product following defined procedure, an RFD is a request for authorization, granted prior to the manufacture of an item, to depart from a particular performance or design requirement of a specification, drawing or other document, for a specific number of units or a specific period of time.....

Market Identification

A "micro-market" can be used to describe a Walkman, more portable, as well as individually and privately recordable; and then Compact Discs ("CDS") brought increased capacity and CD-R offered individual private recording...and so the process goes. The below section on the "technology lifecycle" is a most appropriate concept in this context. Most of the context is not in English so you may need a translator.

In short, termination is not always the end of the cycle; it can be the end of a micro-entrant within the grander scope of a macro-environment. The auto industry, fast-food industry, petro-chemical industry, are just a few that demonstrate a macro-environment that overall has not terminated even while micro-entrants over time have come and gone.

Lessons of the Product Life Cycle (PLC)

It is claimed that every product has a life period, It is launched, it grows, and at some point, may die. A fair comment is that-at least in the short term-not all products or services die. Jeans may die, but clothes probably will not. Legal services or medical services may die, but depending on the social and political climate, probably will not.

Even though its validity is questionable, it can offer a useful 'model' for managers to keep at the back of their mind. Indeed, if their products are in the introductory or growth phases, or in that of decline, it perhaps should be at the front of their mind; for the predominant features of these phases may be those revolving around such life and death. Between these two extremes, it is salutary for them to have that vision of mortality in front of them.

However, the most important aspect of product life-cycles is that, even under normal conditions, to all practical intents and purposes they often do not exist (hence, there needs to be more emphasis on model/reality mappings). In most markets the majority of the major brands have held their position for at least two decades. The dominant product life-cycle, that of the brand leaders which almost monopolize many markets, is therefore one of continuity.

In the Criticism of the Product Life Cycle, Dhalla & Yuspeh State

The PLC is a dependent variable which is determined by market actions; it is not an independent variable to which companies should adapt their marketing programs. Marketing management itself can alter the shape and duration of a brand's life cycle. Thus, the life cycle may be useful as a description, but not as a predictor; and usually should be firmly under the control of the marketer.

The important point is that in many markets the product or brand life cycle is significantly longer than the planning cycle of the organisations involved. Thus, it offers little practical value for most marketers. Even if the PLC (and the related PLM support) exists for them, their plans will be based just upon that piece of the curve where they currently reside (most probably in the 'mature' stage); and their view of that part of it will almost certainly be 'linear' (and limited), and will not encompass the whole range from growth to decline.

Limitations

The PLC model is of some degree of usefulness to marketing managers, in that it is based on factual assumptions. Nevertheless, it is difficult for marketing management to gauge accurately where a product is on its PLC graph. A rise in sales *per se* is not necessarily evidence of growth. A fall in sales *per se* does not typify decline. Furthermore, some products do not (and to date, at the least, have not) experienced a decline.

Coca Cola and Pepsi are examples of two products that have existed for many decades, but are still popular products all over the world. Both modes of cola have been in maturity for some years. Another factor is that differing products would possess different PLC "shapes".

A fad product would hold a steep sloped growth stage, a short maturity stage, and a steep sloped decline stage. A product such as Coca Cola and Pepsi would experience growth, but also a constant level of sales over a number of decades. It can probably be said that a given product (or products collectively within an industry) may hold a unique PLC shape, and the typical PLC model can only be used as a rough guide for marketing management. The Product Life Cycle (PLC) is based upon the biological life cycle.

For example, a seed is planted (introduction); it begins to sprout (growth); it shoots out leaves and puts down roots as it becomes an adult (maturity); after a long period as an adult the plant begins to shrink and die out (decline). In theory it's the same for a product. After a period of development it is introduced or launched into the market; it gains more and more customers as it grows; eventually the market stabilises and the product becomes mature; then after a period of time the product is overtaken by development and the introduction of superior competitors, it goes into decline and is eventually withdrawn.

Strategies for the Differing Stages of the Product Life Cycle

The need for immediate profit is not a pressure. The product is promoted to create awareness. If the product has no or few competitors, a skimming price strategy is employed. Limited numbers of product are available in few channels of distribution.

Growth

Competitors are attracted into the market with very similar offerings. Products become more profitable and companies form alliances, joint ventures and take each other over. Advertising spend is high and focuses upon building brand. Market share tends to stabilise.

Maturity

Those products that survive the earlier stages tend to spend longest in this phase. Sales grow at a decreasing rate and then stabilise. Producers attempt to differentiate products and brands are key to this. Price wars and intense competition occur. At this point the market reaches saturation. Producers begin to leave the market due to poor margins. Promotion becomes more widespread and use a greater variety of media.

Research and Development

The phrase research and development (also R and D or, more often, R&D), according to the Organization for Economic Co-operation and Development, refers to "creative work undertaken on a systematic basis in order to increase the stock of knowledge, including knowledge of man, culture and society, and the use of this stock of knowledge to devise new applications".

R&D

New product design and development is more often than not a crucial factor in the survival of a company. In an industry that is fast changing, firms must continually revise their design and range of products. This is necessary due to continuous technology change and development as well as other competitors and the changing preference of customers. A system driven by marketing is one that puts the customer needs first, and only produces goods that are known to sell. Market research is carried out, which establishes what is needed. If the development is technology driven then it is a matter of selling what it is possible to make. The product range is developed so that production processes are as efficient as possible and the products are technically superior, hence possessing a natural advantage in the market place.

R&D has a special economic significance apart from its conventional association with scientific and technological development. R&D investment generally reflects a government's or organization's willingness to forgo current operations or profit to improve future performance or returns, and its abilities to conduct research and development. In 2006, the world's four largest spenders of R&D were the United States (US$343 billion), the EU (US$231 billion), China (US$136 billion), and Japan (US$130 billion). In terms of percentage of GDP, the order of these spenders for 2006 was China (US$115 billion of US$2,668 billion GDP), Japan, United States, EU with approximate percentages of 4.3, 3.2, 2.6, and 1.8 respectively. The top 10 spenders in terms of percentage of GDP were Israel (4.53%), Sweden (3.73%), Finland (3.45%), Japan (3.39%), South Korea (3.23%), Switzerland (2.9%), Iceland (2.78%), United States (2.62%), Germany (2.53%) and Austria (2.45%). In general, R&D activities are conducted by specialized units or centres belonging to companies, universities and state agencies.

In the context of commerce, "research and development" normally refers to future-oriented, longer-term activities in science or technology, using similar techniques to scientific research without predetermined outcomes and with broad forecasts of commercial yield. Statistics on organizations devoted to "R&D" may express the state of an industry, the degree of competition or the lure of progress. Some common measures include: budgets, numbers of patents or on rates of peer-reviewed publications.

Bank ratios are one of the best measures, because they are continuously maintained, public and reflect risk. In the U.S., a typical ratio of research and development for an industrial company is about 3.5% of revenues. A high technology company such as a computer manufacturer might spend 7%. Although Allergan (a biotech company) tops the spending table 43.4% investment, anything over 15% is remarkable and usually gains a reputation for being a high technology company. Companies in this category include pharmaceutical companies such as Merck & Co. (14.1%) or Novartis (15.1%), and engineering companies like Ericsson (24.9%). Such companies are often seen as poor credit risks because their spending ratios are so unusual.

Generally such firms prosper only in markets whose customers have extreme needs, such as medicine, scientific instruments, safety-critical mechanisms (aircraft) or high technology military armaments. The extreme needs justify the high risk of failure and consequently high gross margins from 60% to 90% of revenues. That is, gross profits will be as much as 90% of the sales cost, with manufacturing costing only 10% of the product price, because so many individual projects yield no exploitable product. Most industrial companies get only 40% revenues. On a technical level, high tech organisations explore ways to re-purpose and repackage advanced technologies as a way of amortizing the high overhead. They often reuse advanced manufacturing processes, expensive safety certifications, specialized embedded software, computer-aided design software, electronic designs and mechanical subsystems. Research has shown that firms with a persistent R&D strategy outperform those with an irregular or no R&D investment programme.

Pharmaceuticals

Research often refers to basic experimental research; development refers to the exploitation of discoveries. Research involves the identification of possible chemical compounds or theoretical mechanisms. In the United States, universities are the main provider of research level products. In the United States, corporations buy licences from universities or hire scientists directly when economically solid research level products emerge and the development phase of drug delivery is almost entirely managed by private enterprise.

Development is concerned with proof of concept, safety testing, and determining ideal levels and delivery mechanisms. Development often occurs in phases that are defined by drug safety regulators in the country of interest. In the United States, the development phase can cost between $10 to $200 million and approximately one in ten compounds identified by basic research pass all development phases and reach market.

R&D Alliance

An R&D alliance is a mutually beneficial formal relationship formed between two or more parties to pursue a set of agreed upon goals while remaining independent organisations, where acquiring new knowledge is a goal by itself. The different parties agree to combine their knowledge to create new innovative products. Thanks to funding from government organizations, like the European Union's Seventh Framework Programme (FP7), and modern advances in technology, such as Eures Tools, R&D alliances have now become more efficient. Research and development is nowadays of great importance in business as the level of competition, production processes and methods are rapidly increasing. It is of special importance in the field of marketing where companies keep an eagle eye on competitors and customers in order to keep pace with modern trends and analyse the needs, demands and desires of their customers.

Unfortunately, research and development are very difficult to manage, since the defining feature of research is that the researchers do not know in advance exactly how to accomplish the desired result. As a result, higher R&D spending and does not guarantee "more creativity, higher profit or a greater market share."

4

Exchange Rate

In finance, the exchange rates (also known as the foreign-exchange rate, forex rate or FX rate) between two currencies specifies how much one currency is worth in terms of the other. It is the value of a foreign nation's currency in terms of the home nation's currency. For example an exchange rate of 91 Japanese yen (JPY, ¥) to the United States dollar (USD, $) means that JPY 91 is worth the same as USD 1. The foreign exchange market is one of the largest markets in the world. By some estimates, about 3.2 trillion USD worth of currency changes hands every day. The spot exchange rate refers to the current exchange rate. The forward exchange rate refers to an exchange rate that is quoted and traded today but for delivery and payment on a specific future date.

Exchange Rate Regime

The exchange rate regime is the way a country manages its currency in respect to foreign currencies and the foreign exchange market. It is closely related to monetary policy and the two are generally dependent on many of the same factors. The basic types are a *floating* exchange rate, where the market dictates the movements of the exchange rate, a *pegged float*, where the central bank keeps the rate from deviating too far from a target band or value, and the *fixed* exchange rate, which ties the currency to another currency, mostly more widespread currencies such as the U.S. dollar or the euro.

Floating Exchange Rate

A floating exchange rate or fluctuating exchange rate is a type of exchange rate regime wherein a currency's value is allowed to fluctuate according to the foreign exchange market. A currency that uses a floating exchange rate is known as a floating currency. It is not possible for a developing country to maintain the stability in the rate of exchange for its currency in the exchange market.

There are two options open for them-Let the exchange rate be allowed to fluctuate in the open market according to the market conditions, or An equilibrium rate may be fixed to be adopted and attempts should be made to maintain it as far as possible. But, if there is a fundamental change in the circumstances, the rate should be changed accordingly.

The rate of exchange under the first alternative is know as fluctuating rate of exchange and under second alternative, it is called flexible rate of exchange. In the modern economic conditions, the flexible rate of exchange system is more appropriate as it does not hamper the foreign trade. There are economists who think that, in most circumstances, floating exchange rates are preferable to fixed exchange rates.

As floating exchange rates automatically adjust, they enable a country to dampen the impact of shocks and foreign business cycles, and to preempt the possibility of having a balance of payments crisis. However, in certain situations, fixed exchange rates may be preferable for their greater stability and certainty. This may not necessarily be true, considering the results of countries that attempt to keep the prices of their currency "strong" or "high" relative to others, such as the UK or the Southeast Asia countries before the Asian currency crisis. The debate of making a choice between fixed and floating exchange rate regimes is set forth by the Mundell-Fleming model, which argues that an economy cannot simultaneously maintain a fixed exchange rate, free capital movement, and an independent monetary policy. It can choose any two for control, and leave third to the market forces.

In cases of extreme appreciation or depreciation, a central bank will normally intervene to stabilize the currency. Thus, the exchange rate regimes of floating currencies may more technically be known as a managed float. A central bank might, for instance, allow a currency price to float freely between an upper and lower bound, a price "ceiling" and "floor". Management by the central bank may take the form of buying or selling large lots in order to provide price support or resistance, or, in the case of some national currencies, there may be legal penalties for trading outside these bounds.

Fear of Floating

A free floating exchange rate increases foreign exchange volatility. There are economists who think that this could cause serious problems, especially in emerging economies. These economies have a financial sector with one or more of following conditions:

- high liability dollarization
- financial fragility
- strong balance sheet effects

When liabilities are denominated in foreign currencies while assets are in the local currency, unexpected depreciations of the exchange rate deteriorate bank and corporate balance sheets and threaten the stability of the domestic financial system.

For this reason emerging countries appear to face greater fear of floating, as they have much smaller variations of the nominal exchange rate, yet face bigger shocks and interest rate and reserve movements. This is the consequence of frequent free floating countries' reaction to exchange rate movements with monetary policy and/or intervention in the foreign exchange market. The number of countries that present fear of floating increased significantly during the nineties.

Fixed Exchange Rate

A fixed exchange rate, sometimes called a pegged exchange rate, is a type of exchange rate regime wherein a currency's value is matched to the value of another single currency or to a basket of other currencies, or to another measure of value, such as gold.

A fixed exchange rate is usually used to stabilize the value of a currency, against the currency it is pegged to. This makes trade and investments between the two countries easier and more predictable, and is especially useful for small economies where external trade forms a large part of their GDP.

It can also be used as a means to control inflation. However, as the reference value rises and falls, so does the currency pegged to it. In addition, according to the Mundell-Fleming model, with perfect capital mobility, a fixed exchange rate prevents a government from using domestic monetary policy in order to achieve macroeconomic stability.

Overview

A former president of the Federal Reserve Bank of New York described fixed currencies as follows:

Fixing value of the domestic currency relative to that of a low-inflation country is one approach central banks have used to pursue price stability. The advantage of an exchange rate target is its clarity, which makes it easily understood by the public. In practice, it obliges the central bank to limit money creation to levels comparable to those of the country to whose currency it is pegged. When credibly maintained, an exchange rate target can lower inflation expectations to the level prevailing in the anchor country. Experiences with fixed exchange rates, however, point to a number of drawbacks. A country that fixes its exchange rate surrenders control of its domestic monetary policy. —William J. McDonough,

In certain situations, fixed exchange rates may be preferable for their greater stability. For example, the Asian financial crisis was improved by the fixed exchange rate of the Chinese renminbi, and the IMF and the World Bank now acknowledge that Malaysia's adoption of a peg to the US dollar in the aftermath of the same crisis was highly successful. Following the devastation of World War II, the Bretton Woods system allowed all the 44 Allied nations of latter World War II to fix exchange rates against the US dollar. The system collapsed in 1970.

With regard to the Asian financial crisis, others argue that the fixed exchange rates (implemented well before the crisis) had become so immovable that it had masked valuable information needed for a market to function properly. That is, the currencies did not represent their true market value. This masking of information created volatility which encouraged speculators to "attack" the pegged currencies and as a response these countries attempted to defend their currency rather than allow it to devalue.

These economists also believe that had these countries instituted floating exchange rates, as opposed to fixed exchange rates, they may very well have avoided the volatility that caused the Asian financial crisis in the first place. Countries like Malaysia adopted increased capital controls, believing that the volatility of capital was the result of technology and globalization, rather than ill-conceived macroeconomic policies.

This resulted not in better stability and growth in the aftermath of the crisis, but sustained pain and stagnation. Countries adopting a fixed exchange rate must exercise careful and strict adherence to policy imperatives, and keep a degree of confidence of the capital markets in the management of such a regime, or otherwise the peg can fail. Such was the case of Argentina, where unchecked state spending and international economic shocks unbalanced the system resulting in an extremely damaging devaluation. On the opposite extreme, China's fixed exchange rate with the US dollar until 2005 led to China's rapid accumulation of foreign reserves, placing an appreciating pressure on the Chinese yuan.

Fixed Exchange Rate Regime Versus Capital Control

The belief that the fixed exchange rate regime brings with it stability is only partly true, since speculative attacks tend to target currencies with fixed exchange rate regimes, and in fact, the stability of the economic system is maintained mainly through capital control. A fixed exchange rate regime should be viewed as a tool in capital control.

For instance, China has allowed free exchange for current account transactions since December 1, 1996. Of more than 40 categories of capital account, about 20 of them are convertible. These convertible accounts are mainly related to foreign direct investment. Because of capital control, even the renminbi is not under the managed floating exchange rate regime, but free to float, and so it is somewhat unnecessary for foreigners to purchase renminbi.

Bilateral vs. Effective Exchange Rate

Bilateral exchange rate involves a currency pair, while effective exchange rate is weighted average of a basket of foreign currencies, and it can be viewed as an overall measure of the country's external competitiveness.

A nominal effective exchange rate (NEER) is weighted with the inverse of the asymptotic trade weights. A real effective exchange rate (REER) adjust NEER by appropriate foreign price level and deflates by the home country price level. Compared to NEER, a GDP weighted effective exchange rate might be more appropriate considering the global investment phenomenon.

Uncovered vs. Covered Interest Parity Example

Let's assume you wanted to pay for something in Yen in a month's time. There are several ways to do this.

- Buy Yen forward 30 days to lock in the exchange rate. Then you may invest in dollars for 30 days until you must convert dollars to Yen in a month. This is called *covering* because you now have covered yourself and have no exchange rate risk.

- Convert spot to Yen today. Invest in a Japanese bond (in Yen) for 30 days (or otherwise loan out Yen for 30 days) then pay your Yen obligation. Under this model, you are sure of the interest you will earn, so you may convert fewer dollars to Yen today, since the Yen will grow via interest. Notice how you have still covered your exchange risk, because you have simply converted to Yen immediately.
- You could also invest the money in dollars and change it for Yen in a month.

According to the interest rate parity, you should get the same number of Yen in all methods. Methods (a) and (b) are covered while (c) is uncovered.

- In method (a) the higher (lower) interest rate in the US is offset by the forward discount (premium).
- In method (b) The higher (lower) interest rate in Japan is offset by the loss (gain) from converting spot instead of using a forward.
- Method (c) is uncovered, however, according to interest rate parity, the spot exchange rate in 30 days *should* become the same as the 30 day forward rate. Obviously there is exchange risk because you must see if this actually happens.

General Rules: If the forward rate is lower than what the interest rate parity indicates, the appropriate strategy would be: borrow Yen, convert to dollars at the spot rate, and lend dollars.

If the forward rate is higher than what interest rate parity indicates, the appropriate strategy would be: borrow dollars, convert to Yen at the spot rate, and lend the Yen.

Balance of Payments

A Balance of payments (BOP) sheet is an accounting record of all monetary transactions between a country and the rest of the world. These transactions include payments for the country's exports and imports of goods, services, and financial capital, as well as financial transfers. The BOP summarises international transactions for a specific period, usually a year, and is prepared in a single currency, typically the domestic currency for the country concerned. Sources of funds for a nation, such as exports or the receipts of loans and investments, are recorded as positive or surplus items. Uses of funds, such as for imports or to invest in foreign countries, are recorded as a negative or deficit item.

When all components of the BOP sheet are included it must balance-that is, it must sum to zero-there can be no overall surplus or deficit. For example, if a country is importing more than it exports, its trade balance will be in deficit, but the shortfall will have to be counter balanced in other ways-such as by funds earned from its foreign investments, by running down reserves or by receiving loans from other countries.

While the overall BOP sheet will always balance when all types of payments are included, imbalances are possible on individual elements of the BOP, such as the current account. This can result in surplus countries accumulating hoards of wealth, while deficit nations become increasingly indebted. Historically there have been different approaches to the question of how to correct imbalances and debate on whether they are something governments should be concerned about. With record imbalances held up as one of the contributing factors to the financial crisis of 2007-2010, plans to address global imbalances are now high on the agenda of policy makers for 2010.

Balancing Mechanisms

One of the three fundamental functions of an international monetary system is to provide mechanisms to correct imbalances.

Broadly speaking, there are three possible methods to correct BOP imbalances, though in practice a mixture including some degree of at least the first two methods tends to be used. These methods are adjustments of exchange rates; adjustment of a nations internal prices along with its levels of demand; and rules based adjustment. Increasing the desirability of exports through other means can also help, though it is generally assumed a nation is always trying to develop and sell its products to the best of its abilities.

Rebalancing by Changing the Exchange Rate

An upwards shift in the value of a nation's currency relative to others will make a nation's exports less competitive and make imports cheaper and so will tend to correct a current account surplus. It also tends to make investment flows into the capital account less attractive so will help with a surplus there too. Conversely a downward shift in the value of a nation's currency makes it more expensive for its citizens to buy imports and increases the competitiveness of their exports, thus helping to correct a deficit (though the solution often doesn't have a positive impact immediately due to the Marshall-Lerner Condition.

Exchange rates can be adjusted by government in a rules based or managed currency regime, and when left to float freely in the market they also tend to change in the direction that will restore balance. When a country is selling more than it imports, the demand for its currency will tend to increase as other countries ultimately need the selling country's currency to make payments for the exports. The extra demand tends to cause a rise of the currencies price relative to others.

When a country is importing more than it exports, the supply of its own currency on the international market tends to increase as it tries to exchange it for foreign currency to pay for its imports, and this extra supply tends to cause the price to fall. BOP effects are not the only market influence on exchange rates however, they are also influenced by differences in national interest rates and by speculative flows.

Rebalancing by Adjusting Internal Prices and Demand

When exchange rates are fixed by a rigid gold standard, or when imbalances exist between members of a currency union such as the Eurozone, the standard approach to correct imbalances is by making changes to the domestic economy. To a large degree, the change is optional for the surplus country, but compulsory for the deficit country. In the case of a gold standard, the mechanism is largely automatic. When a country has a favourable trade balance, as a consequence of selling more than it buys it will experience a net inflow of gold. The natural effect of this will be to increase the money supply, which leads to inflation and an increase in prices, which then tends to make its goods less competitive and so will decrease its trade surplus.

However the nation has the option of taking the gold out of economy (sterilising the inflationary effect) thus building up a hoard of gold and retaining its favourable balance of payments. On the other hand, if a country has an adverse BOP its will experience a net loss of gold, which will automatically have a deflationary effect, unless it chooses to leave the gold standard. Prices will be reduced, making its exports more competitive, and thus correcting the imbalance. While the gold standard is generally considered to have been successful up until 1914, correction by deflation to the degree required by the large imbalances that arose after WWI proved painful, with deflationary policies contributing to prolonged unemployment but not re-establishing balance. Apart from the US most former members had left the gold standard by the mid 1930s.

A possible method for surplus countries such as Germany to contribute to re-balancing efforts when exchange rate adjustment is not suitable, is to increase its level of internal demand (i.e. its spending on goods). While a current account surplus is commonly understood as the excess of earnings over spending, and alternative expression is that it is the excess of savings over investment. That is:

{where CA = current account, NS = national savings (private plus government sector), NI = national investment.}

If a nation is earning more than it spends the net effect will be to build up savings, except to the extent that those savings are being used for investment. If consumers can be encouraged to spend more instead of saving, or if the government runs a fiscal deficit to offset private savings, or if investment is increased, then any current account surplus will tend to be reduced. However in 2009 Germany amended her constitution to prohibit running a deficit greater than 0.35% of her GDP and calls to reduce her surplus by increasing demand have not been welcome by officials, adding to fears that the 2010s will not be an easy decade for the eurozone.

History of Balance of Payments Issues

Historically, accurate balance of payments figures were not generally available. However, this did not prevent a number of switches in opinion on questions relating to whether or not a nations government should use policy to encourage a favourable balance.

Pre 1820: Mercantilism

Up until the early 19th century, measures to promote a trade surplus such as tariffs were generally favoured. Power was associated with wealth, and with low levels of growth, nations were best able to accumulate funds either by running trade surpluses or by forcefully confiscating the wealth of others. From about the 16th century, Mercantilism was a prevalent theory influencing European rulers, who sometimes strove to have their countries out sell competitors and so build up a "war chest" of gold. This era saw low levels of economic growth; average global per capita income is not considered to have significantly risen in the whole 800 years leading up to 1820, and is estimated to have increased on average by less than 0.1% per year between 1700-1820.

1820-1914: Free Trade

From the late 18th century, mercantilism was challenged by the ideas of Adam Smith and other economic thinkers favouring free trade. After victory in the Napoleonic wars Great Britain began promoting free trade, unilaterally reducing her trade tariffs. Hoarding of gold was no longer encouraged, and in fact Britain exported more capital as a percentage of her national income than any other creditor nation has since.

Great Britain's capital exports further helped to correct global imbalances as they tended to be counter cyclical, rising when Britain's economy went into recession, thus compensating other states for income lost from export of goods. According to historian Carroll Quigley, Great Britain could afford to act benevolently in the 19th century due to the advantages of her geographical location, her naval power and her economic ascendancy as the first nation to enjoy an industrial revolution.

Though Current Account controls were still widely used (in fact all industrial nations apart from Great Britain and the Netherlands actually increased their tariffs and quotas in the decades leading up to 1914, though this was motivated more by a desire to protect "infant industries" than to encourage a trade surplus), capital controls were largely absent, and people were generally free to cross international borders without requiring passports. A gold standard enjoyed wide international participation especially from 1870, further contributing to close economic integration between nations. The period saw substantial global growth, in particular for the volume of international trade which grew tenfold between 1820-1870 and then by about 4% annually from 1870 to 1914.

1914-1945: Deglobalisation

The favourable economic conditions that had prevailed up until 1914 were shattered by the first world war, and efforts to re-establish them in the 1920s were not successful. Several countries rejoined the gold standard around 1925. But surplus countries didn't "play by the rules", sterilising gold inflows to a much greater degree than had been the case in the prewar period.

Deficit nations such as Great Britain found it harder to adjust by deflation as workers were more enfranchised and unions in particular were able to resist downwards pressure on wages. During the great depression most countries abandoned the gold standard, but imbalances remained an issue and international trade declined sharply. There was a return to mercantilist type "beggar thy neighbour" policies, with countries competitively devaluing their exchange rates, thus effectively competing to export unemployment.

1945-1971: Bretton Woods

Following World War II, the Bretton Woods institutions (the International Monetary Fund and World Bank) were set up to support an international monetary system designed to encourage free trade while also offer states options to correct imbalances without having to defalte their economies. Fixed but flexible exchange rates were established, with the system anchored by the dollar which alone remained convertible into gold, The Bretton Woods system ushered in a period of high global growth, known as the Golden Age of Capitalism, however it came under pressure due to imbalances related to the central role of the dollar, with imbalances causing gold to flow out of the US and a loss of confidence in the United States ability to supply gold for all future claims by dollar holders.

1971-2009: Transition, Washington Consensus, Bretton Woods II

The Bretton Woods system came to an end between 1971 and 1973. There were attempts to repair the system of fixed exchanged rates over the next few years, but these were soon abandoned, as were determined efforts for the US to avoid BOP imbalances. Part of the reason was displacement of the previous dominant economic paradigm-Keynesianism-by the Washington Consensus, with economists and economics writers such as Murray Rothbard and Milton Friedman arguing that there was no great need to be concerned about BOP issues. According to Rothbard:

Fortunately, the absurdity of worrying about the balance of payments is made evident by focusing on interstate trade. For nobody worries about the balance of payments between New York and New Jersey, or, for that matter, between Manhattan and Brooklyn, because there are no customs officials recording such trade and such balances.

In the immediate aftermath of the Bretton Woods collapse, countries generally tried to retain some control over their exchange rate by independently managing it, or by intervening in the Forex as part of a regional bloc, such as the Snake which formed in 1971. *The Snake* was a group of European countries who tried to retain stable rates at least with each other; the group eventually evolved into the ERM by 1979. From the mid 1970s however, and especially in the 1980s and early 90s, many other countries followed the US in liberalising controls on both their capital and current accounts, in adopting a somewhat relaxed attitude to their balance of payments and in allowing the value of their currency to float relatively freely with exchange rates determined mostly by the market. Developing countries who chose to allow the market to determine their exchange rates would often develop sizeable current account deficits, financed by capital account inflows such as loans and investments, though this often ended in crises when investors lost confidence.

A turning point was the 1997 Asian Financial Crisis, where unsympathetic responses by western powers caused policy makers in emerging economies to re-assess the wisdom of relying on the free market; by 1999 the developing world as a whole stopped running current account deficits while the US current account deficit began to rise sharply. This new form of imbalance began to develop in part due to the practice of emerging economies (principally China) in pegging their currency against the dollar, rather than allowing the value to freely float. The resulting state of affairs has been referred to as Bretton Woods II. According to economics writer Martin Wolf, in the eight years leading up to 2007, "three quarters of the foreign currency reserves accumulated since the beginning of time have been piled up".

2009 and Later: Post Washington Consensus

Speaking after the 2009 G-20 London summit, Gordon Brown announced "the Washington Consensus is over". There is now broad agreement that large imbalances between different countries do matter; for example mainstream US economist C. Fred Bergsten has argued the US deficit and the associated large inbound capital flows into the US was one of the causes of the financial crisis of 2007-2010. In 2007 when the crises began, the total BOP imbalance was $1680bn. On the credit side, the biggest current account surplus was China with approx. $362Bn, followed by Japan at $213Bn and Germany at £185BN, with oil producing countries such as Saudi Arabia also having large surpluses. On the debit side, the US had the biggest current account deficit at over £700Bn, with the UK, Spain and Australia together accounting for close to a further $300Bn. While there have been warnings of future cuts in public spending, deficit countries on the whole did not make these in 2009, in fact the opposite happened with increased public spending contributing to recovery as part of global efforts to increase demand. The emphases has instead been on the surplus countries, with the IMF, EU and nations such as the US, Brazil and Russia asking them to assist with the adjustments to correct the imbalances.

Economists such as Gregor Irwin and Philip R. Lane have suggested that increased use of pooled reserves could help emerging economies not to require such large reserves and thus have less need for current account surpluses. Writing for the FT in Jan 2009, Gillian Tett says she exspects to see policy makers becoming increasingly concerned about exchange rates over the comming year. Japan has allowed her currency to appreciate, but has only limited scope to contribute to the rebalancing efforts thanks in part to her ageing population. The Euro used by Germany is allowed to float fairly freely in value, however further appreciation would be problematic for other members of the currency union such as Spain, Greece and Ireland who run large deficits.

Therefore Germany has instead been asked to contribute by further promoting internal demand, but this hasn't been welcomed by German officials. China has been requested to allow the Renminbi to appreciate but has so far refused, the position expressed by her premier Wen Jiabao being that by keeping the value of the Renimbi stable against the dollar China has been helping the global recovery, and that calls to let her currency rise in value have been motivated by a desire to hold back China's development. After China reported favourable results for her December 2009 exports however, the Financial Times reported that analysts are optimistic that China will allow some appreciation of her currency around mid 2010. 2008 and 2009 did see some reduction in imbalances, but early indications towards the end of 2009 were that major imbalances such as the US current account deficit are set to begin increasing again, leaving the prospects for their resolution uncertain.

Capital Asset Pricing Model

In finance, the capital asset pricing model (CAPM) is used to determine a theoretically appropriate required rate of return of an asset, if that asset is to be added to an already well-diversified portfolio, given that asset's non-diversifiable risk. The model takes into account the asset's sensitivity to non-diversifiable risk (also known as systematic risk or market risk), often represented by the quantity beta (a) in the financial industry, as well as the expected return of the market and the expected return of a theoretical risk-free asset.

The model was introduced by Jack Treynor (1961, 1962), William Sharpe (1964), John Lintner (1965a,b) and Jan Mossin (1966) independently, building on the earlier work of Harry Markowitz on diversification and modern portfolio theory. Sharpe, Markowitz and Merton Miller jointly received the Nobel Memorial Prize in Economics for this contribution to the field of financial economics.

Asset-specific Required Return

The CAPM returns the asset-appropriate required return or discount rate-i.e. the rate at which future cash flows produced by the asset should be discounted given that asset's relative riskiness. Betas exceeding one signify more than average "riskiness"; betas below one indicate lower than average. Thus a more risky stock will have a higher beta and will be discounted at a higher rate; less sensitive stocks will have lower betas and be discounted at a lower rate. Given the accepted concave utility function, the CAPM is consistent with intuition-investors (should) require a higher return for holding a more risky asset.

Since beta reflects asset-specific sensitivity to non-diversifiable, i.e. market risk, the market as a whole, by definition, has a beta of one. Stock market indices are frequently used as local proxies for the market-and in that case (by definition) have a beta of one. An investor in a large, diversified portfolio (such as a mutual fund) therefore expects performance in line with the market.

The Market Portfolio

An investor might choose to invest a proportion of his or her wealth in a portfolio of risky assets with the remainder in cash-earning interest at the risk free rate (or indeed may borrow money to fund his or her purchase of risky assets in which case there is a negative cash weighting). Here, the ratio of risky assets to risk free asset does not determine overall return-this relationship is clearly linear. It is thus possible to achieve a particular return in one of two ways:

1. By investing all of one's wealth in a risky portfolio,
2. or by investing a proportion in a risky portfolio and the remainder in cash (either borrowed or invested).

For a given level of return, however, only one of these portfolios will be optimal (in the sense of lowest risk). Since the risk free asset is, by definition, uncorrelated with any other asset, option 2 will generally have the lower variance and hence be the more efficient of the two. This relationship also holds for portfolios along the efficient frontier: a higher return portfolio plus cash is more efficient than a lower return portfolio alone for that lower level of return. For a given risk free rate, there is only one optimal portfolio which can be combined with cash to achieve the lowest level of risk for any possible return. This is the market portfolio.

Net Capital Outflow

The importance of NCO. The domestic real interest rate determined in the domestic market for loanable funds moves along the NCO curve to determine the quantity of currency available for foreign exchange. This in turn determines the real exchange rate.

Net Capital Outflow (NCO) is the net flow of funds being invested abroad by a country during a certain period of time (usually a year). A positive NCO means that the country invests outside more than the world invests in it; a negative one, that the world invests in the country more than the country invests in the world. NCO is one of two major ways of characterizing the nature of a country's financial and economic interaction with the rest of the world (the other being the balance of trade).

Mundell-Fleming Model

The Mundell-Fleming model is an economic model first set forth by Robert Mundell and Marcus Fleming. The model is an extension of the IS-LM model. Whereas IS-LM deals with economy under autarky, the Mundell-Fleming model tries to describe an open economy.

Typically, the Mundell-Fleming model portrays the relationship between the nominal exchange rate and an economy's output (unlike the relationship between interest rate and the output in the IS-LM model) in the short run. The Mundell-Fleming model has been used to argue that an economy cannot simultaneously maintain a fixed exchange rate, free capital movement, and an independent monetary policy. This principle is frequently called "the Unholy Trinity," the "Irreconcilable Trinity," the "Inconsistent trinity" or the Mundell-Fleming "trilemma."

Mechanics of the Model

One important assumption is the equalization of the local interest rate to the global interest rate.

Under Flexible Exchange Rate Regime

We speak of a system of flexible exchange rates when governments (or central banks) allow the exchange rate to be determined by market forces alone.

Changes in Money Supply

An increase in money supply will shift the LM curve downward. This directly reduces the local interest rate and in turn forces the local interest rate lower than the global interest rate. This depreciates the exchange rate of local currency through capital outflow. (Hot money flows out to take advantage of higher interest rate abroad and hence currency depreciates.) The depreciation makes local goods cheaper compared to foreign goods and increases export and decreases import. Hence, net export is increased. Increased net export leads to the shifting of the IS curve (which is Y = C + I + G + NX) to the right to the point where the local interest rate will equalize with the global rate. At the same time, the BoP is supposed to shift too, as to reflect (1) depreciation of home currency and (2) an increase in current account or in other word, the increase in net export. These increases the overall income in the local economy. A decrease in money supply will cause the exact opposite of the process.

Changes in Government Spending

An increase in government expenditure shifts the IS curve to the right. The shift will cause the local interest rate to go above the global rate. The increase in local interest will cause capital inflow and the inflow will make the local currency stronger compared to foreign currencies. Strong exchange rate also makes foreign goods cheaper compared to local goods. This encourages greater import and discourages export and hence, lower net export. As a result, the IS will return to its original location where the local interest rate is equal to the global interest rate. The level of income of the local economy stays the same. The LM curve is not at all affected.

A decrease in government expenditure will reverse the process.

Changes in Global Interest Rate

An increase in the global interest rate will cause an upward pressure on the local interest rate. The pressure will subside as the local rate closes in on the global rate. When a positive differential between the global and the local rate occurs, holding the LM curve constant, capital will flow out of the local economy. This depreciates the local currency and helps boost net export. Increasing net export shifts the IS to the right. This shift will continue to the right until the local interest rate becomes as high as the global rate. A decrease in global interest rate will cause the reverse to occur.

Under Fixed Exchange Rate Regime

We speak of a system of fixed exchange rates when governments (or central banks) announce an exchange rate (the parity rate) at which they are prepared to buy or sell any amount of domestic currency.

Changes in Money Supply

Under the fixed exchange rate system, the local central bank or any monetary authority will only change the money supply in order to maintain a level of exchange rate. If there is a pressure to appreciate the exchange rate, the local authority will buy domestic currency in order to decrease the money supply to raise the exchange rate back to its original level. If there is pressure to depreciate the exchange rate, the local authority will buy foreign currency with domestic currency in order to increase the money supply and lower the exchange rate back to its original level. A revaluation occurs when there is a permanent increase in exchange rate and hence, decrease in money supply. Devaluation is the exact opposite of revaluation.

Changes in Government Expenditure

Increased government expenditure shifts the IS curve to the right. The shift results are a rise in the interest rate and hence, an appreciation of the exchange rate. However, the exchange rate is controlled by the local monetary authority in the framework of a fixed system. In order to maintain the exchange rate and eliminate the pressure from it, the monetary authority will purchase foreign currencies with local currencies until the pressure is gone i.e. back to the original level. Such action shifts the LM curve in tandem with the direction of the IS shift. This action increases the local currency supply in the market and lowers the exchange rate—or rather, return the rate back to its original state. In the end, the exchange rate stays the same but the general income in the economy increases.

The reverse is true when government expenditure decreases.

Changes in Global Interest Rate

To maintain the fixed exchange rate, the central bank must offset the capital flows (in or out) which are caused by the change of the global interest rate to the domestic rate. The central bank must restore the situation where the real domestic interest rate is equal to the real global interest rate to stop net capital flows from changing the exchange rate.

If the global interest rate increases above the domestic rate, capital will flow out to take advantage of this opportunity. (Hot money flows out of the economy) This would depreciate the home currency, so the central bank may buy the home currency and sell some of its foreign currency reserves to offset this outflow. This decrease in the money supply shifts the LM curve to the left until the domestic interest rate is the global interest rate. If the global interest rate declines below the domestic rate, the opposite occurs. Hot money flows in, the home currency appreciates, so the central bank offsets this by increasing the money supply (sell domestic currency, buy foreign currency), the LM curve shifts to the right, and the domestic interest rate becomes the global interest rate.

Differences from IS-LM

It is worth noting that some of the result from this model differs from the IS-LM because of the open economy assumption. Result for large open economy on the other hand falls within the result predicted by the IS-LM and the Mundell-Fleming models. The reason for such result is because a large open economy has both the characteristics of an autarky and a small open economy.

In the IS-LM, interest rate will be the key component in making both the money market and the good market in equilibrium. Under the Mundell-Fleming framework of small economy, interest rate is fixed and equilibrium in both market can only be achieved by a change of nominal exchange rate.

Example

A much simplified version of the Mundell-Fleming model can be illustrated by a small open economy, in which the domestic interest rate is exogenously predetermined by the *world interest rate* (r=r*).

Consider an exogenous increase in government expenditure, the IS curve will shift upward, with LM curve intact, causing the interest rate and the output to rise (partial crowding out effect) under the IS-LM model.

Nevertheless, as interest rate is predetermined in a small open economy, the LM* curve (of exchange rate and output) is vertical, which means there is exactly one output that can make the money market in the equilibrium under that interest rate. Even though the IS* curve still shift up, it will result in a higher exchange rate and same level of output (complete crowding out effect, which is different in the IS-LM model).

The example above makes an implicit assumption of flexible exchange rate. The Mundell-Fleming model can have completely different implications under different exchange rate regimes. For instance, under a fixed exchange rate system, with perfect capital mobility, monetary policy becomes ineffective. An expansionary monetary policy resulting in an outward shift of the LM curve would in turn make capital flow out of the economy. The central bank under a fixed exchange rate system would have to intervene by selling foreign money in exchange for domestic money to depreciate the foreign currency and appreciate the domestic currency. Selling foreign money and receiving domestic money would reduce real balances in the economy, until the LM curve shifts back to the left, and the interest rates come back to the world rate of interest i*.

Optimum Currency Area

In economics, an optimum currency area (OCA), also known as an optimal currency region (OCR), is a geographical region in which it would maximize economic efficiency to have the entire region share a single currency. It describes the optimal characteristics for the merger of currencies or the creation of a new currency. The theory is used often to argue whether or not a certain region is ready to become a monetary union, one of the final stages in economic integration.

An optimal currency area is often larger than a country. For instance, part of the rationale behind the creation of the euro is that the individual countries of Europe do not each form an optimal currency area, but that Europe as a whole does form an optimal currency area. The creation of the euro is often cited because it provides the most modern and largest-scale case study of the engineering of an optimum currency area, and provides a comparative before-and-after model by which to test the principles of the theory.

In theory, an optimal currency area could also be smaller than a country. Some economists have argued that the United States, for example, really consists of two optimal currency areas and that the United States should have two currencies, one for the western half and one for the eastern half. The theory of the optimal currency area was pioneered by economist Robert Mundell. Credit often goes to Mundell as the originator of the idea, but others point to earlier work done in the area by Abba Lerner.

OCA with Stationary Expectations

Published by Mundell in 1961, this is the most cited by economists. Here asymmetric shocks are considered to undermine the real economy, so if they are too important and cannot be controlled, a regime with floating rates is considered better, because the global monetary policy (interest rates) will not be fine tuned for the particular situation of each constituent region.

The four often cited criteria for a successful currency union are:

- Labour mobility across the region. This includes physical ability to travel (visas, workers' rights, etc.), lack of cultural barriers to free movement (such as different languages) and institutional arrangements (such as the ability to have superannuation transferred throughout the region) (Robert A. Mundell). In the case of the Eurozone, while capital is quite mobile, labour mobility is relatively low, especially when compared to the U.S. and Japan.
- Openness with capital mobility and price and wage flexibility across the region. This is so that the market forces of supply and demand automatically distribute money and goods to where they are needed. In practice this does not work perfectly as there is no true wage flexibility. (Ronald McKinnon). The Eurozone members trade heavily with each other (intra-European trade is greater than international trade), and most recent empirical analyses of the 'euro effect' suggest that the single currency has increased trade by 5 to 15 percent in the euro-zone when compared to trade between non-euro countries.
- A risk sharing system such as an automatic fiscal transfer mechanism to redistribute money to areas/sectors which have been adversely affected by the first two characteristics. This usually takes the form of taxation redistribution to less developed areas of a country/region. This policy, though theoretically accepted, is politically difficult to implement as the better-off regions rarely give up their revenue easily. Theoretically, Europe has no bailout clause in the Stability and Growth Pact, meaning that fiscal transfers are not allowed, but it is impossible to know what will happen in practice.
- Participant counties have similar business cycles. When on country experiences a boom or recession, other countries in the union are likely to follow. This allows the shared central bank to promote growth in downturns and to contain inflation in booms.

While Europe scores well on some of the measures characterising an OCA, it has lower labour mobility than the United States and similarly cannot rely on fiscal federalism to smooth out regional economic disturbances. Also, its Gini coefficient of 31 should have a stabilizing effect; in comparison, the USA has a Gini index of 46.9 (a lower measure indicates a more even distribution of wealth).

Additional criteria suggested are:

- Production diversification (Peter Kenen)
- Homogeneous preferences
- Commonality of destiny.

This theory has been most frequently applied in recent years to the euro and the European Union. Despite the promenience of the EU as the primary case study of a OCA, many have argued that the EU does actually not meet the criteria for an OCA. By these criteria the European Union does not constitute an Optimal Currency Area and therefore the euro should be a suboptimum union of currencies. However it is hoped that the creation of the euro will in itself help encourage the conditions enumerated by Mundell.

The primary criticism of Mundell's theory is that the only area that has optimal conditions for a single currency is one that *already has* a single currency, a circular argument. Furthermore, many existing currency areas do not fulfill these requirements.

OCA with International Risk Sharing

Here Mundell tries to model how exchange rate uncertainty will interfere with the economy; this model is less often cited (publication in 1973).

Supposing that the currency is managed properly, the larger the area, the better. In contrast with the previous model, asymmetric shocks are not considered to undermine the common currency because of the existence of the common currency. This spreads the shocks in the area because all regions share claims on each other in the same currency and can use them for dumping the shock, while in a flexible exchange rate regime, the cost will be concentrated on the individual regions, since the devaluation will reduce its buying power. So despite a less fine tuned monetary policy the real economy should do better.

A harvest failure, strikes, or war, in one of the countries causes a loss of real income, but the use of a common currency (or foreign exchange reserves) allows the country to run down its currency holdings and cushion the impact of the loss, drawing on the resources of the other country until the cost of the adjustment has been efficiently spread over the future. If, on the other hand, the two countries use separate monies with flexible exchange rates, the whole loss has to be borne alone; the common currency cannot serve as a shock absorber for the nation as a whole except insofar as the dumping of inconvertible currencies on foreign markets attracts a speculative capital inflow in favour of the depreciating currency. (Mundell, 1973, *Uncommon Arguments for Common Currencies*)

Robert A. Mundell is found in both sides of the debate about the euro. Most economists cite preferentially the first (stationary expectations) and conclude against the euro, yet Mundell advocates this one, and concludes in favour of the euro.

Rather than moving toward more flexibility in exchange rates within Europe the economic arguments suggest less flexibility and a closer integration of capital markets. These economic arguments are supported by social arguments as well. On every occasion when a social disturbance leads to the threat of a strike, and the strike to an increase in wages unjustified by increases in productivity and thence to devaluation, the national currency becomes threatened. Long-run costs for the nation as a whole are bartered away by governments for what they presume to be shortrun political benefits. If instead, the European currencies were bound together disturbances in the country would be cushioned, with the shock weakened by capital movements.

Business Cycle

The term business cycle (or economic cycle) refers to economy-wide fluctuations in production or economic activity over several months or years. These fluctuations occur around a long-term growth trend, and typically involve shifts over time between periods of relatively rapid economic growth (expansion or boom), and periods of relative stagnation or decline (contraction or recession).

These fluctuations are often measured using the growth rate of real gross domestic product. Despite being termed cycles, most of these fluctuations in economic activity do not follow a mechanical or predictable periodic pattern.

Clement Juglar

Clement Juglar (15 October 1819 in Paris – 28 February 1905 in Paris) was a French doctor and statistician.

Juglar Cycles

He was one of the first to develop an economic theory of business cycles. He identified the 7-11 year fixed investment cycle that is now associated with his name. Within the Juglar cycle one can observe oscillations of investments into fixed capital and not just changes in the level of employment of the fixed capital (and respective changes in inventories), as is observed with respect to Kitchin cycles. The recent research employing spectral analysis has confirmed the presence of Juglar cycles in the world GDP dynamics up to the present time.

Juglar's Impact

Juglar's publications led to other business cycle theories by later economists such as Joseph Schumpeter.

Publications of Clement Juglar

- "Des crises commerciales", 1856, in *Annuaire de l'economie politique.*
- *Des Crises commerciales et leur retour periodique en France, en Angleterre, et aux Etats-Unis.* Paris: Guillaumin, 1862.
- *Du Change et de la liberte d'emission*, 1868.
- *Les Banques de depot, d'escompte et d'emission*, 1884.

Kuznets Swing

Kuznets swing is a claimed medium-range economic wave with a period of 15-25 years found in 1930 by Simon Kuznets. Kuznets connected these waves with demographic processes, in particular with immigrant inflows/outflows and the changes in construction intensity that they caused, that is why he denoted them as "demographic" or "building" cycles/swings. Kuznets swings have been also interpreted as infrastructural investment cycles.

Kuznet's finding was debunked by Howrey (1968). Howrey showed that the apparent business cycle found by Kuznets was an artifact of the filter Kuznets used. Howrey showed that the same cyclical pattern could be found in white noise series when the Kuznets filter was applied.

Kondratiev Wave

Kondratiev waves—also called Supercycles, surges, long waves or K-waves—are described as regular, sinusoidal-like cycles in the modern (capitalist) world economy. Averaging fifty and ranging from approximately forty to sixty years in length, the cycles consist of alternating periods between high sectoral growth and periods of relatively slow growth. Unlike the short-term business cycle which in various forms has been familiar since the nineteenth century, the long wave of this theory does not belong within current orthodox economics and is sometimes categorized as part of heterodox economics (a catch-all term for alternative ideas to economic ideologies in force).

The Russian economist Nikolai Kondratiev (also written Kondratieff) was the first to bring these observations to international attention in his book *The Major Economic Cycles* (1925) alongside other works written in the same decade. Two Dutch economists, Jacob van Gelderen and Samuel de Wolff, had previously argued for the existence of 50 to 60 year cycles in 1913. However, the work of de Wolff and van Gelderen has only recently been translated from Dutch to reach a wider audience.

Kondratiev was a Soviet economist, but his economic conclusions were disliked by the Soviet leadership and upon their release he was quickly dismissed from his post as director of the Institute for the Study of Business Activity in the Soviet Union in 1928. His conclusions were seen as a criticism of Stalin's intentions for the Soviet economy: as a result he was sentenced to the Soviet Gulag and later received the death penalty in 1938.

Later, in *Business Cycles* (1939), Joseph Schumpeter suggested naming the cycles, "Kondratieff waves", in honour of the economist who first noticed them. In the 1950s, French economist Francois Simiand proposed naming the ascendant period of the cycle "Phase A" and the downward period "Phase B". Some market commentators divide the Kondratiev wave into four 'seasons', namely, the Kondratiev Spring (improvement or plateau) and Summer (acceleration or prosperity) of the ascendant period and the Kondratiev Fall (recession or plateau) and Winter (acceleration or depression) of the downward period.

Characteristics of the Cycle

The cycle is supposedly more visible in international production data than in individual national economies. It affects all the sectors of an economy, and concerns mainly output rather than prices (although Kondratieff had made observations focusing more on prices, inflation and interest rates). According to Kondratieff, the ascendant phase is characterized by an increase in prices and low interest rates, while the other phase consists of a decrease in prices and high interest rates.

Kondratieff identified three phases in the cycle: expansion, stagnation, recession. More common today is the division into four periods with a turning point (collapse) between the first and second phases. Writing in the 1920s, Kondratieff proposed to apply the theory to the 19th century:

- 1790 – 1849 with a turning point in 1815.

- 1850 – 1896 with a turning point in 1873.
- Kondratieff supposed that in 1896, a new cycle had started.

The phases of Kondratieff's waves also carry with them social shifts and changes in the public mood. The first stage of expansion and growth, the "Spring" stage, encompasses a social shift in which the wealth, capital accumulation, and innovation that are present in this first period of the cycle create upheavals and displacements in society. The economic changes result in redefining work and the role of participants in society. In the next phase, the "Summer" stagflation, there is a mood of affluence from the previous growth stage that change the attitude towards work in society, creating inefficiencies. After this stage comes the season of deflationary growth, or the plateau period. The popular mood changes during this period as well. It shifts toward stability, normalcy, and isolationism after the policies and economics during unpopular excesses of war. Finally, the "Winter" stage, that of severe depression, includes the integration of previous social shifts and changes into the social fabric of society, supported by the shifts in innovation and technology.

A fourth cycle may have roughly coincided with the Cold War: beginning in 1949, turning with the economic peak of the mid-1960s and the Vietnam War escalation, hitting a trough in 1982 amidst growing predictions in the United States of worldwide Soviet domination and ending with the fall of the Berlin Wall in 1989. The current cycle most likely peaked in 1999 with a possible winter phase beginning in late 2008. The Austrian-school economists point out that extreme price inflation in the absence of economic growth is a form of capital destruction, allowing either stagflation (as in the 1970s and much of the 2000s during the gold and oil price run-ups) or deflation (as in the 1930s and possibly following the crash in commodity prices beginning in 2008) to represent a recession or depression phase of the Kondratieff theory.

Tentative Explanations of the Cycle

Early on, four schools of thought emerged as to why capitalist economies have these long waves. These schools of thought centered on innovations, capital investment, war and capitalist crisis. According to the innovation theory, these waves arise from the bunching of basic innovations that launch technological revolutions that in turn create leading industrial or commercial sectors. Kondratiev's ideas were taken up by Joseph Schumpeter in the 1930s. The theory hypothesized the existence of very long-run macroeconomic and price cycles, originally estimated to last 50–54 years. A rough schematic drawing showing the "World Economy" over time according to the Kondratiev theory.

Since the inception of the theories, various studies have expanded the range of possible cycles, finding longer or shorter cycles in the data. The Marxist scholar Ernest Mandel revived interest in long wave theory with his 1964 essay predicting the end of the long boom after five years and in his Alfred Marshall lectures in 1979. However, in Mandel's theory, there are no long "cycles", only distinct epochs of faster and slower growth spanning 20–25 years. More recently, investment theorist Ian Gordon has advocated a 4 season Kondratiev model in which spring is moderate growth from a stock market and inflationary bottom, summer is characterized by accelerating growth and high inflation, autumn is characterized by declining inflation and asset bubbles, and winter involves the collapse of the asset bubbles.

Long wave theory is not accepted by most academic economists, but it is one of the bases of innovation-based, development, and evolutionary economics, i.e. the main heterodox stream in economics. Among economists who accept it, there has been no universal agreement about the start and the end years of particular waves. This points to another criticism of the theory: that it amounts to seeing patterns in a mass of statistics that aren't really there.

Moreover, there is a lack of agreement over the cause of this phenomenon. How much this matters is disputed: some scientific patterns have in the past been identified before an explanation could be advanced. (The best known example is that of the precursors to the periodic table, which were in fact rejected by many scientists precisely on the grounds of lack of explanation.)

There is controversy over the validity of Kondratiev's theory among many scholars. Some believe that not enough is attributed to actual human errors that have created some of the economic situations of history, and too much to the inevitability of the characteristics of the phases of the waves. They claim that many of the situations were entirely avoidable, not the consequences of an unstoppable wave pattern. Others doubt the legitimacy of Kondratiev's waves because they believe that every wave is a structural cycle that has unique characteristics and cannot be repeated. There is also controversy over Kondratiev's research—many believe that the conclusions and results of his research are biased because he highlighted and used only certain events to reach his conclusions and left out other important data and events that could have affected his outcomes.

Credit/Debt Cycle

The credit cycle is the expansion and contraction of access to credit over the course of the business cycle. Some economists, including Barry Eichengreen, Hyman Minsky, and other Post-Keynesian economists, and some members of the Austrian school, regard credit cycles as the fundamental process driving the business cycle. However, mainstream economists believe that the credit cycle can only partially explain the phenomenon of business cycles.

During the upward phase in the credit cycle, asset prices experience bouts of competitive, leveraged bidding, inducing asset price inflation in a particular asset market due to the recursive "ballooning" nature inherent in fractional reserve banking. This can then cause an unsustainable, speculative price "bubble" to develop. As this upswing in new debt creation also increases the money supply and stimulates economic activity, it tends to temporarily raise economic growth and employment.

When new borrowers cannot be found to purchase at inflated prices, a price collapse can occur in the market segment inflated by excess debt, along with a dramatic reduction in liquidity in that market. This can then cause insolvency, bankruptcy, and foreclosure for those borrowers who came in late to that market. If widespread, this can then damage the solvency and profitability of the private banking system itself, resulting in a dramatic reduction in new lending as lenders attempt to protect their balance sheets from further losses. This in turn results in a contraction in the growth of the money supply, often referred to as a "credit squeeze" or a "drying up of liquidity".

In the Kiyotaki-Moore model of the business cycle, collateral constraints amplify the effects of shocks to the real economy. Prime examples of this "boom-bust" cycle of credit creation and destruction can be found in the United States housing bubble and the subsequent subprime mortgage crisis, the dotcom bubble and the Japanese asset price bubble.

Debt Deflation

Debt deflation is a theory of economic cycles, which holds that recessions and depressions are due to the overall level of debt shrinking (deflating): the credit cycle is the cause of the economic cycle.

The theory was developed by Irving Fisher following the Wall Street Crash of 1929 and the ensuing Great Depression. Debt deflation was largely ignored in favour of the ideas of John Maynard Keynes in Keynesian economics, but has enjoyed a resurgence of interest since the 1980s, both in mainstream economics and in the heterodox school of Post-Keynesian economics, and has subsequently been developed by such Post-Keynesian economists as Hyman Minsky and Steve Keen.

Fisher's Formulation

In Fisher's formulation of debt deflation, when the debt bubble bursts the following sequence of events occurs:

Assuming, accordingly, that, at some point of time, a state of over-indebtedness exists, this will tend to lead to liquidation, through the alarm either of debtors or creditors or both. Then we may deduce the following chain of consequences in nine links:

1. Debt liquidation leads to distress selling and to
2. Contraction of deposit currency, as bank loans are paid off, and to a slowing down of velocity of circulation. This contraction of deposits and of their velocity, precipitated by distress selling, causes
3. A fall in the level of prices, in other words, a swelling of the dollar. Assuming, as above stated, that this fall of prices is not interfered with by reflation or otherwise, there must be
4. A still greater fall in the net worths of business, precipitating bankruptcies and
5. A like fall in profits, which in a "capitalistic," that is, a private-profit society, leads the concerns which are running at a loss to make
6. A reduction in output, in trade and in employment of labour. These losses, bankruptcies and unemployment, lead to
7. pessimism and loss of confidence, which in turn lead to
8. Hoarding and slowing down still more the velocity of circulation.
9. Complicated disturbances in the rates of interest, in particular, a fall in the nominal, or money, rates and a rise in the real, or commodity, rates of interest.

Rejection of Previous Assumptions

Prior to his theory of debt deflation, Fisher had subscribed to the then-prevailing, and still mainstream, theory of general equilibrium. In order to apply this to financial markets, which involve transactions across time in the form of debt-receiving money now in exchange for something in future-he made two further assumptions:

(A) The market must be cleared—and cleared with respect to every interval of time.

(B) The debts must be paid.

In view of the Depression, he rejected equilibrium, and noted that in fact debts might not be paid, but instead defaulted on:

It is as absurd to assume that, for any long period of time, the variables in the economic organization, or any part of them, will "stay put," in perfect equilibrium, as to assume that the Atlantic Ocean can ever be without a wave.

He further rejected the notion that over-confidence alone, rather than the resulting debt, was a significant factor in the Depression:

I fancy that over-confidence seldom does any great harm except when, as, and if, it beguiles its victims into debt.

In the context of this quote and the development of his theory and the central role it places on debt, it is of note that Fisher was personally ruined due to his having assumed debt due to his over-confidence prior to the crash, by buying stocks on margin.

Subsequent Developments

Debt deflation has been studied and developed largely in the Post-Keynesian school.

The Financial Instability Hypothesis of Hyman Minsky, developed in the 1980s, complements Fisher's theory in providing an explanation of how credit bubbles form:

FIH explains how bubbles form, while DD explains how they burst and the resulting economic effects. Mathematical models of debt deflation have recently been developed by Australian economist Steve Keen.

Debt deflation has been referred to alliteratively as the "D-process" by Ray Dalio of Bridgewater Associates, who suggests it as the template for understanding the financial crisis of 2007-2010.

Mainstream Interest

Initially Fisher's work was largely ignored, in favour of the work of Keynes. The following decades saw occasional mention of deflationary spirals due to debt in the mainstream, notably in *The Great Crash, 1929* of John Kenneth Galbraith in 1954, and the credit cycle has occasionally been cited as a leading cause of economic cycles in the post-WWII era, as in (Eckstein & Sinai 1990), but private debt remained absent from mainstream macroeconomic models. James Tobin cited Fisher as instrumental in his theory of economic instability.

The lack of influence of debt-deflation in academic economics is thus described by Ben Bernanke in Bernanke:

Fisher's idea was less influential in academic circles, though, because of the counterargument that debt-deflation represented no more than a redistribution from one group (debtors) to another (creditors). Absent implausibly large differences in marginal spending propensities among the groups, it was suggested, pure redistributions should have no significant macroeconomic effects.

Bernanke's dismissal of debt deflation is criticized as improperly applying the theory of general equilibrium-in equilibrium, marginal redistribution of income produces no macroeconomic effects, but financial crises are characterized by *not* being in equilibrium and markets failing to clear-debt ceasing to grow and instead falling, debtors defaulting, rising unemployment-and thus, it is argued, equilibrium analysis is inapplicable and misleading.

There was a renewal of interest in debt deflation in academia in the 1980s and 1990s, and a further renewal of interest in debt deflation due to the Financial crisis of 2007-2010 and the ensuing Late-2000s recession.

Bernanke's interpretation of debt deflation has been criticized by proponents of debt deflation, notably with his characterization of Fisher's work omitting the fundamental role of *debt,* leading to deflation, instead skipping debt altogether and starting with deflation:

Fisher envisioned a dynamic process in which falling asset and commodity prices created pressure on nominal debtors, forcing them into distress sales of assets, which in turn led to further price declines and financial difficulties. Bernanke.

Real Business Cycle Theory

Real business cycle theory (or RBC theory) is a class of macroeconomic models in which business cycle fluctuations to a large extent can be accounted for by real (in contrast to nominal) shocks. (The four primary economic fluctuations are secular (trend), business cycle, seasonal, and random.) Unlike other leading theories of the business cycle, it sees recessions and periods of economic growth as the efficient response to exogenous changes in the real economic environment. That is, the level of national output necessarily maximizes *expected* utility, and government should therefore concentrate on the long-run structural policy changes and not intervene through discretionary fiscal or monetary policy designed to actively smooth economic short-term fluctuations.

According to RBC theory, business cycles are therefore "real" in that they do not represent a failure of markets to clear, but rather reflect the most efficient possible operation of the economy, given the structure of the economy. It differs in this way from other theories of the business cycle, like Keynesian economics and Monetarism, which see recessions as the failure of some market to clear. RBC theory is associated with freshwater economics (the Chicago school of economics, in the neoclassical tradition), and is rejected and harshly criticized by other schools within mainstream economics, notably Keynesians.

Business Cycles

If we were to take snapshots of an economy at different points in time, no two photos would look alike. This occurs for two reasons:

1. Many advanced economies exhibit sustained growth over time. That is, snapshots taken many years apart will most likely depict higher levels of economy activity in the later period
2. There exist seemingly random fluctuations around this growth trend. Thus given two snapshots in time, predicting the later with the earlier is nearly impossible.

A common way to observe such behaviour is by looking at a time series of an economy's output, more specifically gross national product (GNP). This is just the value of the goods and services produced by a country's businesses and workers.

While we see continuous growth of output, it is not a steady increase. There are times of faster growth and times of slower growth. A common method to obtain this trend is the Hodrick-Prescott filter. The basic idea is to find a balance between the extent to which general growth trend follows the cyclical movement (since long term growth rate is not likely to be perfectly constant) and how smooth it is. The HP filter identifies the longer term fluctuations as part of the growth trend while classifying the more jumpy fluctuations as part of the cyclical component.

Observe the difference between this growth component and the jerkier data. Economists refer to these cyclical movements about the trend as business cycles. A point on this line indicates at that year, there is no deviation from the trend. All other points above and below the line imply deviations. By using log real GNP the distance between any point and the 0 line roughly equals the percentage deviation from the long run growth trend.

We call relatively large positive deviations (those above the 0 axis) peaks. We call relatively large negative deviations (those below the 0 axis) troughs. A series of positive deviations leading to peaks are booms and a series of negative deviations leading to troughs are recessions.

At a glance, the deviations just look like a string of waves bunched together—nothing about it appears consistent. To explain causes of such fluctuations may appear rather difficult given these irregularities. However, if we consider other macroeconomic variables, we will observe patterns in these irregularities. Observe how the peaks and troughs align at almost the same places and how the upturns and downturns coincide.

We might predict that other similar data may exhibit similar qualities. For example, (a) labour, hours worked (b) productivity, how effective firms use such capital or labour, (c) investment, amount of capital saved to help future endeavors, and (d) capital stock, value of machines, buildings and other equipment that help firms produce their goods.

Stylized Facts

By eyeballing the data, we can infer several regularities, sometimes called stylized facts. One is persistence. For example, if we take any point in the series above the trend, the probability the next period is still above the trend is very high. However, this persistence wears out over time. That is, economic activity in the short run is quite predictable but due to the irregular long-term nature of fluctuations, forecasting in the long run is much more difficult if not impossible.

The magnitude of fluctuations in output and hours worked are nearly equal. Consumption and productivity are similarly much smoother than output while investment fluctuates much more than output. Capital stock is the least volatile of the indicators.

Yet another regularity is the co-movement between output and the other macroeconomic variables. Procyclical variables have positive correlations since it usually increases during booms and decreases during recessions. Vice versa, a countercyclical variable associates with negative correlations. Acyclical, correlations close to zero, implies no systematic relationship to the business cycle. We find that productivity is slightly procyclical. This implies workers and capital are more productive when the economy is experiencing a boom. They aren't quite as productive when the economy is experiencing a slowdown. Similar explanations follow for consumption and investment, which are strongly procyclical. Labour is also procyclical while capital stock appears acyclical.

Observing these similarities yet seemingly non-deterministic fluctuations about trend, we come to the burning question of why any of this occurs. It's common sense that people prefer economic booms over recessions. It follows that if all people in the economy make optimal decisions, these fluctuations are caused by something outside the decision-making process. So the key question really is: *what main factor influences and subsequently changes the decisions of all actors in an economy?*

Austrian Business Cycle Theory

The Austrian business cycle theory is an explanation of the phenomenon of business cycles held by the Austrian School of economics. The theory views business cycles (or, as some Austrians prefer, "credit cycles") as the inevitable consequence of excessive growth in bank credit, exacerbated by inherently damaging and ineffective central bank policies, which cause interest rates to remain too low for too long, resulting in excessive credit creation, speculative economic bubbles and lowered savings.

The theory proposes that a sustained period of low interest rates and excessive credit creation results in a volatile and unstable imbalance between saving and investment. According to the theory, the business cycle unfolds in the following way. Low interest rates tend to stimulate borrowing from the banking system. This expansion of credit causes an expansion of the supply of money, through the money creation process in a fractional reserve banking system. This in turn leads to an unsustainable credit-sourced boom during which the artificially stimulated borrowing seeks out diminishing investment opportunities. This credit-sourced boom results in widespread malinvestments, causing capital resources to be misallocated into areas that would not attract investment if the money supply remained stable. A correction or "credit crunch" – commonly called a "recession" or "bust" – occurs when exponential credit creation cannot be sustained. Then the money supply suddenly and sharply contracts when markets finally "clear", causing resources to be reallocated back towards more efficient uses. The main proponents of the Austrian business cycle theory historically were Ludwig von Mises and Friedrich Hayek. Hayek won a Nobel Prize in economics in 1974 (shared with Gunnar Myrdal) in part for his work on this theory.

Austrian business cycle theory contradicts mainstream economic understanding of business cycles, and is generally rejected by mainstream economists. Economists such as Milton Friedman, Gordon Tullock, Bryan Caplan, and Paul Krugman have said that they regard the theory as incorrect.

Origin

The trade cycle argument first appeared in the last few pages of Ludwig von Mises's *The Theory of Money and Credit* (1912). This early development of Austrian business cycle theory was a direct manifestation of Mises's rejection of the concept of neutral money and emerged as an almost incidental by-product of his exploration of the theory of banking. David Laidler has observed in a chapter on the theory that the origins lie in the ideas of Knut Wicksell.

Austrian economist Roger Garrison explains the origins of the theory: Grounded in the economic theory set out in Carl Menger's *Principles of Economics* and built on the vision of a capital-using production process developed in Eugen von Bohm-Bawerk's *Capital and Interest*, the Austrian theory of the business cycle remains sufficiently distinct to justify its national identification. But even in its earliest rendition in Ludwig von Mises' *Theory of Money and Credit* and in subsequent exposition and extension in F. A. Hayek's *Prices and Production*, the theory incorporated important elements from Swedish and British economics.

Knut Wicksell's *Interest and Prices*, which showed how prices respond to a discrepancy between the bank rate and the real rate of interest, provided the basis for the Austrian account of the misallocation of capital during the boom.

The market process that eventually reveals the intertemporal misallocation and turns boom into bust resembles an analogous process described by the British Currency School, in which international misallocations induced by credit expansion are subsequently eliminated by changes in the terms of trade and hence in specie flow.

A popularized version of the theory is presented in Murray Rothbard's pamphlet *Economic Depressions: Their Cause and Cure*, which explains the business cycle by focusing on excessive bank-sourced credit expansion and centralized government intervention (through the actions of a central bank). Rothbard went into much greater detail in his book *What Has Government Done to Our Money?*.

Financial Crisis of 2007–2010

Economist Tyler Cowen in 2005 said that Austrian business cycle theory should be refocused to result in a viable synthesis of Keynesian and Hayekian theories. In 2005 Cowen also said that if he believed in Austrian business cycle theory he would say that U.S. economy is overinvested in housing and a massive shock (sectoral shift toward exports) will result.

After the United States housing bubble began its decline in 2006, Peter Schiff made some predictions regarding a housing crash in the US, though (as of early 2009) Schiff's investment firm had not been able to profit from strategies based on his predictions:

Today's home prices are completely unsustainable... What's going to happen in 2007 is that... these sky-high real estate prices are going to come crashing back to earth as well as the knock-on effects for the financial sector in 2007:

It's not just sub-prime... This is going to be an enormous credit crunch... The fundamentals are not sound... The worst is yet to come. Stay away from the financials – they're toxic.

And for the wider economy in 2008:

By November it'll be obvious that we're in a pretty big recession... it's not going to be months, it's going to be years.

The financial crisis of 2007-2010 has resulted in a revival of interest in the Austrian business cycle theory, but has also resulted in a revival of interest of theories more critical of Austrian theory, such as Keynesianism.

Similar Theories

The Austrian theory is considered one of the precursors to the modern credit cycle theory, which is emphasized by Post-Keynesian economists, economists at the Bank for International Settlements, and by a few mainstream academics such as Hyman Minsky and Charles P. Kindleberger. These two emphasize asymmetric information and agency problems. (Henry George, another precursor, emphasized the negative impact of speculative increases in the value of land, which places a heavy burden of mortgage payments on consumers and companies.)

A different theory of credit cycles is the debt-deflation theory of Irving Fisher, which is today placed in the Post-Keynesian tradition. The difference between these may be stated as debt-deflation being a *demand*-side theory, which emphasizes the period *after* the peak – the end of a credit bubble and contraction of debt causing a fall in *aggregate demand* – while the Austrian theory is a *supply*-side theory, which emphasizes the period *before* the peak – the growth of debt during the growth phase causing malinvestment. The theories may thus be seen as complementary, addressing different aspects of the issue, and are so-considered by some economists.

In 2003 Barry Eichengreen laid out modern credit boom theory as a cycle in which loans increase as the economy expands, particularly where regulation is weak, and through these loans money supply increases. Inflation remains low, however, because of either a pegged exchange rate or a supply shock, and thus the central bank does not tighten credit and money. Increasingly speculative loans are made as diminishing returns lead to reduced yields. Eventually inflation begins or the economy slows, and when asset prices decline, a bubble is pricked which encourages a macroeconomic bust.

In 2006 William White argued that "financial liberalization has increased the likelihood of boom-bust cycles of the Austrian sort". While White conceded that the status quo policy had been successful in reducing the impacts of busts, he commented that the view on inflation should perhaps be longer term and that the excesses of the time seemed dangerous. In addition, White believes that the Austrian explanation of the business cycle might be relevant once again in an environment of excessively low interest rates. According to the theory, a sustained period of low interest rates and excessive credit creation results in a volatile and unstable imbalance between saving and investment.

However, the explanations offered by these credit cycle theories do not depend on an ideological opposition to central banking, in the way that Austrian theory does.

Empirical Research

In 1969, Nobel Laureate Milton Friedman, after examining the history of business cycles in the US, concluded that "The Hayek-Mises explanation of the business cycle is contradicted by the evidence. It is, I believe, false." He analysed the issue using newer data in 1993, and again reached the same conclusions.

In 2001, Austrian economist James P. Keeler stated that the hypotheses of the theory are consistent with his preliminary empirical research.

Critiques

The Austrian theory of the business cycle is now rarely discussed by mainstream economists, but was more actively debated in the 20th century. Nobel laureate Hayek's formulation of the theory in the 1930s was harshly criticized by John Maynard Keynes, Piero Sraffa and Nicholas Kaldor. In 1932, Piero Sraffa argued that Hayek's formulation of the business cycle required a kind of money that was entirely neutral, and was in effect a simple commodity, unable to act as a store of value or be loaned at interest. Hayek reformulated his theory in response to those objections, but his reformulation was then criticised by Nicholas Kaldor in 1939 and again in 1942.

More recently, mainstream economists like Nobel laureate Milton Friedman, Gordon Tullock, Bryan Caplan, and Paul Krugman have stated that they regard the theory as incorrect. David Laidler views the theory as motivated by the political leanings of its major proponents, as Austrian economists are known for their strong opposition to government involvement in the economy, and argues that the theory was discredited because of its association with "nihilistic policy prescriptions" for the Great Depression. On the other hand, Laidler also stated that its core insights were materially worthwhile, especially as related to the work of Dennis Robertson.

In 1988 Gordon Tullock explained his disagreement with the theory. His main point is that "if the process that Rothbard describes did occur, there would be many corporate bankruptcies and business people jumping out of the windows of office buildings, but there would be only minor transitional unemployment. In fact, measured GNP would be higher as a result."

This is because the Austrian theory implies fluctuations in investment, but not in the production decisions of firms. Nobel laureate Paul Krugman also made a similar argument when he stated that the theory implies that consumption would increase during downturns and cannot explain the empirical observation that spending in *all sectors* of the economy falls during a recession. Mainstream economists argue that the theory requires bankers and investors to exhibit a kind of irrationality – that they be regularly fooled into making unprofitable investments by temporarily low interest rates.

Critics have also argued that, as the theory points to the actions of fractional-reserve banks and central banks to explain business cycles, it fails to explain the existence of business cycles before the establishment of Federal Reserve in 1913.

For example, the Panic of 1873 would initiate the Long Depression in US and much of Europe. Additionally, there were also severe market crashes in the United States of the magnitude of the 1929 crash in 1869, 1882, 1884, 1896, 1901, and 1907; there was no central bank or national monetary policy in the US during these crises. In fact, the movement to establish central banking in the United States was in part a response to the business cycle, particularly the Panic of 1907.

Mainstream economists believe that economies have experienced less severe boom-bust cycles after World War II, since central banks have started using monetary policy to stabilize economies.

Notable Responses

With regards to the criticism which concludes that the Austrian Business Cycle theory requires widespread irrationality about the future of interest rates, Austrian thinkers Carilli and Dempster have offered a response. They have argued that a prisoner's dilemma framework can explain the apparent failure of investors to learn from previous experience.

In response to several severe economic crashes that occurred without a central bank, historian Thomas Woods argues in his book *Meltdown* that the crashes were caused by various privately-owned banks (with state charters) which issued paper money, supposedly convertible to gold, in amounts greatly exceeding their gold reserves.

Mitigating

Most social indicators (mental health, crimes, suicides) worsen during economic recessions. As periods of economic stagnation are painful for the many who lose their jobs, there is often political pressure for governments to mitigate recessions. Since the 1940s, following the Keynesian revolution, most governments of developed nations have seen the mitigation of the business cycle as part of the responsibility of government, under the rubric of stabilization policy.

Since in the Keynesian view, recessions are caused by inadequate aggregate demand, when a recession occurs the government should increase the amount of aggregate demand and bring the economy back into equilibrium. This the government can do in two ways, firstly by increasing the money supply (expansionary monetary policy) and secondly by increasing government spending or cutting taxes (expansionary fiscal policy).

By contrast, some economists, notably New classical economist Robert Lucas, argue that the welfare cost of business cycles are very small to negligible, and that governments should focus on long-term growth instead of stabilization. However, even according to Keynesian theory, managing economic policy to smooth out the cycle is a difficult task in a society with a complex economy. Some theorists, notably those who believe in Marxian economics, believe that this difficulty is insurmountable. Karl Marx claimed that recurrent business cycle crises were an inevitable result of the operations of the capitalistic system. In this view, all that the government can do is to change the *timing* of economic crises. The crisis could also show up in a different *form*, for example as severe inflation or a steadily increasing government deficit. Worse, by delaying a crisis, government policy is seen as making it *more dramatic* and thus more painful.

Additionally, since the 1960s neoclassical economists have played down the ability of Keynesian policies to manage an economy. Since the 1960s, economists like Nobel Laureates Milton Friedman and Edmund Phelps have made ground in their arguments that inflationary expectations negate the Phillips curve in the long run. The stagflation of the 1970s provided striking support for their theories, defying the simple Keynesian prediction that recessions and inflation cannot occur together. Friedman has gone so far as to argue that all the central bank of a country should do is to avoid making large mistakes, as he believes they did by contracting the money supply very rapidly in the face of the Wall Street Crash of 1929, in which they made what would have been a recession into the Great Depression. In macroeconomics, the welfare cost of business cycles refers to the decrease in social welfare, if any, caused by business cycle fluctuations.

Nobel economist Robert Lucas proposed measuring the cost of business cycles as the percentage increase in consumption that would be necessary to make a representative consumer indifferent between a smooth, non-fluctuating, consumption trend and one that is subject to business cycles.

Under the assumption that business cycles represent random shocks around a trend growth path, Robert Lucas argued that the cost of business cycles is extremely small and as a result the focus of both academic economists and policy makers on economic stabilization policy rather than on long term growth has been misplaced. Lucas himself, after calculating this cost back in 1987, re-oriented his own macroeconomic research program away from the study of short run fluctuations.

However, Lucas' conclusion is controversial. In particular, Keynesian economists typically argue that business cycles should not be understood as fluctuations above and below a trend. Instead, they argue that booms are times when the economy is near its potential output trend, and that recessions are times when the economy is substantially below trend, so that there is a large output gap. Under this viewpoint, the welfare cost of business cycles is larger, because an economy with cycles not only suffers more variable consumption, but also lower consumption on average.

Basic Intuition

If we consider two consumption paths, each with the same trend and the same initial level of consumption-and as a result same level of consumption per period on average-but with different levels of volatility, then, according to economic theory, the less volatile consumption path will be preferred to the more volatile one. This is due to Risk aversion on part of individual agents. One way to calculate how costly this greater volatility is in terms of individual (or, under some restrictive conditions, social) welfare is to ask what percentage of her annual average consumption would an individual be willing to sacrifice in order to eliminate this volatility entirely.

Another way to express this is by asking how much an individual with a smooth consumption path would have to be compensated in terms of average consumption in order to accept the volatile path instead of the one without the volatility. The resulting amount of compensation, expressed as a percentage of average annual consumption, is the cost of the fluctuations calculated by Lucas. It is a function of people's degree of risk aversion and of the magnitude of the fluctuations which are to be eliminated, as measured by the standard deviation of the natural log of consumption.

Risk Aversion and the Equity Premium Puzzle

However, a major problem related to the above way of estimating (hence and in fact, possibly to Lucas' entire approach is the so-called Equity premium puzzle, first observed by Rajnish Mehra and Edward Prescott. The analysis above implies that since macroeconomic risk is unimportant, the premium associated with systematic risk, that is, risk in returns to an asset that is correlated with aggregate consumption should be small (less than 0.5 percentage points for the values of risk aversion considered above). In fact the premium has averaged around six percentage points.

In a survey of the implications of the equity premium, Simon Grant and John Quiggin note that 'A high cost of risk means that recessions are extremely destructive'.

5

Accounting Management

Accounting, Accountability and the Account

Businesses exist to provide goods or services to customers in exchange for a financial reward. Public-sector and not-for-profit organisations also provide services, although their funding comes not from customers but from government or charitable donations.

While this book is primarily concerned with profit-oriented businesses, most of the principles are equally applicable to the public and not-for-profit sectors. Business is not about accounting. It is about markets, people and operations (the delivery of products or services), although accounting is implicated in all of these decisions because it is the financial representation of business activity.

The American Accounting Association defined accounting in 1966 as:

The process of identifying, measuring and communicating economic information to permit informed judgements and decisions by users of the information.

This is an important definition because:

- it recognizes that accounting is a process: that process is concerned with capturing business events, recording their financial effect, summarizing and reporting the result of those effects and interpreting those results;
- it is concerned with economic information: while this is predominantly financial, it also allows for non-financial information;

- its purpose is to support 'informed judgements and decisions' by users: this emphasizes the decision usefulness of accounting information and the broad spectrum of 'users' of that information.

The notion of accounting for a narrow (shareholders and financiers) or a broad (societal) group of users is an important philosophical debate to which we will return throughout this book. This debate derives from questions of accountability: to whom is the business accountable and for what and what is the role of accounting in that accountability?

Boland and Schultze defined accountability as: The capacity and willingness to give explanations for conduct, stating how one has discharged one's responsibilities, an explaining of conduct with a credible story of what happened and a calculation and balancing of competing obligations, including moral ones. Hoskin suggested that accountability is: more total and insistent... [it] ranges more freely over space and time, focusing as much on future potential as past accomplishment. Boland and Schultze argued that accountability entails both a narration of what transpired and a reckoning of money, both meanings deriving from the original meanings of the word account.

Accounting is a collection of systems and processes used to record, report and interpret business transactions. Accounting provides an account – an explanation or report in financial terms – about the transactions of an organisation. It enables managers to satisfy the stakeholders in the organisation (owners, government, financiers, suppliers, customers, employees etc.) that they have acted in the best interests of stakeholders rather than themselves.

This is the notion of accountability to others, a result of the stewardship function of managers that takes place through the process of accounting. Stewardship is an important concept because in all but very small businesses, the owners of businesses are not the same as the managers. This separation of ownership from control makes accounting particularly influential due to the emphasis given to increasing shareholder wealth (or shareholder value). Accountability results in the production of financial statements, primarily for those interested parties who are external to the business. This function is called financial accounting.

Accounting is traditionally seen as fulfilling three functions:

- *Scorekeeping:* Capturing, recording, summarizing and reporting financial performance.

- *Attention-directing:* Drawing the attention of managers to and assisting in the interpretation of, business performance, particularly in terms of the comparison between actual and planned performance.
- *Problem-solving:* Identifying the best choice from a range of alternative actions.

Here we acknowledge the role of the scorekeeping function while emphasizing attention-directing and problem-solving as taking place through three inter-related functions, all part of the role of functional as well as financial managers:

- *Planning:* Establishing goals and strategies to achieve those goals.
- *Decision-making:* Using financial information to make decisions consistent with those goals and strategies.
- *Control:* Using financial information to maintain performance as close as possible to plan, or using the information to modify the plan itself.

Planning, decision-making and control are particularly relevant as increasingly businesses have been decentralized into many business units, where much of the planning, decision-making and control is focused. Managers need financial and non-financial information to develop and implement strategy by planning for the future (budgeting); making decisions about products, services, prices and what costs to incur (decision-making using cost information); and ensuring that plans are put into action and are achieved (control). This function is called management accounting.

A Short History of Accounting

The history of accounting is intertwined with the development of trade between tribes and there are records of commercial transactions on stone tablets dating back to 3600 BC. The early accountants were 'scribes' who also practiced law. Stone noted:

In ancient Egypt in the pharaoh's central finance department... scribes prepared records of receipts and disbursements of silver, corn and other commodities. One recorded on papyrus the amount brought to the warehouse and another checked the emptying of the containers on the roof as it was poured into the storage building. Audit was performed by a third scribe who compared these two records.

However, accounting as we know it today began in the fourteenth century in the Italian city-states of Florence, Genoa and Venice as a result of the growth of maritime trade and banking institutions. The first bank with customer facilities opened in Venice in 1149. The Lombards were Italian merchants who were established as moneylenders in England at the end of the twelfth century. Balance sheets were evident from around 1400 and the Medici family had accounting records of 'cloth manufactured and sold'. The first treatise on accounting was the work of a monk, Luca Pacioli, in 1494.

The first professional accounting body was formed in Venice in 1581. Much of the language of accounting is derived from Latin roots. 'Debtor' comes from the Latin debitum, something that is owed; 'assets' from the Latin ad + satis, to enough, i.e. to pay obligations; 'liability' from ligare, to bind; 'capital' from caput, a head (of wealth). Even 'account' derives initially from the Latin computare, to count, while 'profit' comes from profectus, advance or progress. 'Sterling' and 'shilling' came from the Italian sterlino and scellino, while the pre-decimal currency abbreviation 'LSD' (pounds, shillings and pence) stood for lire, soldi, denarii. Chandler traced the development of the modern industrial enterprise from its agricultural and commercial roots as a result of the Industrial Revolution in the last half of the nineteenth century. By 1870, the leading industrial nations – the United States, Great Britain and Germany – accounted for two-thirds of the world's industrial output. One of the consequences of growth was the separation of ownership from management.

Although the corporation, as distinct from its owners, had been in existence in Britain since 1650, the separation of ownership and control was enabled by the first British Companies Act, which formalized the law in relation to 'joint stock companies' and introduced the limited liability of shareholders during the 1850s. The London Stock Exchange had been formed earlier in 1773 by stockbrokers, who had previously worked from coffee houses.

The second consequence of growth was the creation of new organisational forms. Based on his extensive historical analysis, Chandler found that in large firms structure followed strategy and strategic growth and diversification led to the creation of decentralized, multidivisional corporations like General Motors, where remotely located managers made decisions on behalf of absent owners and central head office functions. Ansoff emphasized that success in the first 30 years of the mass-production era went to firms that had the lowest prices. However, in the 1930s General Motors 'triggered a shift from production to a market focus'.

In large firms such as General Motors, budgets were developed to co-ordinate diverse activities. In the first decades of the twentieth century, the DuPont company developed a model to measure the return on investment (ROI). ROI was used to make capital investment decisions and to evaluate the performance of business units, including the managerial responsibility to use capital efficiently.

The Role of Management Accounting

The advent of mechanized production following the Industrial Revolution increased the size and complexity of production processes, which employed more people and required larger sums of capital to finance machinery. Accounting historians suggest that the increase in the number of limited companies that led to the separation of ownership from control caused the attention of cost accounting to shift from determining cost to exercising control by absent owners over their managers.

The predecessor of management accounting, 'cost accounting', was reflected in the earlier title of management accountants as cost or works accountants. Typically situated in factories, these accountants tended to know the business and advise non-financial managers in relation to operational decisions. Cost accounting was concerned with determining the cost of an object, whether a product, an activity, a division of the organisation or market segment. The first book on cost accounting is believed to be Garcke and Fell's Factory Accounts, which was published in 1897. Historians have argued that the new corporate structures that were developed in the twentieth century – multidivisional organisations, conglomerates and multinationals – placed increased demands on accounting. These demands included divisional performance evaluation and budgeting. It has also been suggested that developments in cost accounting were driven by government demands for cost information during both World Wars. It appears that 'management accounting' is a term used only after the Second World War.

In their acclaimed book Relevance Lost, Johnson and Kaplan traced the development of management accounting from its origins in the Industrial Revolution supporting process-type industries such as textile and steel conversion, transportation and distribution. These systems were concerned with evaluating the efficiency of internal processes, rather than measuring organisational profitability. Financial reports were produced using a separate transactions-based system that reported financial performance. Johnson and Kaplan argued that by 1925 'virtually all management accounting practices used today had been developed'. They also described how the early manufacturing firms attempted to improve performance via economies of scale by reducing unit cost through increasing the volume of output. This led to a concern with measuring the efficiency of the production process. Calculating the cost of different products was unnecessary because the product range was homogeneous.

Over time, the product range expanded and businesses sought economies of scope through producing two or more products in a single facility. This led to the need for better information about how the mix of products could improve total profits. However, after 1900 the production of accounting information was largely for external reporting to shareholders and not to assist managerial decision-making. Johnson and Kaplan described how a management accounting system must provide timely and accurate information to facilitate efforts to control costs, to measure and improve productivity and to devise improved production processes. The management accounting system must also report accurate product costs so that pricing decisions, introduction of new products, abandonment of obsolete products and response to rival products can be made.

The Chartered Institute of Management Accountants' definition of the core activities of management accounting includes:

- participation in the planning process at both strategic and operational levels, involving the establishment of policies and the formulation of budgets;
- the initiation of and provision of guidance for management decisions, involving the generation, analysis, presentation and interpretation of relevant information;
- contributing to the monitoring and control of performance through the provision of reports including comparisons of actual with budgeted performance and their analysis and interpretation.

One of the earliest writers on management accounting described 'different costs for different purposes'. This theme was developed by one of the earliest texts on management accounting. Vatter distinguished the information needs of managers from those of external shareholders and emphasized that it was preferable to get less precise data to managers quickly than complete information too late to influence decision-making. Johnson and Kaplan commented that even today, organisations with access to far more computational power...

rarely distinguish between information needed promptly for managerial control and information provided periodically for summary financial statements.

They argued that the developments in accounting theory in the first decades of the twentieth century came about by academics who emphasized simple decision-making models in highly simplified firms – those producing one or only a few products, usually in a onstage production process. The academics developed their ideas by logic and deductive reasoning. They did not attempt to study the problems actually faced by managers of organisations producing hundreds or thousands of products in complex production processes.

They concluded: Not surprisingly, in this situation actual management accounting systems provided few benefits to organisations. In some instances, the information reported by existing management accounting systems not only inhibited good decision-making by managers, it might actually have encouraged bad decisions.

Johnson and Kaplan described how the global competition that has taken place since the 1980s has left management accounting behind in terms of its decision usefulness. Developments such as total quality management, just-in-time inventory, computer-integrated manufacturing, shorter product life cycles and the decline of manufacturing and rise of service industries have led to the need for 'accurate knowledge of product costs, excellent cost control and coherent performance measurement'. And 'the challenge for today's competitive environment is to develop new and more flexible approaches to the design of effective cost accounting, management control and performance measurement systems'.

Recent Developments in Management Accounting

Partly as a result of the stimulus of Relevance Lost but perhaps more so as a consequence of rapidly changing business conditions, management accounting has moved beyond its traditional concern with a narrow range of numbers to incorporate wider issues of performance measurement and management. Management accounting is now implicated, to greater or lesser degrees in different organisations, with:

- value-based management;
- non-financial performance measurement systems;
- quality management approaches;
- activity-based management; and

- strategic management accounting.

Value-based management is in brief a concern with improving the value of the business to its shareholders. Management accounting is implicated in this, as a fundamental role of non-financial managers is to make decisions that contribute to increasing the value of the business.

The limitations of accounting information, particularly as a lagging indicator of performance, have led to an increasing emphasis on non-financial performance measures. Non-financial measures are a major concern of both accountants and non-financial managers, as they tend to be leading indicators of the financial performance that will be reported at some future time.

Improving the quality of products and services is also a major concern, since advances in production technology and the need to improve performance by reducing waste have led to management tools such as total quality management (TQM), just-in-time (JIT), business process re-engineering (BPR) and continuous improvement processes such as Six Sigma and the Business Excellence model.

Management accounting has a role to play in these techniques and non-financial managers need to understand the relationships between accounting and new management techniques. Activity-based management is an approach that emphasizes the underlying business processes that are required to produce goods and services and the need to identify the drivers or causes of those activities in order to be able to budget for and control costs more effectively.

Strategic management accounting, is an attempt to shift the perceptions of accountants and non-financial managers from an inward-looking to an outward-looking one, recognizing the need to look beyond the business along the value chain to its suppliers and customers and to seek ways of achieving and maintaining competitive advantage.

These changes to the narrow view of accountants, from 'bean-counters' to more active participants in formulating and implementing business strategy, have been accompanied by a shift in the collection, reporting and analysis of routine financial information from accountants to non-financial line managers. This decentring of accounting is evidenced by the delegation of responsibility for budgets and cost control to line managers and is the underlying reason that non-financial managers need a better understanding of accounting information and how that information can be used in decision-making.

A Critical Perspective

Although the concepts and assumptions underlying accounting are yet to be introduced, having begun this book with an introduction to accounting history it is worthwhile considering a contrasting viewpoint. While this viewpoint is one that may not be accepted by many practising managers, it is worth knowing, because it does lie at the very basis of the capitalist economic system in which we live and in which accounting plays such an important role.

The Marxist historian Hobsbawm argued that colonialism had been created by the cotton industry that dominated the UK economy and this resulted in a shift from domestic production to factory production. Sales increased but profits shrank, so labour (which was three times the cost of materials) was replaced by mechanization during the Industrial Revolution. Entrepreneurs started with borrowings and small items of machinery and growth was largely financed by borrowings. The Industrial Revolution produced 'such vast quantities and at such rapidly diminishing cost, as to be no longer dependent on existing demand, but to create its own market'.

Advances in mass production followed the development of the assembly line, supported by railways and shipping to transport goods and communications through the electric telegraph. At the same time, agriculture diminished in importance. Due to the appetite of the railways for iron and steel, coal, heavy machinery, labour and capital investment, 'the comfortable and rich classes accumulated income so fast and in such vast quantities as to exceed all available possibilities of spending and investment'.

While the rich accumulated profits, labour was exploited with wages at subsistence levels. Labour had to learn how to work, unlike agriculture or craft industries, in a manner suited to industry and the result was a draconian master/servant relationship. In the 1840s a depression led to unemployment and high food prices and 1848 saw the rise of the labouring poor in European cities, who threatened both the weak and obsolete regimes and the rich.

This resulted in a clash between the political and industrial revolutions, the 'triumph of bourgeois-liberal capitalism' and the domination of the globe by a few western regimes, especially the British in the mid-nineteenth century, which became a 'world hegemony'.

This 'global triumph' of capitalism in the 1850s was a consequence of the combination of cheap capital and rising prices. Stability and prosperity overtook political questions about the legitimacy of existing dynasties and technology cheapened manufactured products. There was high demand but the cost of living did not fall, so labour became dominated by the interests of the new owners of the means of production.

'Economic liberalism' became the recipe for economic growth as the market ruled labour and helped national economic expansion. Industrialization made wealth and industrial capacity decisive in international power, especially in the US, Japan and Germany.

This 'British' capitalist system was exported throughout the world, not least with the support of a colonial expansionist Empire that lent large sums of money in return for adopting the British system. This system has since been taken over by multinational corporations, largely based in the United States. Armstrong traced the historical factors behind the comparative (in relation to other professions) pre-eminence of accountants in British management hierarchies and the emphasis on financial control. He concluded that accounting controls were installed by accountants as a result of their power base in global capital markets, which was achieved through their role in the allocation of the profit surplus to shareholders.

Armstrong argued that mergers led to control problems that were tackled by American management consultants who tended to recommend the multidivisional form of organisation... [which] entirely divorce headquarters management from operations. Functional departments and their managers are subjected to a battery of financial indicators and budgetary controls... [and] a subordination of operational to financial decision-making and a major influx of accountants into senior management positions.

Roberts suggested that organisational accounting embodies the separation of instrumental and moral consequences, which is questionable. He argued:

The mystification of accounting information helps to fix, elevate and then impose upon others its own particular instrumental interests, without regard to the wider social and environmental consequences of the pursuit of such interests. Accounting thus serves as a vehicle whereby others are called to account, while the interests it embodies escape such accountability. This is a more critical perspective than that associated with the traditional notion of accounting as a report to shareholders and managers, which is a result of the historical development of capitalism in the West.

While this book is designed to help non-financial managers understand the tools and techniques of accounting, it is also intended to make readers think critically about the role of accounting and the limitations of accounting, some of which have been historically defined.

One intention is to reinforce to readers that: accounting information provides a window through which the real activities of the organisation may be monitored, but it should be noted also that other windows are used that do not rely upon accounting information.

Shareholder Value and Business Structure

Capital and Product Markets

Since the seventeenth century, companies have been formed by shareholders in order to consolidate resources and invest in opportunities. Shareholders had limited liability through which their personal liability in the event of business failure was limited to their investment in shares.

Shareholders appointed directors to manage the business, who in turn employed managers. Shareholders have few direct rights in relation to the conduct of the business. Their main powers are to elect the directors and appoint the auditors in an annual general meeting of shareholders. They are also entitled to an annual report containing details of the company's financial performance.

The market in which investors buy and sell the shares of companies is called the capital market, which is normally associated with the Stock Exchange. Companies obtain funds raised from shareholders (equity) and borrowings from financiers (debt). Both of these constitute the capital employed in the business.

The cost of capital represents the cost incurred by the organisation to fund all its investments, comprising the cost of equity and the cost of debt weighted by the mix of debt and equity. The cost of debt is interest, which is the price charged by the lender.

The cost of equity is partly dividend and partly capital growth, because most shareholders expect both regular income from profits (the dividend) and an increase in the value of their shares over time in the capital market. Thus the different costs of each form of capital, weighted by the proportions of different forms of debt and equity, constitute the weighted average cost of capital. The management of the business relationship with capital markets is called financial management or corporate finance.

Companies use their capital to invest in technologies, people and materials in order to make, buy and sell products or services to customers. This is called the product market. The focus of shareholder wealth, according to Rappaport, is to obtain funds at competitive rates from capital markets and invest those funds to exploit imperfections in product markets. Where this takes place, shareholder wealth is increased through dividends and increases in the share price. The 1990s saw a growing concern with the role of accounting in improving shareholder wealth.

Value-based Management

Since the mid-1980s, there has been more and more emphasis on increasing the value of the business to its shareholders. Traditionally, business performance has been measured through accounting ratios such as return on capital employed (ROCE), return on investment (ROI), earnings per share and so on. However, it has been argued that these are historical rather than current measures and they vary between companies as a result of different accounting treatments.

Rappaport described how companies with strong cash flows diversified in the mid-twentieth century, often into uneconomic businesses, which led to the 'value gap' – the difference between the market value of the shares and the value of the business if it had been managed to maximize shareholder value. The consequence was the takeover movement and subsequent asset stripping of the 1980s, which provided a powerful incentive for managers to focus on creating value for shareholders. The takeover movement itself led to problems as high acquisition premiums (the excess paid over and above the calculated value of the business, i.e. the goodwill) were paid to the owners and financed by high levels of debt. During the 1990s institutional investors (pension funds, insurance companies, investment trusts etc.), through their dominance of share ownership, increased their pressure on management to improve the financial performance of companies.

Value-based management (VBM) emphasizes shareholder value, on the assumption that this is the primary goal of every business. VBM approaches include total shareholder return, market value added, shareholder value added and economic value added. Recent research into the use of value-based management approaches by UK companies is covered by Cooper et al..

Total shareholder return (TSR) compares the dividends received by shareholders and the increase in the share price with the original shareholder investment, expressing the TSR as a percentage of the initial investment. Market value added (MVA) is the difference between total market capitalization (number of shares issued times share price plus the market value of debt) and the total capital invested in the business by debt and equity providers. This is a measure of the value generated by managers for shareholders.

Rappaport coined shareholder value added (SVA) to refer to the increase in shareholder value over time. He defines shareholder value as the economic value of an investment, which can be calculated by using the cost of capital to discount forecast future cash flows (which he called free cash flows) into present values. The business must generate profits in product markets that exceed the cost of capital in the capital market for value to be created (if not, shareholder value is eroded). Rappaport developed a shareholder value network. Through this diagram, he identified seven drivers of shareholder value: sales growth rate, operating profit margin, income tax rate, working capital investment, fixed capital investment, cost of capital and forecast duration. Managers make three types of decisions that influence these value drivers and lead to shareholder value:

- Operating decisions – product mix, pricing, promotion, customer service etc., which are then reflected in the sales growth rate, operating profit margin and income tax rate.
- Investment decisions – in both inventory and capacity, which are then reflected in both working capital and fixed capital investment.
- Financing decisions – the mix of debt and equity and the choice of financial instrument determine the cost of capital, which is assessed by capital markets in terms of business risk.

The value growth duration is the estimated number of years over which the return from investments is expected to exceed the cost of capital.

The seven value drivers determine the cash flow from operations, the level of debt and the cost of capital, all of which determine shareholder value. A detrimental consequence of the emphasis on shareholder value is that it has led to a continued focus on short-term financial performance at the expense of longer-term strategy.

Economic Value Added (EVA) is a financial performance measure developed by consultants Stern Stewart & Co. It claims to capture the economic profit of a business that leads to shareholder value creation. In simple terms, EVA is net operating profit after deducting a charge to cover the opportunity cost of the capital invested in the business. EVA's 'economic profit' is the amount by which earnings exceed (or fall short of) the minimum rate of return that shareholders and financiers could get by investing in other securities with a comparable risk.

EVA accepts the assumption that the primary financial objective of any business is to maximize the wealth of its shareholders. The value of the business depends on the extent to which investors expect future profits to be greater or less than the cost of capital. Returns over and above the cost of capital increase shareholder wealth, while returns below the cost of capital erode shareholder wealth. Stern Stewart argues that managers understand this measure because it is based on operating profits. By introducing a notional charge based on assets held by the business, managers (whether at a corporate or divisional level) manage those assets as well as the profit generated.

EVA also has its critics. For example, the calculation of EVA allows up to 164 adjustments to reported accounting profits in order to remove distortions caused by arbitrary accounting rules and estimates the risk-adjusted cost of capital, both of which can be argued as subjective, although Stern Stewart argues that most organisations need only about a dozen of these. The increase in shareholder value is reflected in compensation strategies for managers whose goals, argues Stern Stewart, are aligned to increasing shareholder wealth through bonus and share option schemes that are paid over a period of time to ensure consistent future performance.

Accounting and Strategy

This book treats accounting as part of the broader business context of strategy, marketing, operations and human resources. The focus of accounting in business organisations is shareholder value – increasing the value of the business to its shareholders – through dividends from profits and/or through capital growth. Strategy both influences and is influenced by shareholder value. Strategy is reflected in the functional business areas of marketing, operations and human resources, through the actions the business wants to take to achieve, maintain and improve competitive advantage.

Financial management is concerned with raising funds from shareholders or financiers to provide the capital the business needs to sell and produce goods and services. Financial accounting represents the stewardship function, that managers are accountable to those with a financial interest in the business and produce financial reports to satisfy that accountability. Management accounting provides the information for planning, decision-making and control. Therefore, the main content of this book is the interaction between the functional areas of marketing, operations and human resources – driven by strategy – and how accounting provides a set of tools and techniques to assist functional managers. Management accounting both influences and is influenced by the functional areas and by business strategy.

The importance of strategy for management accounting and the information it provides is that a strategic perspective involves taking a longer-term view about the business than is usually provided by traditional accounting reports. Management accounting comprises a set of tools and techniques to support planning, decisionmaking and control in business organisations. Accounting is – or at least should be – integrated with business strategy. However, these same accounting tools and techniques can be used to help evaluate the performance of customers, suppliers and competitors in order to improve competitive advantage.

Accounting should also extend beyond a narrow concern with financial measurement and encompass non-financial performance measurement, a subject of steadily increasing importance for those managers who are responsible for achieving performance targets, as well as for accountants.

Strategy is concerned with long-term direction, achieving and maintaining competitive advantage, identifying the scope and boundaries of the organisation and matching the activities of the organisation to its environment. Strategy is also about building on resources and competences to create new opportunities and take advantage of those opportunities and manage change within the organisation. There is also a link between strategy and operational decisions in order to turn strategy formulation into strategy implementation.

An economic perspective is added by Grant, who saw the value created by firms distributed among customers, suppliers and equity risk-takers. In order to provide this value, business firms establish profit as the single dominant objective. The purpose of strategy 'is to pursue profit over the long term'. Strategy is thus linked to performance by setting performance targets for the business as a whole and for individual business units and then measuring performance against those targets. It is to the divisionalized organisational form that we now turn.

Structure of Business Organisations

Organisations are typically considered to be of three types:

- the private sector, comprising businesses whose prime goal is profit;
- the public sector, which is government funded (through various kinds of taxation), providing services for the public, such as in health, education, law and order etc.; and
- the 'third sector' of not-for-profit organisations, providing a range of charitable or social services, funded by donations, lottery grants etc.

The accounting described in this book is primarily concerned with for-profit businesses, although many of the concepts are equally applicable to the other two sectors. Business organisations can be further subdivided into a number of major types:

- agriculture, or primary production;
- manufacturing, or secondary production;
- services, or tertiary production.

Again, our concern is with all businesses other than agriculture as the means of production and the accounting requirements of that type of business are significantly different from the latter two, which in any event dominate the economy. Manufacturing and service businesses are concerned with satisfying customer demand for products or services. Businesses produce products/services through a variety of organisational forms, but predominantly through either a functional structure or a divisionalized structure.

The functional structure locates decision-making at the top of the corporate hierarchy, with functional responsibilities for marketing, operations, human resources, finance and so on allocated to departments. In the functional structure, accounting provides a staff function to the line functions, simplified here as marketing, operations and human resources.

Accounting knowledge tends to be centralized in the accounting department, which collects, produces, reports and analyses accounting information on behalf of its (internal) customer departments. The functional structure may be suitable for smaller organisations with a narrow geographic spread and a limited product/service range, but it is not generally suitable for larger organisations.

The divisional structure is based on a head office with corporate specialists supporting the chief executive, with divisions established for major elements of the business. These divisions may be based on geographic territories or different products/services and each division will typically have responsibility for all the functional areas: marketing, operations, human resources and accounting.

The advantage of the divisional structure is that while planning is centrally coordinated, the implementation of plans, decision-making and control is devolved to local management who should have a better understanding of their local operations. The divisions are often referred to as strategic business units (SBUs) to describe their devolved responsibility for a segment of the business. These SBUs are, in accounting, termed responsibility centres.

Responsibility centres, through their managers, are held responsible for achieving certain standards of performance. There are three types of responsibility centres:

- cost centres, which are responsible for controlling costs;
- profit centres, which are responsible for achieving profit targets; and
- investment centres, which are responsible for achieving an adequate return on the capital invested in the division.

Management within divisions will carry out a significant function in analyzing and interpreting financial information as part of their local management responsibilities, typically supported by locally based accounting support staff. Accounting influences and is influenced by the structure adopted and the extent of managerial responsibility for business unit performance, which considers how the performance of business units and their managers can be evaluated. Emmanuel et al. described organisational structure as: a potent form of control because, by arranging people in a hierarchy with defined patterns of authority and responsibility, a great deal of their behaviour can be influenced or even pre-determined. Child defined organisation structure as 'the formal allocation of work roles and the administrative mechanisms to control and integrate work activities', emphasizing that structure depends on the decision-makers' evaluation of environmental impacts, the standard of required performance and the level of performance actually achieved. This stresses the role of decision-makers, defined as the 'power-holding group'.

Galbraith and Nathanson suggested that the choice of organisational form was the result of choices about five design variables: task, people, structure, reward systems and information and decision processes. These choices should be consistent with the firm's product-market strategy, i.e. there should be 'fit' or 'congruence'. Galbraith and Nathanson applied Chandler's four growth strategies – expansion of volume, geographic dispersion, vertical integration and product diversification – to see how each affects the form of organisational structure, based on Chandler's thesis that structure follows strategy. They argued: Variation in strategy should be matched with variation in processes and systems as well as in structure, in order for organisations to implement strategies successfully.

Galbraith and Nathanson further built on Chandler's research, adding that diversification leads to multidivisional forms, with competition as an important variable.

A Critical Perspective

The shareholder value movement has subsumed much consideration of the wider accountability of business to other stakeholders. Shareholders' interests dominate business and accountants occupy a privileged position as those who establish the rules and report business performance. This can be seen as a historical development.

Stakeholder theory looks beyond shareholders to those groups who influence, or are influenced by, the organisation. Shareholders are not representative of society and stakes are held in the organisation by employees, customers, suppliers, government and the community. Stakeholder theory is concerned with how the power of stakeholders, with their competing interests, is managed by the organisation in terms of its broader accountability. Dermer suggested a broader view of organisations with interdependent but conflicting stakeholders, arguing: Cognitive and/or political models view organisations as non-goal-oriented, non-instrumental social systems, enmeshed in broader socio-political contexts.

Dermer contrasted the presumption of managerial authority and unitary purpose with a pluralistic governance model comprising four elements: leadership (management); citizenship (stakeholders); institutions (formal and informal patterns of relating); and ideologies (patterns of belief).

Given that accountability is the duty to provide an explanation – an account – of the actions for which an organisation is responsible, this implies a social accounting and a right to information by various stakeholder groups in a democracy. Strategy is also open to criticism. Mintzberg was critical of strategic planning because it is a 'calculating style of management' resulting in strategies that are extrapolated from the past or copied from others. Rather, Mintzberg saw some strategy as deliberate but other strategy as an emergent process, which should lead to learning. He argued:

Strategic planning often spoils strategic thinking, causing managers to confuse real vision with the manipulation of numbers. A critical stance can also be applied to the divisionalized form of organisation. Roberts and Scapens argued that in a divisionalized company there is distance between the division and the head office, such that 'the context within which accounting information is gathered will typically be quite different from the context in which it is interpreted'. This may result in manipulating the appearance of accounting reports. Roberts and Scapens concluded: The image of an organisation which is given through Accounts will be from a particular point of view, at a particular point in time and will be selective in its focus. Events, actions, etc. which are significant for the organisation may be out of focus, or not in the picture at all... the image conveyed by the Accounts may misrepresent the actual flow of events and practices that it is intended to record.

The separation of management from control, the creation of decentralized business units and the pursuit of shareholder value imply a particular goal-oriented, economic and rational theory of management behaviour and organisational action.

6

Basics of Finance Theory

What are the financial markets? If you are confused, there is a good reason. That's because financial markets go by many terms, including capital markets, Wall Street, even the markets. Some experts even simply refer to it as the stock market, even though they are referring to stocks, bonds and commodities.

Quite simply, that is what the financial markets are-any type of financial transaction that you can think of that helps businesses grow and investors make money. Here is an overview of the financial markets, from the simple to the complex.

Overview Financial Markets

Markets are interrelated, and a problem in one market can have its source in a different market. This finding is a starting point for macroeconomics. To limit the number of markets they must explore, economists conventionally lump together or aggregate the vast number of markets in a modern economy into only four: markets for goods and services, financial assets, money balances, and resources.

The examination of these four aggregated markets is central to macroeconomics. Macroeconomists ask two central questions as they examine each: "Is this market a likely source of instability that shows up as inflation or recession," and "Will the adjustment process in this market cause problems for the overall adjustment of the economy."

This group of readings begins our exploration of aggregated markets by looking at financial markets. We begin by introducing basic concepts of financial markets, continue by examining the role of speculators in financial markets and introducing the concept of efficient markets, and finish in the foreign exchange market, explaining the difference between floating and fixed exchange rates.

Changes in one part of the economy are rapidly transmitted to other parts through financial markets. The ability of financial markets to transmit is highlighted in the market for foreign exchange, where we show that a tariff designed to protect jobs in one part of the economy can cost jobs in other parts. Such transmission is not limited to questions of tariffs or to the market for foreign exchange; all financial markets transmit.

From a microeconomic point of view, the primary purpose of financial markets is to allocate available savings to the most productive use. A well-functioning financial sector increases economic growth. If an economy does not allocate savings to the most productive uses, it will grow more slowly than it can grow. Since we are looking at financial markets from the viewpoint of macroeconomics, this group of readings largely ignores the importance of financial markets in allocating funds.

Intermediaries

Most people do not enter financial markets directly but use intermediaries or middlemen. Commercial banks are the financial intermediary we meet most often in macroeconomics, but mutual funds, pension funds, credit unions, savings and loan associations, and to some extent insurance companies are also important financial intermediaries. When people deposit money in a bank, the bank uses the funds to make loans to home buyers for mortgages, to students so they can pay for their education, to business to finance inventories, and to anyone else who needs to borrow. A person who has extra money could, of course, seek out borrowers himself and bypass the intermediary. By eliminating the middleman, the saver could get a higher return. Why, then, do so many people use financial intermediaries? Financial intermediaries provide two important advantages to savers.

First, lending through an intermediary is usually less risky than lending directly. The major reason for reduced risk is that a financial intermediary can diversify. It makes a great many loans, and even though some of those loans will be mistakes, the losses will be largely offset by loans that are sound. In contrast, an average saver could directly make only a few loans, and any bad loans would substantially affect his wealth. Because an intermediary can put its "eggs" in many "baskets," it insures its depositors from substantial losses. Another reason financial intermediaries reduce risk is that by making many loans, they learn how to better predict which of the people who want to borrow money will be able to repay. Someone who does not specialize in this lending may be a poor judge of which loans are worth making and which are not, though even a specialist will make some mistakes.

A second advantage financial intermediaries give savers is liquidity. Liquidity is the ability to convert assets into a spendable form—money—quickly. A house is an illiquid asset; selling one can take a great deal of time. If an individual saver has lent money directly to another person, the loan can also be an illiquid asset. If the lender suddenly needs cash, he must either persuade the borrower to repay quickly, which may not be possible, or he must find someone else who will buy the loan from him, which may be very difficult. Although the intermediary may use its funds to make illiquid loans, its size allows it to hold some funds idle as cash to provide liquidity to individual depositors. Only when a great many depositors want to withdraw deposits at the same time, which happens when there is a "run" on the institution, will the financial intermediary be unable to provide liquidity. Unless it can obtain help from the government or other institutions, it will be forced to suspend payments to depositors.

In addition to lending money to individuals and groups, there are other ways in which banks are part of financial markets. Banks borrow and lend funds among themselves in the federal-funds market. They buy and sell foreign exchange. They buy and sell government and commercial debt. And finally, one form of bank debt serves as money in modern economies, and banks create this debt as a result of their financial transactions.

Economists are concerned that financial intermediaries can be a source of shocks to the economy, bumps that can disrupt the normal flow of economic life. This concern arises for at least two reasons. First, bank debt serves as money, so disruptions to banks can affect the amount of money in circulation. Second, financial intermediaries are tied together through chains of debts and assets. Because of these linkages, the failure of one financial intermediary can weaken others, increasing their chances of failure. As a result, there is the possibility that if a key financial intermediary fails, that failure can create a domino effect that could cause other financial institutions to fail, ultimately causing the financial sector to "seize up" and stop functioning. Serious disruption of the financial markets will disrupt the rest of the economy.

Instruments and Rates

When most people think of financial markets, they think of the stock market. A stock is a share in the ownership of a corporation, and through the stock market one can buy and sell ownership in most large businesses in the world. The stock market has high visibility because it is open to anyone who can collect several hundred dollars together. However, the stock market is only a very small part of the total financial market and plays only a minor role in macroeconomic theory.

Markets for debt are much larger than the stock market in terms of their daily transactions. These markets have less visibility because many require hundreds of thousands or even millions of dollars to enter directly. As a result, individuals generally do not enter the debt market directly; most transactions involve financial intermediaries. There are many kinds of transactions that take place in debt markets, and some of these markets do play an important role in macroeconomic theory. Whenever economists include an interest rate in their discussion, a market for debt is playing a role in their thinking.

Prices in the debt market are interest rates, what one pays (or receives) for the use of funds for some period of time. Because they aggregate financial markets, economists often talk about "the interest rate." In fact there are many interest rates. Rates differ depending on factors such as the risk of default, the liquidity and time to maturity of the debt, and the tax status of the interest payments.

The press commonly reports several interest rates. The prime rate was once the interest rate that large commercial banks charged their most creditworthy customers for short-term loans. In recent years banks have usually given their best customers discounts from the prime, so this definition is no longer accurate. A good definition of the prime is hard to give other than it is a rate that banks publicize.

Portfolio Choice

Portfolio choice involves decisions about the way we want to hold our assets (or to structure our liabilities). It is a fancy term for something we do all the time. For example, a yard sale is an example of portfolio adjustment. People holding a yard sale are attempting to convert assets in the form clothing and household items into cash. They are not changing the amount of assets they have, but rather the form in which they hold them.

From a macroeconomic perspective, most important cases of portfolio adjustment involve financial assets. When we look at financial assets, there are three characteristics that most people want to have in their assets. First, they like assets with low risk. Second, they want assets that are liquid, assets that can easily be converted to money and spent. Third, they like assets that give them a high rate of return. Because no asset combines all three characteristics, people face tradeoffs. If they want a higher return, they usually have to accept more risk or less liquidity. For example, over the past half century the average return on holding common stocks has been higher than the return on holding passbook savings in a bank. However, the high average return on common stocks is the result of some stocks performing very well while others perform poorly. Investment in stocks can be quite risky.

Speculators and Markets

Suppose that you receive an advertisement in the mail offering you a book that tells you how you can beat the stock market and become rich. If this book is offered to you for a mere $50, should you buy it? A little reflection should suggest that you be very, suspicious. If there was a way to beat the market, the person who had the way should keep quiet and use it. Once the method becomes publicly known, its use will eliminate any source of profit.

A financial market is an "efficient market" if its prices take into account all knowledge that people have about that market. (Notice that the use of the word "efficiency" in this context is not the same as the use of the word in most of microeconomics.)

If there is knowledge that is not being used, unexploited profit opportunities exist, and in financial markets these opportunities should be quickly taken. If one knows that a stock or bond is undervalued and that it will rise in value, one will make a large amount of money by buying until it does rise. Because profit opportunities are quickly exploited once they become known, one cannot "beat" an efficient market unless one has special information that is unavailable to others.

If the stock market is an efficient market, movements of stock prices from day to day will be random. Knowing the past movements of the stock does not help one predict what the future price will be. This idea contradicts the technique of picking stocks used by "chartists" or "technicians" who believe that past movements can reveal patterns. A variety of studies that have compared randomly picked portfolios of stocks with stocks chosen by various technical rules supports the idea that information about past movements of stock prices does not help predict the future. The idea of efficient markets suggests that one should not place a great deal of faith in any forecasts about interest rates or stock prices, because if the person making the forecast really does know what will happen, he could keep quiet and get rich.

Speculators play a useful role in an efficient market where prices adjust very quickly to new information. They are coolly rational individuals looking at the fundamental values of items, buying when prices are too low and helping lift these prices, and selling when prices are too high and helping to lower these prices. As a result, prices correctly transmit information about values that people can then use to make decisions. An efficient market will not be the source of economic disturbances. It can, however, transmit disturbances, and this alone would be enough to interest economists.

However, there are some who argue that financial markets are not efficient and do not always adjust to economic conditions. They argue that those trading in financial markets are not always calmly rational in the way that those who believe in efficient markets picture them. Rather traders can go on speculative binges, ignoring reality. An important reason people buy items in financial markets is in the hope of selling them at a profit. Thus trading in these markets involves not only an analysis of the fundamental value of an asset, but also an analysis of how other people will react. If people are confident that others will buy the item for more than they paid for it, then they will buy it even if it has little value to them.

The idea described above has been called the "greater-fool" theory. It implies that although one may be a fool for buying an asset that is overpriced, one can profit if there are still greater fools who will pay even more for it. The idea is an example of the model of contingent behaviour. In contingent behaviour, people's actions are based on the way they expect others to act. To the extent that people act in this way and that "greater-fool" speculating influences prices in financial markets, financial markets can serve as a source of economic disturbances rather than as mere transmitters.

There are many cases in which markets clearly were on speculative binges. One of the earliest and most famous was the Dutch tulip market of the 1990s. The tulip was introduced into Holland in the middle of the 16th century from Constantinople. It immediately became a status symbol among the very rich, and then as it became a bit less rare, among the middle classes. According to Charles Mackay, "Until the year 1634 the tulip annually increased in reputation, until it was deemed a proof of bad taste in any man of fortune to be without a collection of them."

After 1630 the price of tulips reflected not only their stylishness, but also speculation. People began to gamble on price changes. As people began to join the speculation, trying to get in at low prices, took off and the market developed a life of its own. People bought tulips at ridiculous prices only because they thought other people would be willing to pay equally ridiculous prices. For example, a single bulb was exchanged for twelve acres of land. Another was sold for a carriage, two horses, and a substantial sum of cash.

The "bulls"—those who expected rising prices—ruled the bulb market until 1636. The boom faded when enough Dutchmen began to wonder if tulip bulbs were really worth what they were being traded for, and decided to get out of the market while they were ahead. As this sentiment spread, the market peaked and began to fall. Speculative markets can crash almost instantly because once prices begin to fall, people realize that there is no fundamental reason for them to be so high. The prices of tulip bulbs fell until they reached a realistic value, which meant that a single bulb was almost worthless.

Looking back at tulipmania, we have a tendency to think, "That is a funny episode, but of no importance. People are smarter today." Yet in 1982 a major speculative binge came to an end, leaving debts in the area of $90 billion. The binge took place in Kuwait in an unregulated over-the-counter market called the Souk al-Manakh. The market was limited to trading in only about 35 companies, most of which were small, and many of which did not even publish annual reports. Activity was clearly speculative, and as prices rose and banks began to refuse to lend money to finance deals, people began to use postdated checks. In effect, people promised to pay based on the belief that they could sell their securities for more than they had paid, and thus redeem the check. Under Kuwaiti law, a check is payable on demand regardless of the date. The collapse came in August of 1982 when someone demanded early payment on a check that could not be paid. With confidence in the system shaken, prices quickly collapsed. Also, greater-fool psychology seems to widespread in the run up of the prices of the dot-com stocks in the late 1990s.

Markets based on "greater-fool" psychology always collapse. Eventually the greatest fool is found, and once he is found, the process cannot continue. In many ways a speculative binge is like a chain letter. Everyone involved in a chain letter believes that he or she will get rich. But since all that is involved is a reshuffling of money, (in technical jargon, a chain letter is a zero-sum game), if someone does get rich, others must get poorer. Like speculative binges, chain letters die when the greatest fools have found and joined the chain.

Speculative binges can affect the production of an economy if they cause enough financial disruption. They will cause bankruptcies, reduce people's trust in others, and cause unemployment for the people who became speculators. However, few periods of inflation or recession can be linked to speculative binges, and, as a result, most economists do not believe that they, or the financial markets, are an important source of macroeconomic disturbance.

Some people argue that the Great Depression was a result of a speculative binge in the stock market in 1928 and 1929. Most economists dismiss this theory because prices in the stock market did not reach levels that were clearly outlandish. Some market watchers have even argued that stock prices were not overvalued at all in 1929 if the 1990s. would have been a normal decade.

Even if one believes that stocks were overvalued in 1929, and that the stock market had gone on a speculative binge, it is hard, and perhaps impossible, to explain why the results of this particular binge were so much more severe than the aftereffects of other, equally large binges in the stock market. In particular, the very large drop in stock market prices on Monday, October 19, 1987 left few traces on production or consumption during the following year. Yet on that one day the value of common stocks, as measured by the Dow Jones Industrial Index, dropped by more than 22%. Clearly a speculative crash in financial markets is not enough, by itself, to trigger a recession.

The Market for Foreign Exchange

In the market for foreign exchange (forex), people trade one country's money for another's. If, for example, you decide to travel to Thailand, you will need to buy some *bahts*, the currency of Thailand, either before you go or once you get there. In your transaction, you will supply dollars to the foreign exchange market and demand bahts.

The foreign exchange market provides an excellent illustration of how financial markets can transmit disturbances. The market is usually considered to be an efficient market, not subject to runaway speculative binges. The heart of the market is the trading by a number of very large banks. A trade worth a million dollars is very small in this market, but it is the prices of these very large bank transactions that newspapers report when they publish exchange rates. When you deal in smaller amounts when you travel to Thailand, you will get less favourable prices.

The market for foreign exchange can be analysed in terms of supply and demand. Americans demand foreign money (and supply dollars) when they buy things abroad, such as vacations, goods, services, factories, and financial assets.

Foreigners supply foreign currency (and demand dollars) when they buy things here, such as vacations, goods, services, factories, and financial assets. Although when you buy a Japanese camera, you do not deal in the foreign exchange market, someone did in the process of bringing the camera to you. It may have been the American importer, who would have sold dollars to buy yen, and then used the yen to buy the camera. Or it may have been the Japanese exporter, who sold cameras for dollars and then sold the dollars for yen. In either case, dollars were supplied to the foreign exchange market and yen were demanded.

The exchange rate, or the price of foreign money, is an important price when we buy things made in other countries. For example, the manufacturer of the camera in the previous paragraph paid its workers in yen. The camera has a yen price. Suppose the price of the camera in yen is 50,000 yen. How much will this camera cost in terms of dollars? To determine this, we must know the value of yen in terms of dollars, or the exchange rate. Suppose one dollar is worth 250 yen. Then to find the value of the camera in dollars, we can use this equation:

Stocks and Stock Investing

Stocks are shares of ownership of a public corporation which are sold to investors to allow the companies to raise a lot of cash at once. The investors profit when the companies increase their earnings which keeps the U.S. economy growing. It is easy to buy stocks, but takes a lot of knowledge to buy stocks in the right company.

What Are the Components of the Stock Market?

To a lot of people, the Dow is the stock market. However, the Dow, which is the nickname for the Dow Jones *Industrial* Average, is just one component among many. There is also the Dow Jones *Transportation* Average and the Dow Jones *Utilities* Average. The stocks that make up these averages are traded on the world's exchanges, two of which include the New York Stock Exchange and the NASDAQ.

What Are Mutual Funds?

Mutual funds give you the ability to buy a lot of stocks at once. In a way this makes them an easier tool to invest in than individual stocks. By reducing stock market volatility, they have also had a calming effect on the U.S. economy. Despite their benefits, you still need to learn how to select a good mutual fund.

What is the Bond Market?

Generally, when stocks go up, bonds go down. However, there are many different types of bonds, including Treasury Bonds, corporate bonds, and municipal bonds. Bonds also provide some of the liquidity that helps keep the U.S. economy lubricated. Their most important effect is on mortgage interest rates.

What are Commodities?

The most important commodity to the U.S. economy is oil, and its price is determined in the commodities futures market. What are futures? They are a way to pay for something today that is delivered tomorrow, which helps to remove some of the volatility in the U.S. economy. However, futures also increase the trader's leverage by allowing him to borrow the money to purchase the commodity. This can have a huge impact on the stock market, and the U.S. economy, if the trader guesses wrong.

What are Hedge Funds?

Recently, hedge funds have increased in popularity due to their supposed higher returns for high-end investors. Since hedge funds invest heavily in futures, some have argued they have decreased the volatility of the stock market and therefore the U.S. economy. However, in 1997 the world's largest hedge fund at the time, Long Term Capital Management, practically brought down the U.S. economy.

Indian Financial System and Capital Market

Overview of Indian Financial System

The Indian financial system comprises a set of financial institutions, financial markets and financial infrastructure. The financial institutions mainly consist of commercial and cooperative banks, regional rural banks (RRBs), all-India financial institutions (AIFIs) and non-banking financial companies (NBFCs). The banking sector which forms the bedrock of the Indian financial system, falls under the regulatory ambit of the Reserve Bank of India under the provisions of the Banking Regulation Act, 1949 and the Reserve Bank of India Act, 1934. The Reserve Bank also regulates select AIFIs. Consequent upon amendments to the Reserve Bank of India (Amendment) Act in 1997, a comprehensive regulatory framework in respect of NBFCs was put in place in January 1997.

The financial market in India comprises the money market, the Government securities market, the foreign exchange market and the capital market. A holistic approach has been adopted in India towards designing and development of a modern, robust, efficient, secure and integrated payment and settlement system. The Reserve Bank set up the Institute for Development and Research in Banking Technology (IDRBT) in 1996, which is an autonomous centre for technology capacity building for banks and providing core IT services.

Financial Institutions

Scheduled commercial banks (SCBs) occupy a predominant position in the financial system accounting for around three fourths of the total assets in the financial system. While the public sector banks (PSBs), consisting of eight banks in the State Bank group and 19 nationalised banks, constitute almost three fourths of the total assets of SCBs, the private sector banks, 30 in number, constitute less than one-fifth of the total assets. The 33 foreign banks operating in India account for about 6-7 per cent of the assets of SCBs. The 196 RRBs play a critical role in extending credit to the poorer sections of the rural society. The ownership of RRBs jointly vests with the Central Government, the State Governments and the sponsor banks. The cooperative banking system, with two broad segments of urban and rural cooperatives, forms an integral part of the Indian financial system. While the urban cooperative banking system has a single tier comprising the Primary Cooperative Banks (commonly known as [1]urban cooperative banks – UCBs), the rural cooperative credit system is divided into long-term and short-term cooperative credit institutions which have a multi-tier structure.

The term-lending institutions are mostly Government-owned and have been the traditional providers of long-term project loans. Non-Banking Financial Companies (NBFCs) encompass an extremely heterogeneous group of intermediaries and provide a gamut of financial services. Primary Dealers (PDs) in the Government securities market constitutes a systemically important segment of the NBFCs. At present, there are a total of 17 PDs playing active role in the Government securities market. A majority of them are promoted by banks.

Apart from this, India has a well-established and vibrant insurance sector within the financial system. The Insurance Regulatory and Development Agency (IRDA) has been established to regulate and supervise the insurance sector.

Pre-reforms Phase

Until the early 1990s, the role of the financial system in India was primarily restricted to the function of channelling resources from the surplus to deficit sectors. Whereas the financial system performed this role reasonably well, its operations came to be marked by some serious deficiencies over the years.

The banking sector suffered from lack of competition, low capital base, low productivity and high intermediation cost. After the nationalisation of large banks in 1969 and 1980, the Government-owned banks dominated the banking sector. The role of technology was minimal and the quality of service was not given adequate importance. Banks also did not follow proper risk management systems and the prudential standards were weak. All these resulted in poor asset quality and low profitability. Among non-banking financial intermediaries, development finance institutions (DFIs) operated in an overprotected environment with most of the funding coming from assured sources at concessional terms. In the insurance sector, there was little competition. The mutual fund industry also suffered from lack of competition and was dominated for long by one institution, viz., the Unit Trust of India. Non-banking financial companies (NBFCs) grew rapidly, but there was no regulation of their asset side.

Financial markets were characterised by control over pricing of financial assets, barriers to entry, high transaction costs and restrictions on movement of funds/participants between the market segments. This apart from inhibiting the development of the markets also affected their efficiency.

Financial Sector Reforms in India

It was in this backdrop that wide-ranging financial sector reforms in India were introduced as an integral part of the economic reforms initiated in the early 1990s with a view to improving the macroeconomic performance of the economy. The reforms in the financial sector focussed on creating efficient and stable financial institutions and markets. The approach to financial sector reforms in India was one of gradual and non-disruptive progress through a consultative process. The Reserve Bank has been consistently working towards setting an enabling regulatory framework with prompt and effective supervision, development of technological and institutional infrastructure, as well as changing the interface with the market participants through a consultative process. Persistent efforts have been made towards adoption of international benchmarks as appropriate to Indian conditions. While certain changes in the legal infrastructure are yet to be effected, the developments so far have brought the Indian financial system closer to global standards.

The reform of the interest regime constitutes an integral part of the financial sector reform. With the onset of financial sector reforms, the interest rate regime has been largely deregulated with a view towards better price discovery and efficient resource allocation. Initially, steps were taken to develop the domestic money market and freeing of the money market rates. The interest rates offered on Government securities were progressively raised so that the Government borrowing could be carried out at market-related rates. In respect of banks, a major effort was undertaken to simplify the administered structure of interest rates. Banks now have sufficient flexibility to decide their deposit and lending rate structures and manage their assets and liabilities accordingly. At present, apart from savings account and NRE deposit on the deposit side and export credit and small loans on the lending side, all other interest rates are deregulated.

Indian banking system operated for a long time with high reserve requirements both in the form of Cash Reserve Ratio (CRR) and Statutory Liquidity Ratio (SLR). This was a consequence of the high fiscal deficit and a high degree of monetisation of fiscal deficit. The efforts in the recent period have been to lower both the CRR and SLR. The statutory minimum of 25 per cent for SLR has already been reached, and while the Reserve Bank continues to pursue its medium-term objective of reducing the CRR to the statutory minimum level of 3.0 per cent, the CRR of SCBs is currently placed at 5.0 per cent of NDTL.

As part of the reforms programme, due attention has been given to diversification of ownership leading to greater market accountability and improved efficiency. Initially, there was infusion of capital by the Government in public sector banks, which was followed by expanding the capital base with equity participation by the private investors.

This was followed by a reduction in the Government shareholding in public sector banks to 51 per cent. Consequently, the share of the public sector banks in the aggregate assets of the banking sector has come down from 90 per cent in 1991 to around 75 per cent in 2004. With a view to enhancing efficiency and productivity through competition, guidelines were laid down for establishment of new banks in the private sector and the foreign banks have been allowed more liberal entry.

Since 1993, twelve new private sector banks have been set up. As a major step towards enhancing competition in the banking sector, foreign direct investment in the private sector banks is now allowed up to 74 per cent, subject to conformity with the guidelines issued from time to time.

As a part of the financial sector reforms, the regulatory framework and supervisory practices have almost converged with the best practices elsewhere in the world. The minimum capital to risk assets ratio (CRAR) has been kept at nine per cent which is one percentage point above the international norm; and additionally, banks are required to maintain a separate Investment Fluctuation Reserve (IFR) out of profits, towards interest rate risk. Impressive institutional and legal reforms have been undertaken in relation to the banking sector. There have been a number of measures for enhancing the transparency and disclosures standards.

The regulatory framework in India, in addition to prescribing prudential guidelines and encouraging market discipline, is increasingly focusing on ensuring good governance through "fit and proper" owners, directors and senior managers of the banks. Transfer of shareholding of five per cent and above requires acknowledgement from the Reserve Bank and such significant shareholders are put through a 'fit and proper' test. Banks have also been asked to ensure that the nominated and elected directors are screened by a nomination committee to satisfy 'fit and proper' criteria. Directors are also required to sign a covenant indicating their roles and responsibilities. The Reserve Bank has recently issued detailed guidelines on ownership and governance in private sector banks emphasizing diversified ownership.

In 1994, a Board for Financial Supervision (BFS) was constituted comprising select members of the Reserve Bank Board with a variety of professional expertise to exercise 'undivided attention to supervision' and ensure an integrated approach to supervision of commercial banks, development finance institutions, non-banking finance companies, urban cooperatives banks and primary dealers. Certain amendments are being considered by the Parliament to enhance Reserve Bank's regulatory and supervisory powers.

Over the last few years, the several policy initiatives undertaken in the form of recapitalisation of the weak RRBs, deregulation of deposits and lending rates and relaxation to lend to nontarget groups, have improved their operational efficiency, governance and regulation and brought them almost at par with the rural branches of commercial banks.

The cooperative banks besides suffering from the problem of multiple supervisory authorities, also face the challenge of reconciling the democratic character with financial discipline and modernising systems and procedures. The Task Force on Cooperatives constituted by the Government (December 2004) has made several suggestions for the revival of the sector to be implemented in consultation with the State Governments. The Reserve Bank has adopted a cautious approach regarding granting licenses for new banks and branches of urban cooperative banks (UCBs), while focusing on consolidation within the sector through mergers and amalgamations. In addition, initiatives have been undertaken to gradually tighten the prudential norms for regulation and supervision of UCBs. As a prelude to revamping the sector, a vision document for UCBs has been released by the Reserve Bank, highlighting the importance of a differentiated regulatory regime for the sector.

The ongoing restructuring of AIFIs is evident in the recent conversion of Industrial Credit and Investment Corporation of India (ICICI) and Industrial Development Bank of India (IDBI) into banks. The Board of Directors of Industrial Finance Corporation of India (IFCI) Ltd. have approved, in principle, the merger with a bank. In view of the deteriorating financial position of Industrial Investment Bank of India (IIBI) Ltd., the Government has undertaken a programme of restructuring its liabilities. Apart from Infrastructure Development Finance Company Ltd. (IDFC), there are three refinancing institutions *viz.*, National Bank of Agriculture and Rural Development (NABARD), Small Industries Development Bank of India (SIDBI) and National Housing Bank (NHB), and EXIM Bank. At the State level, the State Financial Corporations registered under the State Financial Corporations Act, 1951 and the State Industrial Development Corporations (SIDCs)-purvey credit to industries/sectors in different States. On balance, the development financial institution (DFI) model has become increasingly unsustainable and AIFIs are fast adopting the business model of a bank for long-term commercial viability.

Non-Banking Financial Companies (NBFCs) encompass an extremely heterogeneous group of intermediaries. The main area of concern has been the substantial growth in deposits of the Residuary Non-Banking Companies (RNBCs), with just two companies accounting for more than 80 per cent of the total deposits held by NBFCs. The Indian banking sector is gradually heading towards consolidation of core competencies of different financial intermediaries, which would engender greater economic efficiency in the form of lower transaction cost, and greater product sophistication.

Financial System: Current Status

There has been a notable reduction in the ratio of non-performing assets (NPAs) to advances in response to various initiatives, such as, improved risk management practices and greater recovery efforts driven, *inter alia,* by the recently enacted Securitisation and Reconstruction of Financial Assets and Enforcement of Security Interest (SARFAESI) Act, 2002. The financial performance of most of the PSBs has improved in recent times as reflected in their comfortable capital adequacy ratios and declining NPL ratios. The CRAR in respect of all categories of banks has improved. New private sector banks have displayed impressive performance particularly in terms of efficiency and customer service

Financial Markets

A major objective of reforms in the financial sector was to develop various segments of the financial market as also eliminate segmentation across various markets in order to smoothen the process of transmission of impulses across markets, easing the liquidity management process and making resource allocation process more efficient across the economy. The strategy adopted for meeting these objectives involved removal of restrictions on pricing of assets, building the institutional structure and technological infrastructure, introduction of new instruments, and fine-tuning of the market microstructure.

The 1990s saw the significant development of various segments of the financial market. At the short end of the spectrum, the money market saw the emergence of a number of new instruments such as CP and CDs and derivative products including FRAs and IRS. Repo operations, which were introduced in the early 1990s and later refined into a Liquidity Adjustment Facility, allow the Reserve Bank to modulate liquidity and transmit interest rate signals to the market on a daily basis. The process of financial market development was buttressed by the evolution of an active government securities market after the Government borrowing programme was put through the auction process in 1992-93.

The development of a market for Government paper enabled the Reserve Bank to modulate the monetisation of the fiscal deficit. The foreign exchange market deepened with the opening up of the economy and the institution of a market-based exchange rate regime in the early 1990s. Although there were occasional episodes of volatility in the foreign exchange market, these were swiftly controlled by appropriate policy measures.

The capital market also underwent some metamorphic changes during the 1990s. The development of the financial markets was well supported by deregulation of balance sheet restrictions in respect of financial institutions, allowing them to operate across markets. This resulted in increased integration among the various segments of the financial markets.

Overview of Indian Capital Market

The Indian capital market is more than a century old. Its history goes back to 1875, when 22 brokers formed the Bombay Stock Exchange (BSE). Over the period, the Indian securities market has evolved continuously to become one of the most dynamic, modern, and efficient securities markets in Asia. Today, Indian market confirms to best international practices and standards both in terms of structure and in terms of operating efficiency.

Indian securities markets are mainly governed by

a) The Company's Act 1956,

b) the Securities Contracts (Regulation) Act 1956 (SCRA Act), and

c) the Securities and Exchange Board of India (SEBI) Act, 1992.

A brief background of these above regulations are given below:

a) The Companies Act 1956 deals with issue, allotment and transfer of securities and various aspects relating to company management. It provides norms for disclosures in the public issues, regulations for underwriting, and the issues pertaining to use of premium and discount on various issues.

b) SCRA provides regulations for direct and indirect control of stock exchanges with an aim to prevent undesirable transactions in securities. It provides regulatory jurisdiction to Central Government over stock exchanges, contracts in securities and listing of securities on stock exchanges.

c) The SEBI Act empowers SEBI to protect the interest of investors in the securities market, to promote the development of securities market and to regulate the security market.

The Indian securities market consists of primary (new issues) as well as secondary (stock) market in both equity and debt. The primary market provides the channel for sale of new securities, while the secondary market deals in trading of securities previously issued. The issuers of securities issue (create and sell) new securities in the primary market to raise funds for investment. They do so either through public issues or private placement. There are two major types of issuers who issue securities. The corporate entities issue mainly debt and equity instruments (shares, debentures, etc.), while the governments (central and state governments) issue debt securities (dated securities, treasury bills). The secondary market enables participants who hold securities to adjust their holdings in response to changes in their assessment of risk and return. A variant of secondary market is the forward market, where securities are traded for future delivery and payment in the form of futures and options. The futures and options can be on individual stocks or basket of stocks like index. Two exchanges, namely National Stock Exchange (NSE) and the Stock Exchange, Mumbai (BSE) provide trading of derivatives in single stock futures, index futures, single stock options and index options. Derivatives trading commenced in India in June 2000.

Major Reforms in the Indian Capital Market

The major reforms in the Indian capital market since the 1990s are presented below:

- As a first step to reform the capital market, the Securities and Exchange Board of India (SEBI), which was earlier set up in April 1988 as a nonstatutory body under an administrative arrangement, was given statutory powers in January 1992 through an enactment of the SEBI Act, 1992 for regulating the securities markets. Twin objectives mandated in the SEBI Act are investor protection and orderly development of the capital market.
- The most significant development in the primary capital market has been the introduction of free pricing. The issuers of securities are now allowed to raise the capital from the market without requiring any consent from any authority either for making the issue or for pricing it. However, the issue of capital has been brought under SEBI's purview in that issuers are

required to meet the SEBI guidelines for Disclosure and Investor Protection, which, in general, cover the eligibility norms for making issues of capital (both public and rights) at par and at a premium by various types of companies, reservation in issues, *etc.*

- The abolition of capital issues control and the freeing of the pricing of issues led to unprecedented upsurge of activity in the primary capital market as the corporates mobilised huge resources. It, *inter alia*, exposed certain inadequacies of the regulations. Therefore, without seeking to control the freedom of the issuers to enter the market and freely price their issues, the SEBI further strengthened the norms for public issues in April 1996. Alongside, SEBI raised the standards of disclosure in public issues to enhance their transparency for improving the levels of investor protection. Issuers of capital are now required to disclose information on various aspects, such as, track record of profitability, risk factors, *etc.* Issuers now also have the option of raising resources through fixed price floatations or the book building process.
- Trading infrastructure in the stock exchanges has been modernised by replacing the open outcry system with on-line screen based electronic trading, unlike several of the developed countries where the two systems still continue to exist on the same exchange. In all, 23 stock exchanges in India have approximately 8,000 trading terminals spread all over the country. This improved the liquidity of the Indian capital market and a better price discovery.
- The trading and settlement cycles were initially shortened from 14 days to 7 days. Subsequently, to further enhance the efficiency of the secondary market, rolling settlement was introduced on a T+5 basis. With effect from April 1, 2002, the settlement cycle was further shortened to T+3 for all listed securities. The settlement cycle is now T+2.
- All stock exchanges in the country have established clearing houses. Consequently, all transactions are settled through the clearing house only and not directly between members, as was practiced earlier.
- Several measures have been undertaken/strengthened to ensure the safety and integrity of the market. These are: margining system, intra-day trading limit, exposure limit and setting up of trade/settlement guarantee fund.

- Securities, which were earlier held in physical form, have been dematerialised and their transfer is done through electronic book entry, which has eliminated some of the disadvantages of securities held in physical form. There are two depositories operating in the country.
- In India, all listed companies are now required to furnish to the stock exchanges and also publish unaudited financial results on a quarterly basis. To enhance the level of continuous disclosure by the listed companies, the SEBI decided to amend the Listing Agreement to incorporate the Segment Reporting, Accounting for Taxes on Income, Consolidated Financial Results, Consolidated Financial Statements, Related Party Disclosures and Compliance with Accounting Standards.
- The Indian capital market is also increasingly integrating with the international capital markets. One of the significant steps towards integrating Indian capital market with the international capital markets was the permission given to Foreign Institutional Investors (FIIs) such as, mutual funds, pension funds and country funds to operate in the Indian markets. Indian firms have also been allowed to operate in the Indian markets. Indian firms have also been allowed to raise capital from international capital markets through issues of Global Depository Receipts (GDRs), American Depository Receipts (ADRs), Euro Convertible Bonds (ECBs), *etc*.
- Boards of various stock exchanges, which in the past included mainly brokers, have been broad-based in order to make them more widely representative so that they represent different interests and not just the interests of their members. Reconstituted Governing Boards have now broker and non-broker representation in the ratio of 50-50 apart from the Executive Director who has a seat on the Board and is required to be a non-broker professional. To remove the influence of brokers in the functioning of stock exchanges, the SEBI decided that no broker member of the stock exchange shall be an office bearer of an exchange or hold the position of President, Vice President, Treasurer, *etc*. Efforts are afoot to demutualise and corporatise the stock exchanges.
- Apart from stock exchanges, various intermediaries, such as mutual funds, stock brokers and sub-brokers merchant

bankers, portfolio managers, registrars to an issue and share transfer agents, underwriters, debenture trustees, bankers to an issue, custodian of securities, venture capital funds and issuers have been brought under the SEBI's regulatory purview.

- There are now regulations in place governing substantial acquisition of shares and takeovers of companies. The Regulations are aimed at making the takeover process more transparent and to protect the interests of minority shareholders.
- Trading in derivative products, such as stock index future, stock index options and futures and options in individual stocks have also been introduced.

Foreign Institutional Investment in India

The liberalisation and consequent reform measures have drawn the attention of foreign investors leading to a rise in portfolio investment in the Indian capital market. Over the recent years, India has emerged as a major recipient of portfolio investment among the emerging market economies. Apart from such large inflows, reflecting the confidence of cross-border investors on the prospects of Indian securities market, except for one year, India received positive portfolio inflows in each year. The stability of portfolio flows towards India is in contrast with large volatility of portfolio flows in most emerging market economies.

The Indian capital market was opened up for foreign institutional investors (FIIs) in 1992. The FIIs started investing in Indian markets in January 1993. The Indian corporate sector has been allowed to tap international capital markets through American Depository Receipts (ADRs), Global Depository Receipts (GDRs), Foreign Currency Convertible Bonds (FCCBs) and External Commercial Borrowings (ECBs). Similarly, non-resident Indians (NRIs) have been allowed to invest in Indian companies. FIIs have been permitted in all types of securities including Government securities and they enjoy full capital convertibility. Mutual funds have been allowed to open offshore funds to invest in equities abroad.

FII investment in India started in 1993, as FIIs were allowed to invest in the Indian debt and equity market in line with the recommendations of the High Level Committee on Balance of Payments. These investment inflows have since then been positive, with the exception of 1998-99, when capital flows to emerging market economies were affected by contagion from the East Asian crisis. These investments account for over 10 per cent of the total market capitalisation of the Indian stock market.

Limits on Foreign Institutional Investors

- Each FII (investing on its own) or sub-account cannot hold more than 10 per cent of the paid-up capital of a company. A sub-account under the foreign corporate/individual category cannot hold more than 5 per cent of the paid up capital of the company.
- The maximum permissible investment in the shares of a company, jointly by all FIIs together is 24 per cent of the paid-up capital of that company. The limit is 20 per cent of the paid-up capital in the case of public sector banks. The ceiling of 24 per cent for FII investment can be raised up to sectoral cap/statutory ceiling, subject to the approval of the board and the general body of the company passing a special resolution to that effect.
- A cap of US $1.75 billion is applicable to FII investment in dated Government securities and treasury bills under 100 per cent and the 70:30 route. Within this ceiling of US $1.75 billion, a sub-ceiling of US $200 million is applicable for the 70:30 route. (FIIs are required to allocate their investment between equity and debt instruments in the ratio of 70:30. However, it is also possible for an FII to declare itself a 100 per cent debt FII in which case it can make its entire investment in debt instruments.)
- A cumulative sub-ceiling of US $500 million outstanding has been fixed on FII investments in corporate debt and this is over and above the subceiling of US $1.75 billion for Government debt.

Growth of Indian Capital Market

The Indian equity market has developed tremendously since the 1990s. The market has grown exponentially in terms of resource mobilisation, number of listed stocks, market capitalisation, trading volumes, turnover and investors' base. Along with this growth, the profiles of the investors, issuers and intermediaries have changed significantly. The market has witnessed a fundamental institutional change resulting in drastic reduction in transaction costs and significant improvement in efficiency, transparency and safety. In the 1990s, reform measures initiated by the SEBI such as, market determined allocation of resources, rolling settlement, sophisticated risk management and derivatives trading have greatly improved the framework and efficiency of trading and settlement.

Almost all equity settlements take place at two depositories. As a result, the Indian capital market has become qualitatively comparable to many developed markets. There are 23 stock exchanges in the country with 9413 listed companies as at end-December 2004. The market capitalization of BSE has grown over the period and is estimated at Rs.16,860 billion as at end-December 2004.

Latest Trends in Indian Stock Markets

Indian stock markets are currently trading at all-time high levels. The BSE Sensex (a BSE index comprising 30 large-cap companies with Base: 1978-79=100) closed at all-time high level of 7859.53 on August 17, 2005. On a point-to-point basis, the BSE Sensex has gained 21.05 per cent during the current financial year so far (up to August 17, 2005). The rally has been supported by strong investment by the FIIs, satisfactory progress of monsoon, firm trends in the international markets and satisfactory financial results by the corporates for Q1 2005-06.

The market capitalization of BSE increased by 24.3 per cent to Rs.21,112 billion (60.7 per cent of GDP) as on August 17, 2005 over the level of March 31, 2005. The market capitalization as a percentage of GDP has increased from 43.5 per cent as at end-March 2004 to 54.6 per cent as at end-March 2005 due mainly to increase in the stock prices as well as listing of new securities. Despite unprecedented price levels, the price-earning ratio for Indian equities has remained attractive due to strong growth in corporate earnings. The P/E ratio of BSE Sensex, however, is marginally higher than that in the other emerging market economies, even though the ratio is much lower than that witnessed in earlier stock market rallies in India.

The gains in the stock markets in the financial year so far have been widespread among blue-chips as well as small and mid-cap stocks. The Indian stock markets have outperformed the other markets. On pointto-point basis, the BSE Sensex witnessed an increase of 21.05 per cent during current financial year so far (up to August 17, 2005) over end-March 2005, as compared with Hong Kong (14.3 per cent), Japan (5.2 per cent), UK (8.1 per cent), US (Dow Jones – 0.4 per cent),

South Korea (15.3 per cent), Taiwan (3.9 per cent), Indonesia (3.1 per cent), and Malaysia (6.3 per cent).

Payment and Settlement System

In recent years, the endeavour of the Reserve Bank has been to improve the efficiency of the financial system by ensuring safe, secure and effective payment and settlement system. In the process, the Reserve Bank apart from performing the regulatory and oversight functions has also played an important role in promoting its functionality and modernisation on an on-going basis. The consolidation of the existing payment systems revolves around strengthening computerised cheque clearing, expanding the reach of Electronic Clearing Services (ECS) and Electronic Funds Transfer (EFT). The critical elements of the developmental strategy are opening of new clearing houses, interconnection of clearing houses through the Indian Financial Network (INFINET); development of Real Time Gross Settlement (RTGS) System, Centralised Funds Management System (CFMS), Negotiated Dealing System (NDS) and the Structured Financial Messaging System (SFMS). Similarly, integration of the various payment products with the systems of individual banks has been another thrust area. A Board for Regulation and Supervision of Payment and Settlement Systems (BPSS) has also been recently constituted to prescribe policies relating to the regulation and supervision of all types of payment and settlement systems, set standards for existing and future systems, authorise the payment and settlement systems and determine criteria for membership to these systems.

The Indian Financial Sector: Some Issues

The Indian financial system has undergone structural transformation over the past decade. The financial sector has acquired strength, efficiency and stability by the combined effect of competition, regulatory measures, and policy environment. While competition, consolidation and convergence have been recognised as the key drivers of the banking sector in the coming years, consolidation of the domestic banking system in both public and private sectors is being combined with gradual enhancement of the presence of foreign banks in a calibrated manner.

There has been improvement in banks' capital position and asset quality as reflected in the overall increase in their capital adequacy ratio and declining NPLs, respectively. Significant improvement in various parameters of efficiency, especially intermediation costs, suggest that competition in the banking industry has intensified. The efficiency of various segments of the financial system also increased.

The major challenges facing the banking sector are the judicious deployment of funds and the management of revenues and costs. Concurrently, the issues of corporate governance and appropriate disclosures for enhancing market discipline have received increased attention for ensuring transparency and greater accountability. Financial sector supervision is increasingly becoming risk based with the emphasis on quality of risk management and adequacy of risk containment.

Consolidation, competition and risk management are no doubt critical to the future of Indian banking, but governance and financial inclusion have also emerged as the key issues for the Indian financial system.

The capital market in India has become efficient and modern over the years. It has also become much safer. However, some of the issues would need to be addressed. Corporate governance needs to be strengthened. Retail investors continue to remain away from the market. The private corporate debt market continues to lag behind the equity segment.

Role of Financial Institutions in India

The Financial Institutions in India mainly comprises of the Central Bank which is better known as the Reserve Bank of India, the commercial banks, the credit rating agencies, the securities and exchange board of India, insurance companies and the specialized financial institutions in India.

Reserve Bank of India

The Reserve Bank of India was established in the year 1935 with a view to organize the financial frame work and facilitate fiscal stability in India. The bank acts as the regulatory authority with regard to the functioning of the various commercial bank and the other financial institutions in India. The bank formulates different rates and policies for the overall improvement of the banking sector. It issue currency notes and offers aids to the central and institutions governments.

Commercial Banks in India

The commercial banks in India are categorized into foreign banks, private banks and the public sector banks. The commercial banks indulge in varied activities such as acceptance of deposits, acting as trustees, offering loans for the different purposes and are even allowed to collect taxes on behalf of the institutions and central government.

Credit Rating Agencies in India

The credit rating agencies in India were mainly formed to assess the condition of the financial sector and to find out avenues for more improvement. The credit rating agencies offer various services as:

- Operation Up gradation
- Training to Employees
- Scrutinize New Projects and find out the weak sections in it
- Rate different sectors.

The two most important credit rating agencies in India are:

- CRISIL
- ICRA.

Securities and Exchange Board of India

The securities and exchange board of India, also referred to as SEBI was founded in the year 1992 in order to protect the interests of the investors and to facilitate the functioning of the market intermediaries. They supervise market conditions, register institutions and indulge in risk management.

Insurance Companies in India

The insurance companies offer protection against losses. They deal in life insurance, marine insurance, vehicle insurance and so on. The insurance companies collect the little saving of the investors and then reinvest those savings in the market. The insurance companies are collaborating with different foreign insurance companies after the liberalization process. This step has been incorporated to expand the Indian Insurance market and make it competitive.

Specialized Financial Institutions in India

The specialized financial institutions in India are government undertakings that were set up to provide assistance to the different sectors and thereby cause overall development of the Indian economy. The significant institutions falling under this category includes:

- Board for Industrial & Financial Reconstruction
- Export-Import Bank of India
- Small Industries Development Bank of India
- National Housing Bank.

Financial Services in India

In last few years, India has emerged as the one of the most rapidly growing economies in the world. India has been categorized with nations like Brazil, Russia and China (BRIC Nations) who are going to be the prime drivers of world economy in next few decades. Since the time, India first opened its gates to foreign investment (FDI & FII), there has been a complete turnaround. Now the traditional Hindu rate of growth is a thing of past and clocking 8%-9% GDP growth rate is the common norm. India along with other Asian powerhouse China makes for the fastest growing nations in the entire world.

Even if we take the case of ongoing global recession, India has managed to perform far better than other nations. Right from banking system to financial regularities, the country has thrived on discipline and out-performance. The booming Indian economy resulted in widespread growth and arrival of new industries. The most sparkling phenomenon is in form of financial market of India.

Financial services in India has taken a giant leap from the days of standing in banks queue for several hours for opening a saving account or trying to get some fixed deposits (FD) done. The financial services have increased manifold and now people have the choice to choose the one that most suitably fits the bill.

There are several services like broking firms, investment services, financial consulting, evergreen national banks, numerous private banks, mutual funds, car and home loans, equity market and other banking services. Services are many and offered by blue chip names of the industry. Most of the companies in financial segment offer taxation services, project consultancy services and all the services of wide financial gamut.

Whether it's taking a car loan or booking your favourite house, going for pension plan or getting your child insured, numerous attractive financial services are available at affordable costs. Personal banking services have acquired an altogether new meaning. Now customers have multiple choices to choose from. One can find all the financial services on the internet that are just a call away.

With market sentiment turning positive due to the formation of a stable newly elected government, the ripple effect is likely to be felt across all the financial services in India. The sectors, including banking and insurance, and mutual funds are all beginning to reap the benefits of a good closure for 2008-09. The Indian economy is estimated to have grown by 6.7 per cent in 2008-09. According to the latest Central Statistical Organisation (CSO) data, financial services and real estate sector rose by 9.5 per cent in the first quarter of 2009-10.

The government has taken a number of steps in recent months to revive the economy, including slashing interest rates, lowering factory levies and more than doubling the limit on foreign investment in corporate bonds. The financial services space is a rapidly growing one in India. The country received US$ 45 billion in foreign currency remittances from non-resident Indians in 2008, the highest in the world.

Foreign institutional investors' (FIIs) net investments in Indian equities crossed US$ 8 billion in calendar year 2009.

The mutual fund industry has seen an 8.7 per cent increase in the asset base for the month of August 2009, against an increase of 2.8 per cent in July 2009, largely due to significant inflows into debt schemes.

The average assets under management of the mutual fund industry stood at US$ 153.89 billion as at end August 2009, according to the data released by Association of Mutual Funds in India (AMFI).

With the capital market showing signs of revival, banks and financial companies that had put their mutual fund plans on hold are gearing up to enter the segment.

At present, nine players from the financial services sector are in various stages of entering the space. The list includes Bank of India, IDBI Bank, Axis Bank, Mahindra and Mahindra Financial Services (M&M Finance), SREI Infrastructure Finance, Bajaj Allianz, Indiabulls Financial Services, L&T Finance and Motilal Oswal.

India has increased its exposure to American debt securities by over three-fold to US$ 38.2 billion till March 2009 as against US$ 11.8 billion in March 2008, according to the data from the US Treasury Department.

The country's foreign exchange reserves rose by US$ 1.28 billion to touch US$ 277.64 billion for the week ended September 4, 2009, according to the figures released in the Reserve Bank of India's Weekly Statistical Supplement.

The World Bank and India have concluded negotiations for loans worth US$ 3.2 billion for recapitalising state-run banks and funding for the India Infrastructure Finance Company Ltd.

Stock Markets

India's market capitalisation (m-cap) has touched US$ 1.04 trillion making it the ninth largest in the world. India's share in the total world m-cap has risen to 2.79 per cent currently. The Indian stock market has currently responded to the optimism of reforms by the new stable government and its continuity in policies.

Fund raising by India Inc through initial public offers (IPOs) rose by a whopping 62 per cent since the beginning of 2008 to May 29, 2008 to US$ 4.2 billion, against US$ 2.6 billion during the same period in 2006, according to global deal data provider, Dealogic. According to Goldman Sachs, Indian companies may raise US$ 4 billion-US$ 6 billion from IPOs in the fiscal year ending March 31, 2010.

Insurance

India is the fifth largest life insurance market in the emerging insurance economies globally and the segment is growing at a healthy 32–34 per cent annually.

According to a report by research firm RNCOS—'Booming Insurance Market in India (2008–2011)'—the total life insurance premium in India is projected to grow to US$ 259.72 billion by 2010–11. Life Insurance Corporation (LIC) is bullish on growth and is targetting business in excess of US$ 59.14 billion by 2011–12.

The government is planning to ease restrictions on foreign investments in insurance, banking and pensions, and allow foreign direct investment (FDI) of 49 per cent from the present 26 per cent.

The 'Mallassurance' delivery channel is first of its kind in India's insurance sector, selling life and general insurance policies through all Future Group retail outlets across the country. For Future Generali Insurance, a sizeable chunk of their customers now comes through the Mallassurance route.

Online sales take place through two major channels through direct sales by the insurers and through online insurance portals which offer a range of products from various insurers. The most active insurers online are ICICI Lombard, Bajaj Allianz etc.

Magma Fincorp is foraying into insurance business. The company has inked an agreement with German insurance major HDI-Gerling International Holding to enter the general insurance sector in India. The new JV plans to seek the necessary Insurance Regulatory & Development Authority (IRDA) and the Reserve Bank of India (RBI) approvals soon.

Banking Services

During 2008-09, State Bank of India (SBI) and associate banks advanced US$ 16.8 billion for infrastructure projects such as power plants and petroleum refineries. The big-sized credits have made SBI and group one of the largest project financiers in the country.

Market Maker

Who Are Market Makers? Many option traders and stock traders ask, who is buying from me when I am selling and who is selling to me when I am buying? What happens when nobody wants to buy a stock or stock option which I am selling? In a normal, liquid market, there are usually someone queuing to sell a stock or stock option when you are buying and someone queuing to buy when you are selling. However, there are times when nobody is queuing to sell when you are buyng and times when nobody is queuing to buy when you are selling, so, how is it that you are still able to buy or sell your stocks or stock options smoothly? This is where Market Makers come in.

A "Market Maker" can be an individual or representatives of a firm whose function is to aid in the making of a market, by making bids and offers for his account in the absence of public buy or sell orders in order to ensure market transactions are as smooth and continuous as possible.

When an option trader places an order to buy a stock option which nobody is queuing to sell, market makers sell that stock option to that option trader from their own portfolio or reserve of that particular stock option. When an option trader places an order to sell a stock option which nobody is queuing to buy, market makers buy that stock option from that option trader and adds it to their own portfolio and reserve. In doing so, market orders are continuously moving, eradicating sudden surges and ditches due to buying and selling imbalance.

You'll most often hear about market makers in the context of the NASDAQ or other "over the counter" (OTC) markets. In contrast to the "Specialist" system that the NYSE employs, NASDAQ has no individuals through which a stock's transaction must pass. Instead, all transactions pass from one market maker to another. In the market maker system, market makers compete with one another to buy or sell stocks & options to investors by displaying quotes and are obligated to buy and sell at their displayed bids and offers. An investor may be dealing with several market makers at once if that investor is placing a very large order which cannot be filled by the inventory of one market maker. An option trader may also deal directly with individual, specific market makers through Level II Quotes.

In reality, Market Makers make up the actual "market". When a stock or option trader places an order with a broker, that broker fills that order by buying or selling with the Market Makers.

Another way of understanding what Market Makers do is that Market Makers are like the book makers in Las Vegas who set the odds and then accomodate individual gamblers who select which side of the bet they want. A Market Maker supplies a bid and ask price and then let the public decide whether to buy or sell at those prices. As an options trader, Market Makers are master position traders who aims to establish and profit from every low risk and risk free opportunities.

Advantage of The Market Maker System

In NYSE, there is one official employee of the exchange to act as market maker for each security. In the Market Maker System, many market makers are assigned to every security. As every Market Maker effectively acts as a "Specialist" like in NYSE, there are effectively many specialists for each stock. This creates a decentralised market place where liquidity and volatility varies. This improves overall liquity and makes market manipulation much more difficult.

What Happens if There are no Market Makers?

Market makers have given option traders quite a negative impression as people who buys at very low prices and sells at very high prices just when an option trader is desperate to buy or sell a position. Let's see what happens when we remove market makers from the markets.

XYZ stock is an extremely bullish stock who has just announced fantastic earnings. You want to buy XYZ stocks but investors who are already holding XYZ stocks are not selling. In order to attract a seller, you begin to bid higher and higher for XYZ stock until at last, a seller is moved to selling the stock. This price could already be extremely high.

Consider again a sudden bad news released from XYZ company, creating a rush to sell XYZ stocks. You are queing to sell but nobody is buying. In order to attract a buyer, you start to push the price lower and lower until at last, the price bottoms out worthless.

As we have seen, in an imbalanced buying and selling situation, market makers play an extremely important role of creating liquidity for prices in between in order to eradicate huge gap ups and downs and to ensure a liquid market for all.

How Does Market Makers Make a Profit?

Market Makers are not paid commissions to buy and sell stock options, so how do they make a profit? Well, most institutional market makers simply earns a salary from the marker maker firm that they represent. Market Maker firms like Goldman Sachs and Morgan Stanley, commit their own capital to maintain an inventory of stocks and options and represent customer orders. On the trading floor, Market Makers make money by maintaining a difference between the price he would buy and the price he would sell a particular stock or stock option. This difference in price is known as the Bid-Ask Spread. A bid-ask spread ensures that if an order to buy and an order to sell arrives simulataneously, the Market Maker makes the difference in Bid-Ask Spread as profit.

Example: XYZ May 30 Call option has a bid price of $1.10 and an ask price of $1.30. Market Maker John recieves simulataneously an order to buy and an order to sell. Market Maker John buys that May 30 Call option from the seller for $1.10 and then sells that same May 30 Call option to the buyer for $1.30, thus making $0.20 in profit completely risk-free.

However, when a Market Maker is not confident that a stock or stock option can be so quickly bought and sold, due to the fact that there are only very few option traders or stock traders trading that security, then there is a risk that a stock or stock option which that Market Maker buys can only be sold when the market price is lower than the prevailing price, therefore resulting in a loss. In order to protect against such a risk, Market Makers, widen the bid-ask spread so that the transaction remains risk free to him over a larger price range.

Conversely, when Market Makers are selling highly active option contracts, they frequently raise the price of the option through increasing the implied volatility of that particular option contract. That results in the Volatility Smile or Volatility Skew.

Apart from market making, market makers also make profits from options arbitrage. An arbitrage opportunity presents itself when a severe deviation from Put Call Parity occurs leading to options pricing discrepancies which can be locked in completely risk-free using options trading strategies such as the Box Spread and the Conversion & Reversal Arbitrage. As any possible profits from arbitrage is extremely low, only Market Makers who need not pay a broker commission can actually make any money out of it.

How Does Market Makers Protect From Risk?

As you can see by now, Market Makers are like you and me, buying and selling stocks and stock options. Doesn't that expose them to certain directional risks? Yes, even though market makers endeavour to be able to buy and sell simultaneously in order to benefit risk-free from bid-ask spread, such ideal situation rarely exist in stocks or stock options which are not extremely liquid. Most of the time, Market Makers end up owning stocks or stock options and that exposed them to directional risk.

Example : Market Maker John buys XYZ May 30 Call option from a seller for $0.80. If XYZ stock falls before Market Maker John manages to find a buyer for it, Market Maker John stands to lose money as the call option decreases in price.

Market Makers protect themselves from directional risks through "Hedging" and flexible use of synthetic positions. A Market Maker hedges his inventory through buying or selling additional stocks or stock options in order to achieve a position whereby stocks and options falls as much as the other rises in order to maintain the overall value of the account.

This is what we call a "Delta-Neutral" position. A Market Maker's positioning strategy, especially in making markets for stock options, is extremely complex and requires to the second calculation and execution. It is because of this complexity in balancing all kinds of risks that some new Market Makers actually lose money to the market despite all the privileges of being a Market Maker.

Risks That Market Makers Face

Market Makers for stock options trading faces 6 forms of risks which, in fact, all option traders face :

Directional Risk/Delta Risk

Directional or Delta risk is the risk that a stock option price will turn against the market maker as the underlying stock value changes. A Market Maker consistent attempts to hedge this risk by going "Delta-Neutral".

Gamma Risk

Gamma risk is the risk that the delta value of a stock option may change over time. This consistently threatens to tip a Market Maker's sensitive Delta-Neutral position to become of positive or negative delta, thereby exposing a Market Maker to directional risk. Gamma risk can be overcome by taking Gamma Neutral Positions.

Volatility Risk

An increase in implied volatility in the market increases the premium value of stock options while a decrease in implied volatility decreases the premium value of stock options due. This is known as the Vega risk. Market Makers who hold an inventory of stock options could sustain a loss if implied volatility decreases.

Time Decay Risk

Time Decay or Theta risk is when stock option premium reduces as expiration date draws nearer even if the underlying stock does not move. A Market Maker with an inventory of long stock options can sustain a loss over time even if the underlying stock does not move.

Interest Rate Risk

Stock options, especially long term ones, are affected slightly by changes in interest rates. This change, although insignificant to most option traders, is significant to Market Makers who hold very large inventory of stock options. This risk is represented by the Options Rho.

Dividend Risk

Dividends declared reduces call option value as holder of the call option do not received the dividends. Such risks are usually hedged by Market Makers by buying the underlying stock ahead of it's dividend declaration. The dividends received then hedge against the decline in call option value. Unlike independent option traders, Market Makers cannot sell off their inventory of stock options simply because they know these stock options are going to go down in value due to any of the above risks, that is why hedging is such an important skill to Market Makers.

Difference Between Market Makers and Brokers

A broker is an intermediary who has a license to buy and sell securities on a client's behalf. Stockbrokers coordinate contracts between buyers and sellers, usually for a commission. A market maker, on the other hand, is an intermediary that is willing and ready to buy and sell securities for a profitable price.

A broker makes money by bringing together securities' buyers and sellers. Brokers have the authorization and expertise to buy securities on an investor's behalf-not just anyone is allowed to walk into the New York Stock Exchange and purchase stocks; therefore, investors must hire licensed brokers to do this for them. A flat fee or percentage-based commission is given to the broker for carrying out a trade and finding the best price for a security. Because brokers are regulated and licensed, they have an obligation to act in the best interests of their clients. Many brokers can also offer advice on what stocks, mutual funds and other securities to buy. Due to the availability of internet-based automated stock brokering systems, clients often do not have any personal contact with their brokerage firms.

A market maker makes a profit by attempting to sell high and buy low. Market makers establish quotes whereby the bid price is set slightly lower than listed prices and the ask price is set slightly higher in order to earn a small margin. Market makers are useful because they are always ready to buy and sell as long as the investor is willing to pay a specific price. This helps to create liquidity and efficiency in the market. Market makers essentially act as wholesalers by buying and selling securities to satisfy the market; the prices they set reflect market supply and demand. When the demand for a security is low and supply is high, the price of the security will be low.

7

Public Revenue

The Development of Public Revenue

Most Demands of the Modern State are Monetary

In supplying the various materials and services which have been considered in the preceding pages, the state has no superhuman power. The funds required for these expenditures must be secured from some existing source. The two most imperative needs of the state are the control over space, from which it can direct its activities, and the control over services and commodities with which to carry out its desires. The modern state differs vastly from the earlier ones in the method by which this control is secured. Under feudalism and other early forms of government the ownership of the land was in the hands of the state, and the first mark of citizenship was obligation to render services to the state. Gradually the lands passed into the ownership of individuals, and the obligation of service was no longer synonymous with citizenship.

The change has continued until the modern state must act very much as an individual in supplying itself with space, services, and commodities. If land is needed for a public building it must be purchased in the open market. Officials are secured to carry out the functions of the state by paying them salaries.

The powers of the state are somewhat stronger than those of individuals, however, in that it can commandeer land for its use, or for the use of individuals it may designate, through the right of eminent domain. It also has the right to coerce services of its citizens. This always follows some well-defined plan, and may be extended to include a large proportion of the citizenship, as in the case of conscription for army and navy services.

The best example, perhaps, in normal times, of coercive service, is in securing men for juries. This is a general practice in the United States. Another form of coercive service which is rapidly disappearing is the requirement of a certain amount of work for the maintenance of highways. With few exceptions, then, it may be said that the demands of the modern state are monetary. It requires its revenue to come in the form of money, and uses this money to secure land, services, and commodities from individuals or governments, instead of requiring them to be supplied gratuitously.

Gratuitous Services to the State are Unsatisfactory

The unsatisfactory character of gratuitous services is one reason why they are so little used at present. In the United States services are sometimes given on boards of directors, or as visitors to public institutions, or occasionally as mayors of small towns. The motives which prompt citizens to offer such gratuitous services are patriotism, distinction, or some such appeal. That patriotism gives a strong appeal was evidenced by the number and caliber of some of the "dollar a year" men in the service of the United States government during the Great War.

The difficulty with most of the motives for gratuitous services is that they are not of sufficient permanence to insure a continued efficient service. The patriotic flash soon dies with the passing of a crisis, while a position of honour may quickly lose such distinction. Men who receive nothing for their services can hardly be expected to give much in return. It is only when they are put on a "value received" basis that the public can successfully hold them responsible for the proper performance of duties.

The motives for gratuitous service, moreover, unless underneath there be a chance for individual gain or pull-and then the service ceases to be gratuitous are ordinarily not strong enough to call men with marked ability. Either they will have accomplished their goal in private life, and are willing to ease off on the public, or will be using the office as a stepping stone, neither of which could give the best results. As a whole, political units have gone to the basis of paying for men to render the required service, and it is the duty of the citizenship to hold officials responsible for the proper conduct of their duties.

Public Revenues Received Many Early Classifications

Almost as soon as states began to rely upon revenues to carry on activities, those interested in fiscal problems became concerned about the importance and justice of the various sources of revenues. Bodin, the French scholar, gave one of the most interesting early classifications. He enumerated seven sources for securing public revenue which, he said, included all that could be thought of. They were: (1) landed domain; (2) conquests from enemies; (3) gifts from friends; (4) tributes from subject states; (5) public trading; (6) customs duties; (7) taxes.

Such a classification is interesting when compared with the important modern sources of revenue. Bodin held that the revenues from public domains were the most just and certain, but that customs duties were wholly just. His reason for the latter was the one commonly held at that time-if any foreigner was to gain by trading, let him pay for it. Taxes were only to be used when all other sources failed to produce a sufficient amount.

Adam Smith divided revenues into those coming from a fund belonging to the state, and from a fund belonging to the citizens. He was not in favour of the state entering industry, and believed that most revenues should come from the citizens. Most of the other early fiscal writers were likewise concerned about the important sources of revenues, and many of these sources were discussed, not only from the fiscal point of view, but from the standpoint of economic principle and ethics as well.

The Question of Public Lands has been Important

The public domain formerly held the most important place in the source of revenues. Much discussion arose as to the wisdom of this, and the result has been that modern states have almost entirely disposed of their landed possessions. A number of reasons have been set forth why the state should retain these lands, and also why the state should dispose of them. The best summary of these arguments has been given, perhaps, by Rau, a German fiscal writer. Some of them are worthy of notice.

Disposal of Public Land: A state should give up its public domain, he said, because it was not fitted to enter industry. In private hands the domains would yield a larger income because an individual owner is more energetic in seeking to get profits than is a public official. As a rule public officials are not so much concerned in making improvements in methods of production as are individuals. The public ownership of land, moreover, gives the government a special interest of its own, which may lessen its activity in undertaking projects which might be needed for the general good of its citizens. Competition with private industry might also lead to dissatisfaction. Experience has shown, moreover, that states that have given up lands have had an ample source of revenue from the citizens, which shows that the retention is unnecessary.

Retention of Public Land: On the other hand, something may be said in favour of the state retaining lands so as to have an independent source of revenue. An income from such a permanent source can be depended upon, and the state does not have to rely upon legislative enactment to procure funds. When legislative enactment is necessary, officials who desire to gain favour with a part of their constituency may curtail the exaction of revenues far beyond legitimate needs. Recognition has sometimes been made of the fact that particular officials may be hostile to, or disinterested in, certain public enterprises, the usefulness of which could be hampered by retrenchment in the revenues for their development. To prevent this situation, provision is sometimes made that a certain part of the revenue collected shall be used for a particular purpose, as, for example, for the state university. If the citizenship lacks public spirit, moreover, and resents the exaction of funds, an independent source of revenue might mean more harmony within the state. The problems of inequality and injustice, which arise when funds are secured from individuals, would also be minimized, it was claimed.

Public credit would be strengthened, it was further contended, if the state had public lands to offer as security. Use was made of lands as a basis for credit to a relatively large extent in the early development of governments. One of the best examples of the use and failure of the public domain as a basis for credit was in France, when John Law used it as the basis for bank note circulation. Not only were the notes based upon the public lands of France, but also upon the lands in the Mississippi Valley. Difficulty arose, however, when attempts were made to redeem the notes.

The reasons set forth for the state's retention of public lands would have more weight if they could be managed as efficiently in the hands of the state as when turned over to individuals. This, however, would seldom be true, especially if agricultural pursuits were followed, since this form of industry does not lend itself well to large scale production. The state can draw upon the resources of its

operations, yet there is at present much agitation for government ownership and operation. It is too much to expect that a government could successfully manage every kind of industry, yet some may be carried on to better advantage than others. No rule can be definitely stated which would mark off the field for state enterprise, yet it may be possible to suggest some conditions which favour the success of state activity in industry.

Conditions Favourable to State Management: An industry suitable for state management must be one which can be closely watched by the public. It is necessarily carried on by public officials, with the temptation always before them of securing benefits to themselves at the expense of the public. Not only must it be an industry which can be closely observed, but it must be one in which the public is interested. The managing officials, otherwise, will not be held responsible for the method in which the business is conducted. An industry which has reached, or nearly reached, its final stage in development is better fitted for government management than a new industry in which much progress is needed to make it efficient. State officials do not have the same motives for progress and efficiency as individual entrepreneurs, since the returns of the business are the rewards to the latter, while the former receive a salary for their services. A mature industry has the further advantage that the necessary operations have been standardized so that it is comparatively easy to assign definite tasks for which the employees can be held responsible. In a new and progressive industry, the entire method of operation may change every few years, while different aspects are continually in the process of change. This makes it difficult to secure men to be held accountable for particular tasks. While many individual exceptions doubtless exist, as a general proposition, however, the government will be more successful in managing a mature industry than one in the formative stage.

The Post Office is a Good Example of Government Enterprise

Some enterprises seem to fall naturally to government management-in fact, so naturally that the situation that they are really government enterprises is often lost sight of. The postal systems of various countries give the best example, perhaps, of an industry conducted by the government. The postal system is so generally conducted by the government that the possibility of its existence under individual management is scarcely given a thought. Not only is it one of the most general forms of public industry, but one of the oldest. Adam Smith referred to it as the only mercantile project which had been successfully managed by every sort of government.

The beginnings of postal systems were usually with individuals connected with mercantile pursuits. Messages were sent from establishment to establishment by a runner, who gradually acquired the habit of carrying messages for individuals who were along his route. An exception to this was the postal system which the Romans established as an adjunct to the military organization. As a whole, however, the system had very little development before it was taken over by the government in various countries.

After the postal system became a government monopoly a number of changes were made in rates of charges, and in the method for their determination. Charges at first were generally very high, and distance of carriage was an important factor to be considered in fixing the rate of charge. Gradually, however, rates were lowered, weight became the sole basis for the charge, while payment was made by affixing stamps. It might be said that the postal system had assumed its present form by 1850. While rates within the various countries were gradually reduced, cheap international postal rates came slowly. The recent establishment of the Postal Union has secured lower rates among the countries which are members.

Postal System in the United States: The growth of the postal system in the United States has followed the general trend of development of this enterprise. Acts passed by the Mother country provided for a Colonial postal system. A three-cent rate was adopted in 1851, and a two-cent rate in 1883. Distance as a basis of charge was given up comparatively early, and weight with payment by stamp was adopted.

This has no doubt imposed a burden upon some parts of the country at the expense of other parts. If statements could be secured which would separate the postal revenues and expenditure of the part of the country east of the Mississippi from those of the territory west of this line, there is no doubt that the eastern part would show a substantial surplus, while the western part would show a large loss. It appears the people in the more thickly settled part of the country are paying an excessive price for their service, while the more sparsely settled regions are securing services at less than cost, with the deficits paid by the former class. If all the indirect gains were considered, however, which have come to the eastern population because of the rapid development which a cheap postal service has fostered, it would no doubt be quite evident that all expenditures for maintaining the system have been very remunerative.

Motives for Conducting Postal System: The aims which a state may have in view in conducting the postal system are not the same in different countries, nor in the same country at different times. In the earlier periods the idea of securing revenue predominated, while the claim of public service received little consideration. In that part of the service where the government has a monopoly, as in carrying letters, the charge will be comparatively high, while in the part of the service where there may be competition, as in carrying parcels, the rates will be fixed more on a competitive basis.

There has been a tendency to minimize the importance of securing the largest possible revenue, however, while public service has been given greater consideration. It is at present the policy of no country, perhaps, to secure more than a good business profit, while some attempt to conduct the industry on a cost basis, or even run with a deficit which must be made up from the common treasury. France and England usually receive a substantial profit, while the United States has practically attempted the cost basis, although in a majority of years a deficit has appeared. Before 1819, in the United States, the annual revenues exceeded expenditures, while a deficit appeared for more than half of the next thirty years. This whole period showed a slight deficit, while a deficit has occurred in practically every year since 1850. During the Great War the revenue aspect received more emphasis. Rates were raised, and distance was adopted as a factor in determining the postage upon second class matter. Since the war the letter rates have been reduced, and as expenditures assume more normal proportions the zone system of charge for second class mail will doubtless be repealed.

States Enter Many Fields of Activity

The ownership and management of the postal system is perhaps the oldest and most general of government enterprises, yet modern state activities reach into many other fields. Many causes have contributed to the development of this situation. The success which attended the various states in the management of the postal system, whatever the aim primarily in view, soon led to the conclusion, among certain classes, that the state could be just as successful in other lines of endeavor. The doctrine of laissez faire, moreover, under which competition was expected to work out justice in charges and services, soon proved to be unsatisfactory. This became increasingly true in the industries with which the public is most deeply interested-the public utilities. From factors inherent in the nature of their business, competition is destructive, and combinations and trade agreements soon began to appear.

Public ownership has been proposed as one method of escape from the abuses perpetrated by these monopolies. It has been carried much farther in some countries than in others. In many European states the telegraph, telephone, railroad, and express companies are owned and operated by the government. In the United States these industries still remain under individual management in spite of increased agitation and pressure from certain classes for government ownership. The extension of the postal system to the carrying of parcels has made the government a competitor with express companies, while the extensive regulation through the Interstate Commerce Commission and the numerous state public utility commissions substantially limits the activities of the individual enterpriser.

Public Ownership has had most Rapid Extension in Municipalities

The larger governmental units of the United States, as has been indicated, have been slow in developing public industries. The opposite tendency has been shown in the municipalities, especially in the smaller ones. The waterworks very early began to be taken over by the cities, and the policy has grown until at present comparatively few individuals are supplying water for cities. A few large cities have taken over the task of supplying gas and electricity, yet unqualified success has not crowned the efforts. Cases have arisen where failure was so marked that the plants have been turned back to private management. In the smaller cities, however, extension of ownership has been much more rapid. Not only is the supply of nearly all the water furnished from public plants, but the cities have frequently undertaken to supply a number of other utilities. In some cases the success has been certain; in others, doubtful, while failure has sometimes resulted. Instances in which smaller cities have given such industries over to individuals are infrequent, which would lead to the belief that the experiment has been fairly satisfactory.

Reasons for Municipal Industries: The reasons for the rapid municipalization of industries are not far to seek. Competition naturally gave way to monopoly, followed by an exploited public. Antagonistic public sentiment was quickly aroused, in the development of which the public press played an important part. A number of magazines devoted to municipal problems rapidly came to the front, which supplemented the agitation already carried on by numerous newspapers. State legislatures influenced the development by facilitating the acquisition of the industries by the cities. Debt limitations frequently have been lifted so that bonds could be issued for construction or purchase.

The above factors have not only caused a rapid extension of municipal ownership, but have had a salutary effect upon the individuals who continue to operate public utilities, in that more consideration is given to the wishes of the public. Where this results in a satisfactory agreement between the operator and the public, the desire for public ownership may be indefinitely postponed. The inauguration of regulation by public boards, in so far as this succeeds in securing just relations between the public and the individuals or corporations supplying its utilities, will postpone and weaken the desire for municipal ownership. However successful public management has been, it does not indicate that a rapid extension may be expected. The agitation has, perhaps, done much to accomplish its purpose through the changes in the service given by individuals, and the past successes of public ownership suggest a plausible alternative if the desired results cannot be obtained through private management.

The United States Census Bureau Classifies Revenues

The classification of revenues which is used by the census bureau is similar to its classification of expenditures, in that it is largely for mechanical purposes. The reports must be based upon official records, and since there is a lack of uniformity in the various political divisions, a detailed classification would be impossible. Only a broad statement of receipts, therefore, has been attempted. A number of classes have been formed with a definite meaning assigned to the terms used to designate them. The meaning assigned has been taken from the usage of the best authorities on fiscal problems, modified in particular instances by some special requirement.

Revenue Receipts: The two primary classes of revenues correspond to the two primary classes of expenditure. They are revenue receipts and nonrevenue receipts, The former applies to all money and wealth received by governmental bodies which increase the aggregate assets without increasing the liabilities. Under this head the following items are listed, a detailed discussion of which will be taken up in succeeding chapters: general property taxes; special property taxes; poll and occupation taxes; special assessments; business and income taxes; business license taxes; nonbusiness license taxes; fines, forfeits, and escheats; highway privileges; interest and rents; subventions and grants; donations and gifts; earnings of general departments; and earnings of public service enterprises.

Nonrevenue Receipts: The class of nonrevenue receipts is described by the census bureau as follows: "The term nonrevenue receipts is applied to all receipts of a civil division other than its revenue receipts, as previously defined. The nonrevenue receipts of a fiscal year of any civil division comprise all receipts recorded during the year from (1) sales of investments and of supplies which have been purchased for sale; (2) issue of debt obligations and transactions which increase the indebtedness without the issue of formal debt obligations; (3) trust and agency transactions; (4) receipts offsetting outlays, as the collections of insurance to be applied to the reconstruction of destroyed property, refunds of erroneous payments, and receipts in error; and (5) such counterbalancing receipts as transfers between the funds or divisions of the governmental unit." From the nature of the items in this second classification, it is readily seen that it occupies a place of comparative unimportance. In so far as the discussion of succeeding chapters deals with revenue, therefore, the revenue receipts will occupy a place of much greater importance than nonrevenue receipts.

Tax

To tax (from the Latin *taxo*; "I estimate", which in turn is from *tango*; "I touch") is to impose a financial charge or other levy upon a taxpayer (an individual or legal entity) by a state or the functional equivalent of a state such that failure to pay is punishable by law.

Taxes are also imposed by many subnational entities. Taxes consist of direct tax or indirect tax, and may be paid in money or as its labour equivalent (often but not always unpaid). A tax may be defined as a "pecuniary burden laid upon individuals or property owners to support the government 1-2 a payment exacted by legislative authority." A tax "is not a voluntary payment or donation, but an enforced contribution, exacted pursuant to legislative authority" and is "any contribution imposed by government 1-2 whether under the name of toll, tribute, tallage, gabel, impost, duty, custom, excise, subsidy, aid, supply, or other name."

The legal definition and the economic definition of taxes differ in that economists do not consider many transfers to governments to be taxes. For example, some transfers to the public sector are comparable to prices. Examples include tuition at public universities and fees for utilities provided by local governments. Governments also obtain resources by creating money (e.g, printing bills and minting coins), through voluntary gifts (e.g., contributions to public universities and museums), by imposing penalties (e.g,, traffic fines), by borrowing, and by confiscating wealth. From the view of economists, a tax is a non-penal, yet compulsory transfer of resources from the private to the public sector levied on a basis of predetermined criteria and without reference to specific benefit received.

In modern taxation systems, taxes are levied in money, but in-kind and *corvee* taxation are characteristic of traditional or pre-capitalist states and their functional equivalents. The method of taxation and the government expenditure of taxes raised is often highly debated in politics and economics. Tax collection is performed by a government agency such as Canada Revenue Agency, the Internal Revenue Service (IRS) in the United States, or Her Majesty's Revenue and Customs (HMRC) in the UK. When taxes are not fully paid, civil penalties (such as fines or forfeiture) or criminal penalties (such as incarceration) may be imposed on the non-paying entity or individual.

Purposes and Effects

Funds provided by taxation have been used by states and their functional equivalents throughout history to carry out many functions. Some of these include expenditures on war, the enforcement of law and public order, protection of property, economic infrastructure (roads, legal tender, enforcement of contracts, etc.), public works, social engineering, and the operation of government itself. Governments also use taxes to fund welfare and public services. These services can include education systems, health care systems, pensions for the elderly, unemployment benefits, and public transportation. Energy, water and waste management systems are also common public utilities. Colonial and modernizing states have also used cash taxes to draw or force reluctant subsistence producers into cash economies.

Governments use different kinds of taxes and vary the tax rates. This is done to distribute the tax burden among individuals or classes of the population involved in taxable activities, such as business, or to redistribute resources between individuals or classes in the population. Historically, the nobility were supported by taxes on the poor; modern social security systems are intended to support the poor, the disabled, or the retired by taxes on those who are still working. In addition, taxes are applied to fund foreign and military aid, to influence the macroeconomic performance of the economy (the government's strategy for doing this is called its fiscal policy), or to modify patterns of consumption or employment within an economy, by making some classes of transaction more or less attractive.

A nation's tax system is often a reflection of its communal values or the values of those in power. To create a system of taxation, a nation must make choices regarding the distribution of the tax burden—who will pay taxes and how much they will pay—and how the taxes collected will be spent. In democratic nations where the public elects those in charge of establishing the tax system, these choices reflect the type of community that the public wishes to create. In countries where the public does not have a significant amount of influence over the system of taxation, that system may be more of a reflection on the values of those in power.

The resource collected from the public through taxation is always greater than the amount which can be used by the government. The difference is called *compliance cost*, and includes for example the labour cost and other expenses incurred in complying with tax laws and rules. The collection of a tax in order to spend it on a specified purpose, for example collecting a tax on alcohol to pay directly for alcoholism rehabilitation centres, is called hypothecation. This practice is often disliked by finance ministers, since it reduces their freedom of action. Some economic theorists consider the concept to be intellectually dishonest since (in reality) money is fungible. Furthermore, it often happens that taxes or excises initially levied to fund some specific government programs are then later diverted to the government general fund. In some cases, such taxes are collected in fundamentally inefficient ways, for example highway tolls.

Some economists, especially Neo-classical economists, argue that all taxation creates market distortion and results in economic inefficiency. They have therefore sought to identify the kind of tax system that would minimize this distortion. Also, one of every government's most fundamental duties is to administer possession and use of land in the geographic area over which it is sovereign, and it is considered economically efficient for government to recover for public purposes the additional value it creates by providing this unique service.

Since governments also resolve commercial disputes, especially in countries with common law, similar arguments are sometimes used to justify a sales tax or value added tax. Others (e.g. libertarians) argue that most or all forms of taxes are immoral due to their involuntary (and therefore eventually coercive/violent) nature. The most extreme anti-tax view is anarcho-capitalism, in which the provision of *all* social services should be voluntarily bought by the person(s) using them.

The Four "R"s

Taxation has four main purposes or effects: Revenue, Redistribution, Repricing, and Representation. The main purpose is revenue: taxes raise money to spend on roads, schools and hospitals, and on more indirect government functions like market regulation or legal systems. This is the most widely known function.

A second is redistribution. Normally, this means transferring wealth from the richer sections of society to poorer sections.

A third purpose of taxation is repricing. Taxes are levied to address externalities: tobacco is taxed, for example, to discourage smoking, and many people advocate policies such as implementing a carbon tax.

A fourth, consequential effect of taxation in its historical setting has been representation. The American revolutionary slogan "no taxation without representation" implied this: rulers tax citizens, and citizens demand accountability from their rulers as the other part of this bargain. Several studies have shown that direct taxation (such as income taxes) generates the greatest degree of accountability and better governance, while indirect taxation tends to have smaller effects.

Proportional Tax

A proportional tax is a tax imposed so that the tax rate is fixed as the amount subject to taxation increases. In simple terms, it imposes an equal burden (relative to resources) on the rich and poor. "Proportional" describes a distribution effect on income or expenditure, referring to the way the rate remains consistent (does not progress from "low to high" or "high to low" as income or consumption changes), where the marginal tax rate is equal to the average tax rate. It can be applied to individual taxes or to a tax system as a whole; a year, multi-year, or lifetime. Proportional taxes maintain equal tax incidence regardless of the ability-to-pay and do not shift the incidence disproportionately to those with a higher or lower economic well-being.

Proportional taxes are uncommon in advanced economies, whose nationwide taxes typically include a graduated tax on household incomes and corporate profits, such that the marginal tax rate rises as the income or profit of the taxed entity rises. Flat taxes, implemented as well as proposed, usually exempt from taxation household income below a statutorily determined level that is a function of the type and size of the household. As a result, such a flat marginal rate is consistent with a progressive average tax rate. A progressive tax is a tax imposed so that the tax rate increases as the amount subject to taxation increases. The opposite of a progressive tax is a regressive tax, where the tax rate decreases as the amount subject to taxation increases.

Proportional Rates

Proportional taxes on consumption are considered by some to be regressive; that is, low income people tend to spend a greater percentage of their income in taxable sales (using a cross section time-frame) than higher income people. However, this calculation is derived when the tax paid is divided not by the tax base (the amount spent) but by income, which is argued to create an arbitrary relationship. The tax rate itself is proportional with higher income people paying more tax but at the same rate as they consume more. If a consumption tax is to be related to income, then the unspent income can be treated as tax-deferred (spending savings at a later point in time), at which time it is taxed creating a proportional rate using an income base. However, consumption taxes like a sales tax can often exclude items or provide rebates in an effort to create progressive effects. In many locations, "necessary" items such as non-prepared food, clothing, or prescription drugs are exempt from sales tax to alleviate the burden on the poor.

Progressive Tax

A progressive tax is a tax by which the tax rate increases as the taxable base amount increases. "Progressive" describes a distribution effect on income or expenditure, referring to the way the rate progresses from low to high, where the average tax rate is less than the marginal tax rate. It can be applied to individual taxes or to a tax system as a whole; a year, multi-year, or lifetime. Progressive taxes attempt to reduce the tax incidence of people with a lower ability-to-pay, as they shift the incidence increasingly to those with a higher ability-to-pay.

The term is frequently applied in reference to personal income taxes, where people with more disposable income pay a higher percentage of that income in tax than do those with less income. It can also apply to adjustment of the tax base by using tax exemptions, tax credits, or selective taxation that would create progressive distributional effects.

For example, a sales tax on luxury goods or the exemption of basic necessities may be described as having progressive effects as it increases a tax burden on high end consumption or decreases a tax burden on low end consumption respectively. The opposite of a progressive tax is a regressive tax, where the tax rate decreases as the amount subject to taxation increases. In between is a proportional tax, where the tax rate is fixed as the amount subject to taxation increases. The opposite of proportional tax is fixed tax.

History of Intellectual Debate

The idea of a progressive tax has garnered support from economists and political scientists of many different ideologies-ranging from Adam Smith to Karl Marx, although there are differences of opinion about the optimal level of progressivity. Some economists trace the origin of modern progressive taxation to Adam Smith, who wrote in *The Wealth of Nations*:

The necessaries of life occasion the great expense of the poor. They find it difficult to get food, and the greater part of their little revenue is spent in getting it. The luxuries and vanities of life occasion the principal expense of the rich, and a magnificent house embellishes and sets off to the best advantage all the other luxuries and vanities which they possess. A tax upon house-rents, therefore, would in general fall heaviest upon the rich; and in this sort of inequality there would not, perhaps, be anything very unreasonable. It is not very unreasonable that the rich should contribute to the public expense, not only in proportion to their revenue, but something more than in that proportion.

The French *Declaration of the Rights of Man and of the Citizen* of 1789 agrees:

A common contribution is essential for the maintenance of the public forces and for the cost of administration. This should be equitably distributed among all the citizens in proportion to their means. In most western European countries and the United States, advocates of progressive taxation tend to be found among the majority of economists and social scientists, many of whom believe that completely proportional taxation is not a possibility. In the U.S., an overwhelming majority of economists (81%) support progressive taxation.

Arguments for Implementation

- A progressive tax maximizes the amount of tax that can be collected, with the minimum number of protests, thereby presenting an easy political solution for governments with budgeting problems.

- In a market economy, the larger an investment is, the higher its rate of return. This is due to both economies of scale and the increased range of investment opportunities. In addition to these economic forces, those who control greater amounts of capital within a society are able to participate more directly in shaping government policy, often in ways that further maximize their wealth. Thus, due to both economic and political realities within a market economy, it is a natural process for the wealthiest individuals and firms in a society to become disproportionately wealthier over time. In order to prevent the political instability resulting from the natural stratification of the populace into an ever smaller and wealthier aristocracy or moneyed class, and an ever larger working class, all free market democracies engage in progressive taxation and programs to enhance economic opportunity for the lower and middle classes.
- In response to the concern that progressive taxation creates an unfair psychological burden on the wealthy, it is argued that if the utility gained from income exhibits diminishing marginal returns, as many psychologists assert, than for the tax burden to be shared in a utilitarian way the tax-bill must increase non-linearly with income.
- As income levels rise, marginal propensity to consume tend to drop. Thus it is often argued that economic demand can be stimulated by reducing the tax burden on lower incomes while raising the burden on higher incomes
- It is also argued that people with higher income tend to have a higher percentage of that in disposable income, and can thus afford a greater tax burden (this is the "vertical equity" argument). Some would claim that a person earning exactly enough money to pay for food and housing cannot afford to pay any taxes without it causing material damage, while someone earning twice as much can afford to pay up to half their income in taxes.
- Some believe that the wealthy have a disproportionately greater interest in maintaining societal goods typically supported by taxation such as security of property rights, defence and infrastructure, as they have much more to lose if these fail

than do the poor. Public investments in defence and foreign aid often support assets abroad whose expropriation is a far greater risk than is the risk involving domestic investments.

- It is inherent in tax policy that it implements economic and social policy. People who are concerned about a runaway, cancerous character in the global economy, greenhouse gases, etc., see benefits in progressive taxation, both in its braking effect on the economy and in helping shape economic activities towards necessities more effectively than purely monetary or fiscal policies.
- As long as after-tax income is a strictly increasing function of gross income, there is a monetary incentive to increase compensation received. Indeed, for any particular income goal, the higher the tax rate, more compensation one must receive to reach that income goal. For this reason, progressive income tax may increase the incentive to produce among the largest producers (if higher production is truly associated with higher compensation).
- A progressive tax reduces income inequality, which has been reported to have a number of societal benefits, such as lower homicide rates at all income levels. Richard Wilkinson argues that in a more unequal society, even middle class people on good incomes are likely to be less healthy, less likely to be involved in community life, more likely to be obese, and more likely to be victims of violence. Amongst the wealthiest quarter of countries, there is no relation between a country's wealth and general population health, but within a country, relative levels can have an effect.

Arguments Against Implementation

- It has been argued that progressive taxation violates the principle of equality under the law.
- Progressive taxes result in high marginal tax rates, which kills the division of labour. For example, in the United States a middle class professional is better off spending the day repairing a $500 appliance by hand than earning $1000 in exchange for something he's actually good at doing. The preceding example (50% take-home pay for each additional dollar) applies to any family in a 28% tax bracket with additional 9% state and local taxes, 7% social security and medicare taxes, and 7% worth of deduction phaseouts for such progressive tax schemes as

Child Tax Credit, Making Work Pay, Alternative Minimum tax, etc.

- Progressive taxes lower savings rates. High-earners have a lower average propensity to consume, so shifting the tax-burden away from them will increase the aggregate savings rate, which should increase steady state growth (if the savings rate is initially below the Golden Rule savings rate).

The classical argument against progressive taxation runs as follows:

The diminishing returns argument applies to the fraction of income used for present consumption. As income rises, diminishing returns implies that a smaller and smaller fraction of income will be spent on consumption goods. The remaining income will (of necessity) be used to purchase capital goods. This acts as a form of positive feedback that in turn yields more income for capital spending. Meanwhile (and because) these capital goods induce a decline in the costs of production which has the effect of raising real wages generally and implicitly raising the general standard of living.

The income paid back on the capital helps create the disincentive to consume that creates capital spending. Thus, those capitalists who effectively manage their property are rewarded and given control of more (newly created) property, of which they are increasingly less inclined to consume and increasingly more inclined to purchase capital goods and thus further elevate the general standard of living by driving down the costs of production. As they acquire more capital goods, eventually their ownership outstrips their ability to manage and oversee what they own; however, they only control as many capital goods as can be attributed to the income of their prior capital— which previously did not exist. Therefore, their ownership does not negatively contribute to the general standard-of-living relative to counterfactual state of them not purchasing those goods. It would thus be misleading to argue that redistributing their capital may yield further increases in the standard-of-living. Doing so may well cause that effect, but doing so neglects that it was the assumption that redistribution would not happen that induced the accumulation of capital. — Eugen von Bohm-Bawerk, *Karl Marx and the Close of his System*, 1896

A belief that progressive taxation shifts the total economic production of society away from capital investments (tools, infrastructure, training, research) and toward present consumption goods. This could happen because high-income earners tend to pay for capital goods (through investment activities) and low-income earners tend to purchase consumables. Smithian and Neo-classical growth theory says that spending more on consumption goods and less on capital goods will slow the rise of the standard of living, and possibly even reduce it since capital goods increase future production possibilities.

- Brain drain and tax avoidance. High progressive taxes may encourage emigration because taxes are not internationally harmonized, so very high earners are sometimes able to relocate in order to pay less tax, or find tax havens for their income. Unlike the opposing income effect and substitution effect of leisure which may make tax progressivity neutral in terms of working hours, the emigration rate can only increase with the top rates of tax.

8

Functional Business Systems

IT in Business

Information systems can be grouped into business function categories; however, in the real world information systems are typically integrated combinations of functional information systems. Functional business systems are composed of a variety of types of information systems (transaction processing, management information, decision support, etc) that support the business functions of:

- Accounting
- Finance
- Marketing
- Productions/operations management

Functional Business System

E-business is the use of the Internet and other networks and information technologies to support electronic commerce, enterprise communications and collaboration, and Web-enabled business processes both within a networked enterprise, and with its customers and business partners.

Analysing Cypress Semiconductor and FleetBoston. We can learn a lot from this case about how information technologies are transforming and improving the management of the business processes of many companies today. Take a few minutes to read it, and we will discuss it. Information systems can be grouped into business function categories; however, in the real world information systems are typically integrated combinations of functional information systems. Functional business systems are composed of a variety of types of information systems (transaction processing, management information, decision support, etc) that support the business functions of:

- Accounting
- Finance
- Marketing
- Productions/operations management
- Human resource management

There is a strong emphasis in many organizations to develop such composite or cross-functional information systems that cross the boundaries of traditional business functions in order to reengineer and improve vital business processes.

These organizations view cross-functional information systems as a strategic way to share information resources and improve the efficiency and effectiveness of a business, thus helping it attain its strategic objectives. Business firms are turning to Internet technologies to integrate the flow of information among their internal business functions and their customers and suppliers. Companies are using the World Wide Web and their intranets and extranets as the technology platform for their cross-functional and inter organizational information systems. The business function of marketing is concerned with the planning, promotion, and sale of existing products in existing markets, and the development of new products and new markets to better serve present and potential customers.

Marketing information systems integrate the information flow required by many marketing activities. Marketing information systems provide information for: Internet/intranet web sites and services make an interactive marketing process possible where customers can become partners in creating, marketing, purchasing, and improving products and services.

Sales force automation systems use mobile computing and Internet technologies to automate many information processing activities for sales support and management. Other marketing systems assist marketing managers in product planning, pricing, and other product management decisions, advertising and sales promotion strategies, and market research and forecasting.

Interactive Marketing: The explosive growth of Internet technologies has had a major impact on the marketing function. The term interactive marketing has been coined to describe a type of marketing that is based on using the Internet, intranets, and extranets to establish two-way interaction between a business and its customers or potential customers. The goal of interactive marketing is to enable a company to profitably use those networks to attract and keep customers who will become partners with the business in creating, purchasing, and improving products and services. Interactive marketing:

- Customers are not passive participants, but are actively engaged in a network-enabled proactive and interactive process.
- Encourages customers to become involved in product development, delivery, and service issues.
- Enabled by various Internet technologies, including chat and discussion groups, web forms and questionnaires, and e-mail correspondence.
- Expected outcomes are a rich mixture of vital marketing data, new product ideas, volume sales and strong customer relationships. Targeted Marketing.

Targeted marketing has become an important tool in developing advertising and promotion strategies for a company's electronic commerce websites. Target marketing is an advertising and promotion management concept that includes five targeting components:

Community: companies can customize their web advertising messages and promotion methods to appeal to people in specific communities. These can be communities of interest, such as virtual communities of online sporting enthusiasts or arts and crafts hobbyists, or geographic communities formed by the websites of a city or local newspaper.

Content: advertising such as electronic billboards or banners can be placed on various website pages, in addition to a company's home page. These messages reach the targeted audience.

Context: advertising appears only in web pages that are relevant to the content of a product or service. So advertising is targeted only at people who are already looking for information about a subject matter that is related to a company's products.

Demographic/Psychographic: marketing efforts can be aimed only at specific types or classes of people: unmarried, twenty-something, middle income, and male college graduates.

Online Behaviour: advertising and promotion efforts can be tailored to each visit to a site by an individual. This strategy is based on "web cookie" files recorded on the visitor's disk drive from previous visits. Cookiefiles enable a company to track a person's online behaviour at a website so marketing efforts can be instantly developed and targeted to that individual at each visit to their website.

Sales Force Automation: Increasingly, computers and networks are providing the basis for sales force automation.

In many companies, the sales force is being outfitted with notebook computers that connect them to Web browsers, and sales contact management software that connect them to marketing websites on the Internet, extranets, and their company intranets. Characteristics of sales force automation include: Increases the personal productivity of sales people.

Dramatically speeds up the capture and analysis of sales data from the field to marketing managers at company headquarters. Allows marketing and sales management to improve the delivery of information and the support they provide to their salespeople. Many companies view sales force automation as a way to gain a strategic advantage in sales productivity and marketing responsiveness.

Manufacturing Systems

Manufacturing information systems support the production/ operations function, which includes all activities concerned with the planning and control of the processes that produce goods or services. The production/operations function is concerned with the management of the operational systems of all business firms. Information systems used for operations management and transaction processing support all firms that must plan, monitor, and control inventories, purchases, and the flow of goods and services.

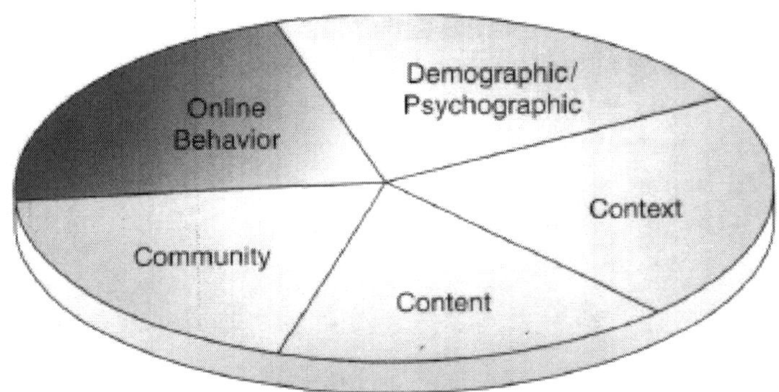

Computer-based manufacturing information systems use several major techniques to support computer-integrated manufacturing (CIM). CIM is an overall concept that stresses that the goals of computer use in factory automation must be to:

- *Simplify:* (reengineer) production processes, product designs, and factory organization as a vital foundation to automation and integration.
- *Automate:* Production processes and the business functions that support them with computers, machines and robots.
- *Integrate:* All production and support processes using computers, telecommunications networks, and other information technologies.

Overall Goal of CIM: Is to create flexible, agile, manufacturing processes that efficiently produce products of the highest quality. Thus, CIM supports the concepts of: Flexible manufacturing systems Agile manufacturing Total quality management

Results of CIM: Implementing such manufacturing concepts enables a company to quickly respond to and fulfill customer requirements with high-quality products and services. Uses of computers in manufacturing include: Computer-aided engineering (CAE) Computer-aided design (CAD) Computer-aided process planning (CAPP) Material requirements planning (MRP) Manufacturing resource planning (MRP-II) Computer-aided manufacturing (CAM). Computer-aided manufacturing - (CAM) systems are those that automate the production process. For example, this could be accomplished by monitoring and controlling the production process in a factory (manufacturing execution systems) or by directly controlling a physical process (process control), a machine tool (machine control), or machines with some human like work capabilities (robots).

Manufacturing execution systems - (MES) are performance monitoring information systems for factory floor operations. They monitor, track, and control the five essential components involved in a production process: Materials Equipment Personnel Instructions and specifications Production facilities. MES includes: Shop floor scheduling and control systems Machine control systems Robotics control systems Process control systems. Some of the benefits of CIM are: Increased efficiency through:-work simplification and automation,- better production schedule planning- better balancing of production workloads in production capacity Improved utilisation of facilities, higher productivity, better quality control through:- continuous monitoring- feedback and control of factory operations, equipment and robots. Reduced investments in production inventories and facilities- work simplification- just-in-time inventory policies- better planning and control of production- better planning and control of finished goods requirements Improved customer service- reducing out-of-stock situations- producing high-quality products that better meet customer requirements

Process Control: Process control is the use of computers to control an ongoing physical process. Process control computers are usedto control physical processes in such areas as:

- Petroleum refineries
- Food product manufacturing plants

Cement plants:

- Pulp and paper mills
- Steel mills
- Electrical power plants
- Chemical plants

Machine Control: Machine control is the use of a computer to control the actions of a machine. This is also popularly called numerical control. The control of machine tools in factories is a typical numerical control application, though it also refers to the control of type setting machines, weaving machines, and other industrial machinery. Machine control computers are used in such areas as: Factories Industrial shops Machine tooling shops.

The human resource management (HRM) function involves the recruitment, placement, evaluation, compensation, and development of the employees of an organization. The goal of HRM is the effective and efficient use of the human resources of a company. Thus, human resource information systems are designed to support: Planning to meet the personnel needs of the business. Development of employees to their full potential. Control of all personnel policies and programs. Traditionally, businesses used computer-based information systems to: Produce paychecks and payroll reports Maintain personnel records Analyse the use of personnel in business operations. Many firms have gone beyond these traditional personnel management functions and have developed human resource information systems (HRIS) that also support: Recruitment, selection and hiring Job placement Performance appraisals Employee benefit analysis Training and development Health, safety, and security HRM and the Internet:

The Internet has become a major force for change in human resource management. For example, companies are:

- Recruiting for employees through recruitment sections of their corporate web sites.
- Using commercial recruiting services and databases on the World Wide Web, posting messages in selected Internet newsgroups, and communicating with job applicants by Internet e-mail. HRM and the Corporate Intranet technologies allow companies to process most common HRM applications over their corporate intranets. For example: Intranets allow the HRM department to provide around-the-clock services to their customers – the employees.

Intranets allow for the dissemination of valuable information faster than through previous company channels. Intranets can collect information online from employees for input to their HRM files Intranets enable employees to perform HRM tasks with little intervention by the HRM department. Intranets can serve as a superior training tool.

Staffing the Organization

The staffing function must be supported by information systems that record and track human resources within a company to maximise their use. These systems are used in personnel record keeping systems, employee skills inventory systems, and personnel requirements forecasting systems. Examples:

- Personnel record keeping system keeps track of additions, deletions, and other changes to the records in a personnel database.
- Changes in job assignments and compensation, or hiring and terminations
- Employee skills inventory system that uses the employee skill data from a personnel database to locate employees within a company who have the skills required for specific assignments and projects.
- Forecasting personnel requirements to assure a business an adequate supply of high-quality human resources.

Training and Development

Information systems help human resource managers: Plan and monitor employee recruitment, training, performance appraisals, and career development by analysing the success history of present programs. Analyse the career development status of each employee to determine whether development methods such as training programs and periodic performance appraisals should be recommended.

Intershop E-Business Modelling Method

A business-process-driven modelling method with reference models based on Intershop Enfinity.

Abstract: As organizations continue to leverage the Internet for business, there is an increasing demand for platforms that support a variety of different business models – including business-to-consumer, business-to-business, business-to-employee and marketplaces. Organizations are looking for common frameworks to support their interactions with their customers, suppliers, distribution channels, and other supply chain partners.

The structure of an eBusiness that will be successful near-term and long-term generally requires an ongoing and comprehensive analysis and definition of the company's cost savings and revenue growth potentials. The challenge is to transform these potentials into a business model and an eBusiness solution with successful performance. Given the complex requirements of eBusiness solutions today, there is a high demand on implementation methods to support all the different participants during an eBusiness solution implementation. This document gives an introduction to the Intershop eBusiness Modelling Method which derives dedicated business cases including business processes and technical workflows from a company's strategic decisions and marketing aspects built on Intershop's eBusiness platform Enfinity.

The Intershop eBusiness Modelling Method is supported by IDS Scheer's modelling tool ARIS for Intershop Enfinity and Intershop's development tool Visual Pipeline Manager which is part of Enfinity. The combination of ARIS for Intershop Enfinity and Intershop's Visual Pipeline Manager provides an effective and seamless transition from the E-Business Solution Definition to the eBusiness Solution Implementation.

In order to provide a professional and effective business requirements mapping, Intershop's eBusiness Components are shipped with reference models. These reference models haven been refined by deploying Intershop's business-process-driven modelling method. This "best practice" approach insures a common base of communication with all participants during the project phases and provides a solid base for further developments of complex eBusiness implementations.

E-Business Market Landscape

The Internet has been accepted as a viable channel for organizations to conduct commerce andextend relationships with customers, employees, business partners and suppliers. By using the Internet as a platform for E-Business, organizations can redefine themselves, transform their business processes and establish new business channels along the value chain.

As a result, the role of IT organizations has shifted from an operational or cost centre to a strategic business unit that is vital for enabling revenue growth and increasing a company's value. This is based on using Internet-based technologies and the right eBusiness platform decision. In addition, business units like Sales, Marketing, Services or NewMedia take charge of getting closer to customers and partners, responding to competitive pressures, boosting revenues – and are thus drivers for eBusiness applications. These business units know what the organization needs to improve the relationships with key trading partners across the company's value chain.

Given this eBusiness climate, there are many new priorities for businesses and their IT organizations today. These priorities include scalability, application integration, return on investment and globalisation. In addition, organizations want to empower their business units to play a role in developing and taking part in business process improvements. For that reason, it is necessary to provide a methodology to easily modify existing business processes based on dynamic requirements, which can be matched to eBusiness applications without extensive IT involvement.

Intershop E-Business Modelling Approach

Intershop's approach to address this market needs, is a scalable platform with a flexible architecture and infrastructure for building custom applications. The eBusiness platform Intershop Enfinity comes along with packaged eBusiness Components (ISH BC) including reference models and a business-process-driven modelling method that supports the customer's solution scoping and definition, speeds design and lowers implementation risks.

Modelling Approach and Methodology - Overview

This chapter describes Intershop's eBusiness Modelling Approach and gives an overview how to derive the customer solution from the customer's vision. This approach is based on Intershop's eBusiness platform Enfinity with eBusiness Components and the eBusiness Modelling Method. Basically there are 3 main phases to derive the customer solution definition from the customer vision which are described in the following 3 chapters.

Solution Analysis

After determining the customer's business vision and strategy including business model and business scenarios, the next step is the Solution Analysis phase. The aim of the Solution Analysis phase is to provide a proposal of the customer's potential eBusiness Solution. In order to detail the customer's requirements, Intershop's business-process- driven modelling method provides a way to refine a model of the proposed Customer eBusiness Solution based on elaborated information.

Solution Definition

During the Solution Definition phase, technical and business related issues are analysed and defined in detail. Most eBusiness Solutions are growing very fast and there is a high risk that these complex systems are not manageable. Because of that, on the one hand it is essential to provide an overview of the whole proposed eBusiness Solution, and on the other hand, also the chance to trace down along an understandable and seamless model to an appropriate level of detail. Intershop's eBusiness Components are shipped with reference models. These reference models haven been refined by deploying Intershop's business-process-driven modelling method. Using ARIS for Intershop Enfinity it is possible to provide such a seamless model of an entire eBusiness solution - from a company's business strategy and marketing aspects over dedicated business cases including business processes, linked to front-end workflows and Intershop Enfinity pipelines. This fact is a big advantage in order to provide reference models of Intershop's eBusiness Components and is the base for professional and effective business requirements mapping.

The result of the Solution Definition phase is the Customer's Requirements Specification (CRS) with the recommended Intershop eBusiness Solution as the basis for the eBusiness Solution design and implementation phase.

Benefits of Intershop's E-Business Modelling Approach

The following section summarises the benefits of deploying Intershop's eBusiness Solutions with its outstanding eBusiness platform Enfinity and the eBusiness Components, straight ahead with the Intershop eBusiness Modelling Method.

Main benefits of Intershop's eBusiness Modelling Approach: a transparent eBusiness Modelling Method derived from project experiences one seamless model from business strategy and marketing aspects, over business scenarios including business processes linked to technical workflows based on Intershop Enfinity reduction of information loss a common base for communication and documentation providing a clear discussion and decision foundation by different model views reduction of project and development risks decreased time to market better maintenance and faster adaptation of implemented solutions reference models of business scenarios for shorter implementation time.

Changes Accelerate in World of e-business

Nothing evolves faster than the field of e-business which means that company managers need to be quick on their feet just to keep up. The ambition of everyone who runs a small company is basically the same - to run a much bigger company! If you are in the world of e-business that can sometimes happen much faster than you expect. It is then necessary to be two things at once: the freewheeling entrepreneur who can drive things forward, and the more cautious corporate leader concerned with structures, strategies and long-term sales projections. Peter Yan, chief executive officer of Global e-Business Services Limited (GO-Business), which was established in 2000, has had just this experience. "We are comparatively young even though our parent company.

Computer and Technologies Holdings Limited, has a long history in the IT industry," he says. "Our most notable success is a pioneering e-tendering system, which is the only one of its kind in the world, and has enabled us to expand rapidly. We developed a comprehensive electronic platform to offer the government and their suppliers, and it includes customer service hotlines and training for the suppliers. That was a breakthrough and we are now responsible for the operation of the system and customer related matters."

Over the past two years, GO-Business has seen a marked increase in its customer base. Besides government bodies like Hong Kong Post, major corporations such as the MTRC, Shui On Construction, Nanyang Commercial Bank and Jones Lang LaSalle have spotted the value of what they have to offer and formed productive new business relationships.

In January 2003, the company was granted the government electronic trading services licence (GETS) and, under the brand name "Ge-TS", subsequently started to collect and process various statutory documents by electronic means for more than 60,000 companies. These included trade declarations, certificates of origin and dutiable commodities permits, and the company's aim is now to further the capability of e-commerce in Hong Kong.

Business turnover and staff numbers have doubled in the past two years. Mr Yan is confident that the same rate of increase can be maintained and is planning accordingly. "In the next six months, we will actively recruit for technical, sales and marketing, and customer service staff at all levels," he says. "We want to provide more tailor-made services to enhance our customers' operational efficiency." A stronger management team is also being formed to provide leadership and attend to career development strategies.

New Style

> *"We used to be able to do almost everything ourselves, but have now learned to delegate more and monitor the quality standards and timeframes set for staff," he adds. "As the company has grown, we have had to ensure a series of smooth business As the company has grown, we have had to ensure a series of smooth business transitions and to implement plans which empower the management team as well as the workforce."*

Changes have been particularly apparent in the broader job responsibilities people have taken on, the quicker pace of work adopted, more diverse methodologies and a greater focus on quality management. Previously the work was concentrated on project development, maintenance and customer service.

Now, as the pace picks up, more must be done in a shorter time and the planning process has become more detailed, including both near and longer-term considerations. Business indicators, potential competitors and general market developments must be tracked more closely and a flexible structure created for the company, so that expansion can be accommodated more easily. "To sustain growth, the structure must be right," Mr Yan explains. "Our management team is very stable and the technical support system is well in place, but we must anticipate rather than just maintain." When potential technical problems are spotted, SMS alerts are now sent to the staff responsible and immediate action is taken to prevent any faults occurring. Key performance indicators have also been established to measure progress and achievements.

Team Tactics

In order to further enhance team spirit and cross-departmental cooperation, social activities are encouraged and regular meetings held at which staff can discuss the company's overall direction and development. The administration of HR issues is being handled by an e-HRM system, which was developed by a sister company and has proved highly efficient.

> *"This unique technology has significantly reduced the time needed for managing human resources and will be a significant benefit as we increase staff numbers," notes Mr Yan. "All employees can gain access to the system via the Internet to check that personal information is updated, and one module allows us to carry out performance assessments far more effectively than before."*

GO-Business is all set for further rapid expansion, but Mr Yan is not yet satisfied. "We can always do better. In this business, speed is everything and to stand still for even one day is the equivalent of going backwards. Success depends on having staff who are dedicated to progress."

Then and Now:

Before

- Business focus on project development and short-term goals
- Management team very hands-on in running projects, operations and business implementation
- No specialised IT system for HR and other administrative functions
- Limited discussion about how to manage growth
- Standard measures of company progress

After

- Planning process more complex and for the long term
- Company leaders must demonstrate management and delegation skills
- An e-HRM system in place to streamline routine processes
- All staff encouraged to give constructive feedback
- Key performance indicators to gauge progress and achievements

- Focus on creating a flexible corporate structure
- Improved team spirit and cross-departmental cooperation

Intershop's Visual Pipeline Manager

The Visual Pipeline Manager (VPM) is a development tool for designing workflows using pipelines. Pipelines are at the centre of Enfinity's ability to separate business logic from code and web design.

A pipeline is a symbolic representation (described in XML) of a workflow. It includes nodes that denote a particular type of execution step in a pipeline. In general, there are three types of nodes:

- pipelet node
- flow control node
- interaction node

The decisive marking points in pipelines are symbolized with flow control nodes, which are listed in the VPM editor in the upper left box. The pipelet nodes are reusable steps that perform specific, discrete functions in a pipeline and are listed in the lower left box in the VPM.

When pipelines are executed, they begin with a "start" node and are executed step-by-step until they reach a stopping point, symbolized by an "end" node, a "jump," or a template symbol (called interaction node). Between the start and the end node is the business logic contained in the pipelets, and the flow control logic that dictates whether, for example, a yes/no branch in the pipeline needs to be followed, another pipeline must be called, or a template should be displayed. The flow control elements are common to all pipelines and can be re-used indefinitely. The following figure shows the 3 types of nodes and an excerpt of a pipeline in Intershop Enfinity's Visual Pipeline Manager.

The Pipeline Process and the Pipeline Dictionary

The following section gives an overview about pipeline processes and the role of the pipeline dictionary. This call can come from an HTTP request embedded in a front-end template, from a call or jump node in another pipeline, or from logic itself (for back office or scheduling pipelines). Once called, the pipeline starts and initializes the pipeline dictionary. Any parameters passed to the start of the pipeline by the request are stored in this pipeline dictionary. The parameter name is the "key" and has an associated "value". These are referred to as key-value pairs. They are maintained in the dictionary until the pipeline ends and clears the dictionary. The pipeline executes each pipelet and flow control action in sequential order. Each pipelet may require a key-value pair (or pairs) to be available in the pipeline dictionary. The pipelet checks the pipeline dictionary; if it finds the necessary key(s), it executes its logic. As a result of executing, the pipelet may add other key-value pairs to the pipeline dictionary. The dictionary cumulatively stores all the key-value pairs from all preceding pipelet activity until it reaches an end-and-clear point. Front-end processes often end with the display of a front-end template. After showing a template, the pipeline can either continue (and eventually show another template) or end and clear the pipeline dictionary.

Note: - that a front-end workflow may include more than one pipeline, including "sub-pipelines" which are called into a process with a call node - that every pipeline or sub-pipeline does not necessarily end in a template

Tool based Modelling with AIRS Toolset

The usage of graphical business process models is with no doubt a means to reduce the complexity of today's business environment. However, the new and increased requirements that arise from the transition from traditional business to eBusiness increases the demand for integrated modelling architectures and modelling tools. The "Architecture of Integrated Information Systems" (ARIS) provides several applications that support the transformation of the company's strategic decision into technically implemented processes. The main reasons for Intershop to base its eBusiness Modelling Method on ARIS were as follows:

1. The ARIS concept provides a lot of different modelling methods that enable the user to describe a business process from various perspectives. The great variety of model types, such as the event driven process chain (EPC) or object oriented methods of the Unified Modelling Language (UML) offer the possibility to describe a business scenario completely. The combination of process and object oriented methods makes ARIS a flexible architecture to address the needs of a fast changing business environment.
2. The ARIS Toolset2 integrates several tools that support an eBusiness implementation approach that is business-process-driven. With the add-on ARIS for Intershop Enfinity it is possible to combine the model-based optimization of a process with the customization of the corresponding workflows within Enfinity. ARIS allows to model a business scenario starting

with the corporate strategy and continuing with the business processes. At the end the technical processes which implement those business processes are represented by Enfinity pipelines.

3. The Intershop eBusiness Modelling Method is built on Intershop's experiences in many eBusiness projects and the special skills that an eBusiness platform like Enfinity requires from the project team. ARIS facilitates the requirements analysis and the definition of the customers' eBusiness solution. Moreover it supports the Intershop methodology in a perfect way and has therefore turned out to be the tool that Intershop prefers as a basis for their eBusiness Modelling Method.

The ARIS add-on component ARIS for Intershop Enfinity is the result of the joint development between IDS Scheer and Intershop Communications.

It integrates the ARIS Toolset with the Enfinity pipeline development tool Visual Pipeline Manager. The foundation of the tool is built by a bi-directional interface which allows a direct data transfer via XML. A seamless modelling from the strategic decision down to the pipeline workflow is possible. With this, the main benefit is that ARIS for Intershop Enfinity enables a "top-down" development of an eBusiness solution based on reference models.

Furthermore ARIS for Intershop Enfinity provides a rich set of features, for example: The import of Enfinity pipelets, templates and pipelines is used to create reference models as implementation basis. It also provides the instrument for a complete documentation of the system. The pipeline export transfers the pipelines XML representation to the Enfinity application server which processes them directly. Together with the connection and modification of business process models and pipelines one can directly customize its eBusiness system. With the extensive reporting abilities of the tool and the fact that there is one source of models, one can generate project documentation during the different phases of a project. Starting at the Solution Scoping phase, continue with a solution proposal, moving forward with the requirement specification the process models are the basis for the technical specification, the project estimation and at last the system documentation.

The following figure shows a window out of ARIS Toolset with an opened toolbar of ARIS for Intershop Enfinity. Furthermore there is a front-end workflow diagram in the left and the linked pipeline diagram in the right. ARIS Toolset with its add-on ARIS for Intershop

Enfinity fits different needs over the project life cycle. The project experiences have shown that ARIS simplifies the work during the requirement analysis and definition - furthermore reduces information loss over the whole project lifetime. In addition, the use of the tool leads to a better maintenance and faster adaptation of the implemented solution.

Reference Models

The Intershop eBusiness Modelling Method supports Enfinity projects during the whole project life cycle, e.g. the requirements definition is worked out in a business process driven way based on that methodology. Moreover, Intershop uses the eBusiness Modelling Method to create reference models of its eBusiness Components corresponding to that methodology. In that way these reference models enable the project team to easily define the requirements of the customer solution and to identify missing parts (DELTA) that need to be customized or developed. The following figure illustrates that approach. Within the Intershop eBusiness Modelling Method processes are structured on four levels. Each level uses a collection of model types used for pre-defined purposes.

Business Scenario

The purpose of the first level is to provide an overview of eBusiness scenarios, common business models and the main business processes in the e-commerce sector. It is focused on the core business functions and their dependencies from a very high business perspective. The models support the first step of identifying an adequate business model for the customer's requirements. By identifying the business model and the related core processes, a first overview to specify detailed processes can be worked out.

The following model types are used on this level: value added chain diagram, process selection matrix/ diagram, business scenario diagram. The major model type which is used on the first level is the value added chain diagram. With this model type, the functions which are directly involved in the creation of a company's added value are identified. These functions are linked to the second level. The used objects can be arranged hierarchically, similar to a function tree. Additional information can be given to the viewer by modelling the functions' operators, with organizational units and information objects.

At this level a segmentation of main processes according to different criteria takes place. The purpose of the models is to get an overview of the core processes of the customer solution and the associated sub-processes and functions. The models help to get a clear view of all customer requirements. The models are the basis for the Customer Requirement Specification and all following specifications. The used model types at this second level are: value added chain diagram, function tree, organizational chart, process selection matrix.

The next figure shows the function tree diagram on the second level. It represents the hierarchical structure of the functions occurring in a company which can be grouped by different criteria. Within the Intershop eBusiness Modelling Method the function tree is used to visualize the features of the customer's eBusiness solution. The model displays a graphical overview of the main features and additionally each object includes a verbal description of the feature. The objects are used in the processes on the third level.

Detailed Business Processes

That level shows models which are focused on the business process. They are modelled in a more detailed form by specifying different business functions. Such a business process is defined by a number of activities in a company which can be executed by different people and supported by different application systems. Used model types on that level are: event driven process chain (EPC). The event driven process chain diagram is used to model the procedural sequence of functions in the sense of business processes. This model type consists of two main objects: functions, which represent activities or technical tasks and events, which trigger functions or are the results of the processing of a function.

The business process model can be extended by a variety of information, such as the actor who executes the function or the application system which supports the execution. In order to keep the models structured and simple, the process chains can be modelled in a modular form. Thus, a core process is modelled in one overview EPC and the fine specifications are done in assigned sub-models.

Workflow Design

At this level the requirements are transferred to the Enfinity pipeline level by using existing pipelines, modifying existing pipelines or creating new pipelines. Via the existing bi-directional XML interface these pipelines can be directly transferred to the Enfinity system. Additionally the front-end workflow, meaning the interaction of the user with the system is modelled on that level. This type of modelling also provides the connection between the business process on the third level and the pipelines. The following model types are used: event driven process chain in column display, Enfinity pipeline diagram.

The modelling of the user interaction with Enfinity is an important task on the fourth level. It links the business processes on level three with the Enfinity pipelines.

EPC Model Type in Column Display.

The actors and the various systems, are modelled in the header of the columns. Each column contains the objects that are related to that actor. Starting with the triggering event of the process a pipeline is called in Enfinity (function in the right column). The result of the processing of that pipeline is the display of an HTML page (middle column) which builds the connection between the user and the system. The functions that are modelled in the left column below the HTML page are those that are available to the user. Mostly, those functions represent links or user inputs into a form. The functions lead to the next pipeline call, a resulting event or a sub-process.

The competition between standard eBusiness software providers is increasing. Customer expectations are not only a scalable and reliable eBusiness solution with a rich feature set out of the box and standardized interfaces to connect to, but also proven business components for supporting their business scenarios and a strong methodology to transform complex requirements into eBusiness technology. Also maintenance costs, efforts for further developments and return on investment of implemented solutions are essential for the customer. Our real life implementation experiences in building successful eBusiness solutions showed us the importance of having the business model and the scenarios precisely defined, the most important business processes fixed, and the integration into existing process and IT landscapes defined and accepted, before starting the implementation of eBusiness systems.

The Intershop eBusiness Modelling Method is the result of eBusiness consulting experiences during lots of successful eBusiness projects. The business-process-driven modelling method is based on Intershop's eBusiness Solutions and ARIS for Intershop Enfinity of IDS Scheer's eBusiness Suite as the business process modelling tool.

During the entire life cycle of an Intershop Enfinity project, the Intershop eBusiness Modelling Method provides a common base of communication with all participants. The business-process-driven modelling method is also used to create reference models for Intershop's eBusiness Solutions. This "best practice" approach builds the bridge for the successful transformation of business requirements into eBusiness technology - based on Intershop Enfinity.

The main reasons for Intershop's choice using ARIS Toolset 5 - E-Business Suite as the business process modelling tool, was the successful cooperation between Intershop an IDS Scheer during their joint development of ARIS for Intershop Enfinity and the great results in deploying Intershop's eBusiness Modelling Method in projects.

With the most recent release ARIS Toolset 6 - Collaborative Suite, IDS Scheer offers various functionality for designing, analysing, implementing and optimizing business processes and disposes of a browser enabled Front-End. This means platform independence for users, worldwide availability, high scalability and low administration costs.

Intershop and IDS Scheer will proceed in working closely together with implementing further improvements on ARIS for Intershop Enfinity and will reinforce the Intershop eBusiness Modelling Method based on successful eBusiness project experience and professional Consulting Services.

Electronic Commerce and Third Party Initiated Transactions: A Conceptual Exploration

The Concept and Models

The key to the proposed model is the role of third parties (that is, the economic exchange facilitators or intermediaries who effect the transfer of ownership of assets, including cash transfers, between sellers and buyers.) They will initiate the accounting for the economic event. For simplicity the model is limited to the buyer/seller relationship. However, as pointed out by Robert K. Elliot "...Other counterparties (employees, shareholders, tax authorities) [have] transactions [which] are mirrored and can contribute to the 'lock-down' of the enterprise in its entire transaction matrix." (1997, e-mail).

The "sales/purchases" transactions will be prepared by the seller, perhaps using direct computer input from the buyer, reflecting the details of the exchange events of interest to both parties and not just the direct financial data. In a recent interview on MS-NBC, Frederick W. Smith, Chief Executive Officer of FedEx, indicated his company's desire to provide more and better information to their customers related to marketing and shipping. The data is recorded in machine-readable form, for example, on a microchip, which is the shipment documentation. The transaction data to be recorded, therefore, belongs to the exchange partners and not the ntermediary.

(Model 1) Independent Database

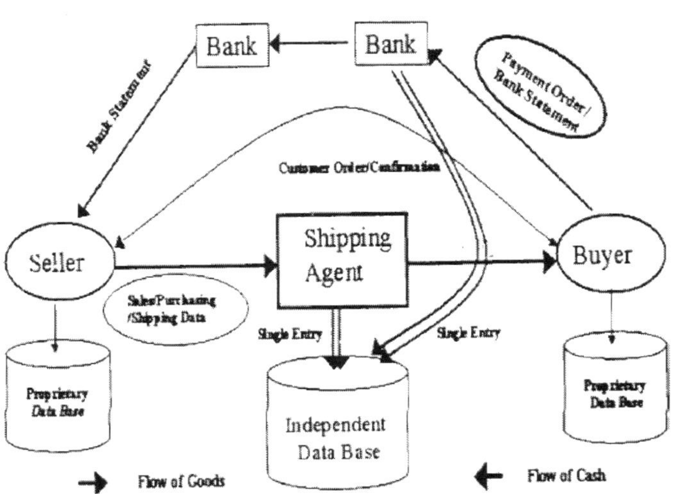

The content of the transactions processed by the model is not limited to just the essential financial accounting elements. Theoretically, anything of interest to the buyer or seller can be included. Robert K. Elliott suggests that a much richer set of information about the buyer/seller relationship is required in the modern management environment (1992, p. 61-85).

Banks or other financial institutions will initiate the cash receipt/ payment transactions, when they transfer funds from one entity to another based on instructions from the payor. The banks will not retain any data beyond their current requirements. They will merely signal recognition that the transfer occurred. The intermediary's role is only to trigger recognition of the actual, real event (i.e., the transfer of ownership of the economic resources when the shipment is picked up or delivered, or the cash is transferred). In these cases, it is essential that the data about the transaction be placed in an environment accessible to both parties immediately and simultaneously. The data storage and retrieval environment for the third party transaction may be separate and distinct from the proprietary database maintained by each entity.

If so, it must be under the control of a third party, independent of the buyer/seller, and payer/payee. Perhaps the initiating intermediary will provide the independent database management function. As shown earlier presents the data storage and extraction environment using an independently maintained database for the "Electronic Commerce" (EC) transactions.

Data Storage & Extraction

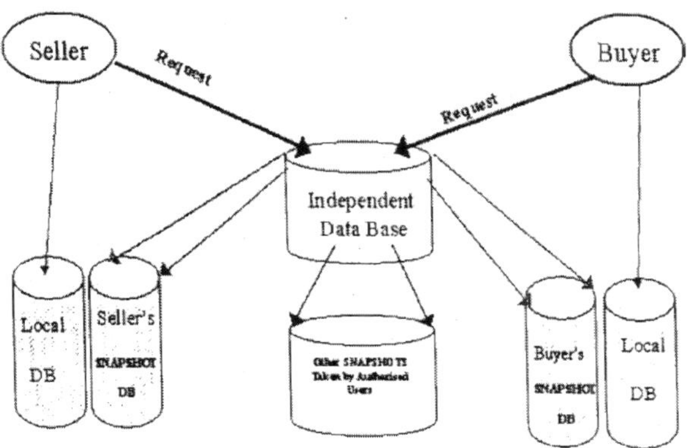

Figure provides an alternative model. As a result of concerns expressed about the structure of wide area based networks and the problems of independent database models (Goldschmidt, 1998, e-mail), this alternative, may provide a viable solution. In this model each entity maintains a portion of its proprietary database exclusively for "independent" externally generated "EC" transactions.

The bifurcation will allow for different levels of security to be imposed on the third party transactions, as opposed to internally generated maintenance transactions. Under either model a separate company level "local" database will contain entity generated accounting transactions and records, e.g., adjustments and subsidiary ledgers, just as they do today. It may also contain copies of data records extracted from the independent database.

Regardless of which database environment is used to capture and store third-party initiated transactions, the control over the integrity of the original data in each transaction and determination of access rights to the data is the responsibility of those in direct relationship. The independent database operator is responsible for protecting the integrity of the data held, the authenticity of the data extracted, and the application of the access limitations set by the data owners. The same control issues are present if a bifurcated, proprietary database structure is used.

(Model 2) Local Database

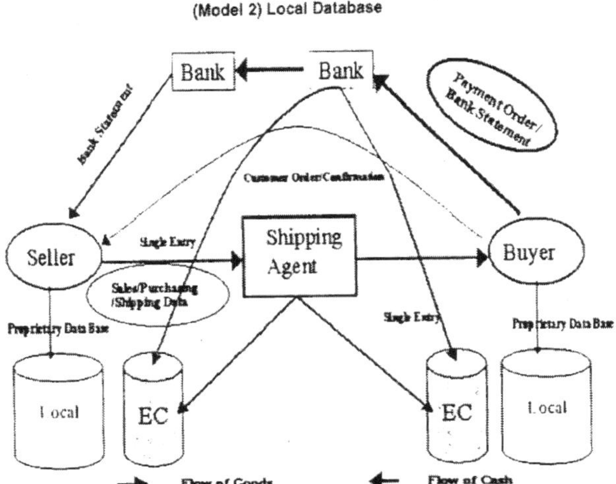

What is required by buyers, sellers, payors, and payees is knowledge about where the data record is and what descriptive and control tags are attached to it to provide for access to the details, security, and authentication. Thus with the appropriate authorization anyone can literally "take a picture of the data", but they cannot alter the contents.

Discussion

The present accounting model has been in existence for over eight centuries. Double entry bookkeeping as it is now known emerged in the Thirteen Hundreds. Luca Pacioli's book, "Summa de Arthimetica Geometria Propartioni et Proportionalita" (review of Arithmetic, Geometry and Proportions), 1494, is the first book on the double entry bookkeeping known to be published.

Mutuality of Interest

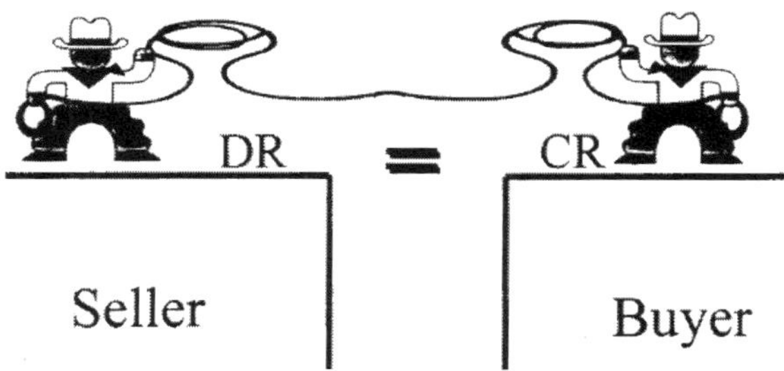

The terms employed today, 'debit' and 'credit', were mentioned by Pacioli as 'debito' (owed to) and 'credito' (owed by). In explaining double entry accounting, Pacioli said, "All entries ... have to be double entries, that is, if you make someone a creditor then you must make someone a debtor". (Kam, 1990).

It is this fundamental premise on which the proposed model is based. Moreover, the proposed model explicitly uses the idea that the creditor is in one entity and the debtor is in another. Figure demonstrates the dynamic tension and equality existing between the parties. They share a mutual interest in the economic event and, therefore, the accounting transaction. One of the advantages of the double entry accounting is that it provides a means by which errors – particularly human errors – can be found readily, because of the necessity for duality and equilibrium of accounts and classifications. It also imposes a requirement for systematic and orderly accounting transactions. In general this applies within the accounting entity, but it is not necessarily true between entities, because each entity does its own recording.

Usually the timing is different and in some cases the information is different—accidentally or intentionally. The "mutuality of interest" that exists between the two parties is assumed in the traditional model. However, because the accounting transactions are recorded independently by each party, the assumed equilibrium may not in fact exist. The proposed model overcomes this serious defect in the current accounting process, which results in information asymmetry.

The asymmetry problem is the result of the complexity of modern economic activity.

Historical Perspective: Economic Events and Accounting

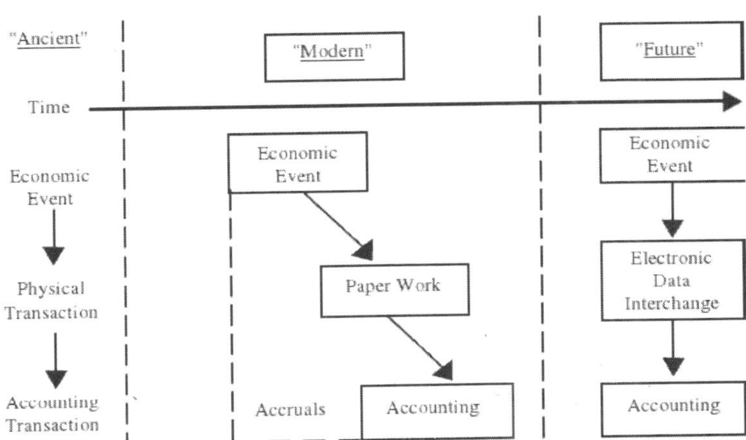

As seen in Figure above, in ancient times (and to some degree today in cash basis and barter economies) economic events are settled immediately and simultaneously at the physical level. The mutuality of interest is immediately evident and effective. However, as economic activity increases in volume and variety, documents are used to capture the essential data about the physical events. Additionally, data about commitments to be settled in the future are also captured on documents (e.g., payables, receivables, and other accruals). The documents are the support for the accounting transactions. Invariably there is a timing difference between when the physical events occur or when the commitments are made and when the related accounting transactions are recorded based on the paperwork.

Timing, however, is only one part of the asymmetry problem. The more critical aspect is the risk that the parties will not record the events or commitments consistently between entities. This is the reliability problem. Accounting information is assumed to be reliable if it is objective and verifiable and accurately maps the real economic event it relates to. Under the current process accounting information between entities may not be "globally" reliable because of the independence in recording. If the cause for the global unreliability is intentional misstatement (i.e., fraud), the mutuality of interest and the singularity of the information set in the proposed model will greatly reduce the likelihood of the misstatement being over looked. Robert K. Elliot commented: "I foresee the day when, through massive redundancy of data collection, it will become extremely difficult to commit a fraud and virtually impossible to conceal it." (1997, e-mail).

The proposed model facilities accounting between entities and enhances the reliability of the data, because both entities simultaneously are given "credit" for their economic interest in the exchange event. Since the economic events are discrete and quantitatively equal to both entities, a single transaction will be viewed from two perspectives accurately and completely. Any attempt to manipulate the subsequent reporting will be readily apparent in the "adjusting" entries found in the local database.

International trade transactions provide an example of possible improving reporting symmetry. They will be balanced automatically and National Current Account reporting will be improved. That is, the balance of payments statistics will be more accurate and complete. The International Monetary Fund (1997) estimated that world-wide the current account balances for 1996 were "out of balance" by at least $100 billion. By anyone's standards this is a rather significant lack of information symmetry. The attest function in financial audit, is intended to provide verification of the reliability of accounting information. However, the difficulty of providing high quality verification services is well understood.

The historic audit problems of understanding the economic event and determining if the proper and most appropriate accounting rules were applied is now exacerbated by the use of increasingly sophisticated electronic data interchange (EDI) to record the event in the accounting record. Numerous observers, including Elliott (1994, 1995, 1996) and Wallman (1995, 1996 a&b, 1997) have addressed this problem. Technology, the demand for ever increasing speed in processing data, and a decline in interest in control over transaction accuracy by preparers has reduced the efficacy of the traditional audit to provide high quality assurance on the reliability of accounting information. The Report of the Special Committee on Assurance Services supports this contention (AICPA, 1997).

It is imperative, therefore, that the idea of mutuality of interest and the recording of a transaction as a way of increasing the reliability of accounting information be taken seriously. EDI essentially restores the direct relationship between the physical economic event and accounting that existed in ancient times. It provides an opportunity to overcome both aspects of the asymmetry problem. A single piece of data sent simultaneously to both parties, when the event occurs, virtually eliminates the problem and re-establishes the "mutuality of interest" in the events. In the future, EDI transactions will dominate as the primary means by which economic events are communicated to accounting systems. Articles about new developments in EDI applications and related technology appear in the popular business press. For example, a recent article described a system under development to provide secure electronic checks, which if successful may be included in a European Union program to provide an electronic market place (Barnes, 1998).

Another article describes the use of "extranets" to reduce the cost of business-to-business commerce using off-the-shelf technology that is being operated by General Electric's information services division (Nairn,1998 (a)). Yet another article describes the development of multi-directional (omni-directional?) information environments which provide horizontal, as well as, vertical communication. Elizabeth Lank, director of knowledge management at ICL in the UK, has identified the critical factor determining the success of all information rich environments: "The technology is the easy bit; what is more difficult is motivating people to share knowledge (Nairn, 1998 (b)).

One of the most ambitious projects based on a model similar to the one proposed is TARGET, the new Pan-European clearing mechanism for high-value payments, which is similar to the system operated by the Federal Reserve Banks in the US. The system will provide for the immediate and irrevocable transfer of funds between banks and the execution will be completed within seconds (ABN AMRO, 1997).

The business information environment suggested by Elliott in 1992 is becoming a reality as the "virtual enterprise." A "virtual company", as suggested in a document published by Andersen Consulting (AC), [is] "a company that relies to a great extent on third parties to conduct its business...." (Zuin and Kutz, 1997). AC suggests that "...As more enterprises conduct more business electronically, large numbers of providers, suppliers and customers will become more closely coupled. Soon, networks of complimentary enterprises will emerge, boasting global reach, reduced cost structures, rapid response times, and highly profitable knowledge assets."

Elliott's assertion that the world is facing a "third wave" of innovation (1992) is discussed by Steven J. Johnson, worldwide managing partner of Andersen Consulting's Retail and Electronic Commerce practice, and Edward M. Schreck, worldwide managing partner of Andersen Consulting's Technology practice. They suggest that: At this point, the 'transformation' period becomes possible, when innovation begins shaping entire markets and, often, fundamental aspects of how we live....

Today, information technology has reached the point of critical mass required for transformation to occur-spurred by the convergence of computing, communications and knowledge, and manifested by electronic commerce.... Today's implementations are transforming or even erasing those boundaries, by integrating business more closely with their suppliers, partners and customers. Thus the changes which have occurred and that are continuing to occur in technology create the need to transform the way the accounting process is conceptualized and modelled. The single entry, third party models suggested above are consistent with the emerging future. EDI and the proposed model also provide an opportunity to revisit the decision alternatives that led to the current financial reporting model. Over the past several hundred years the way commercial activity is conducted has changed.

The individual tradesmen or craftsmen have increasingly joined forces to form complex organizations. Some have remained owner-managers, but others have become employees. Many organizations have required large infusions of capital obtained from investors and banks. As enterprises have became larger and more diverse and obtained investment capital from a large number of individuals, not directly involved in managing the entity, there has arose a need to communicate with a variety of stakeholders and to provide them with information for monitoring the performance of management and the entity. Kam suggests that there are two alternative approaches to this requirement for information (1990):

- Provide access to the raw data necessary for an observer to understand the business. For example, permit appropriate individuals and parties (that is, stakeholders), access to ledgers and books of original entry of the entity; or
- Compile the information in a format transmittable to and usable by others using a standardized format and produced under the control of the entity.

As a practical matter, the second alternative was chosen by the authors and developed into a model to provide comparability and standardization, so that multiple parties could understand and work with the accounting information. However, since each nation has its own set of GAAP and there is an International set also, the proposed model does not deal with the issue of multiple standards for measuring and reporting economic events. Information technology has brought us to a point where the earlier decision about how to provide needed information must be re-examined. The choice to develop a standardized set of financial statements prepared by the entity is based on practicality. It simply is not possible to provide raw data to all interested parties. Corporate financial reporting and corporate disclosure exists in the context of a dynamic, constantly changing business world. Competitive challenge and business opportunities arise quickly. Firms have an advantage if they are agile in adapting corporate structure and developing or utilising innovative and sophisticated financial instruments. In the middle of this evolving business world stands the accounting profession that needs to assure the continued utility and integrity of financial reporting.

As we approach the end of the 20th Century, financial accounting and disclosure is not keeping pace with the rapid change in the business world. Not only is accounting and disclosure increasingly at risk of failing to satisfy its promise to society, but also they are becoming deterrent to economic environment. "The value and worth of financial reporting lies, in almost exclusive way, in its usefulness to users" (FASB Concept Statement, para. 34, 1998). Not all users have the same needs. For example, an analyst attempting to discern or predict earnings or cash flows needs different information than managers reviewing the allocation and utilisation of deployed assets. Investors attempting to employ relatively new measures such as Economic Value Add (EVA) need still different information. The diversity of users complicates the task of peering into future. Thus it becomes important to develop both analytical systems for thinking about what the future might bring and the mechanisms and information structures to respond appropriately. During the past 30 years, the information in financial statements has been aggregated and compressed to such a degree that the real information value is questionable. Furthermore, there is some evidence that the Financial Accounting Standards Board's efforts to enhance communication by requiring ever more complex disclosures has lead to an unwillingness or inability by some analysts to use the new information (Kang, 1997).

Timeliness (i.e., the speed of delivery or accessibility of information), is another factor becoming increasingly important in the business environment today. Annual or even quarterly reports do not capture material developments in sufficient time to meet market informational needs. Product cycles have shortened and company strategies become obsolete much more quickly now than ever before. The current system of periodic reports has been in place for decades, but the business environment has changed dramatically. The financial reporting systems need to use technology to respond to these changes.

The efficient market hypothesis should have a comparable expression in financial reporting. Today the technology exists to enable anyone authorized to do so to obtain desired, authenticated accounting data at the transaction level and accumulate or manipulate it to meet their own needs, whenever they want to. Ultimately, accounting data will become a highly reliable consumer product, in contrast to the current financial statements which are a product of the producer and, perhaps not a very good one, who has a - "one size fits all, take it or leave it" attitude. The data storage and extraction component of the model provides the context for the development of a totally different paradigm for financial reporting.

9

Financial Statements and Auditing

Balance Sheet

In financial accounting, a balance sheet or statement of financial position is a summary of the financial balances of a sole proprietorship, a business partnership or a company. Assets, liabilities and ownership equity are listed as of a specific date, such as the end of its financial year. A balance sheet is often described as a "snapshot of a company's financial condition". Of the four basic financial statements, the balance sheet is the only statement which applies to a single point in time.

A standard company balance sheet has three parts: assets, liabilities and ownership equity. The main categories of assets are usually listed first, and typically in order of liquidity. Assets are followed by the liabilities. The difference between the assets and the liabilities is known as equity or the net assets or the net worth or capital of the company and according to the accounting equation, net worth must equal assets minus liabilities.

Another way to look at the same equation is that assets equals liabilities plus owner's equity. Looking at the equation in this way shows how assets were financed: either by borrowing money (liability) or by using the owner's money (owner's equity). Balance sheets are usually presented with assets in one section and liabilities and net worth in the other section with the two sections "balancing."

Records of the values of each account or line in the balance sheet are usually maintained using a system of accounting known as the double-entry bookkeeping system. A business operating entirely in cash can measure its profits by withdrawing the entire bank balance at the end of the period, plus any cash in hand. However, many businesses are not paid immediately; they build up inventories of goods and they acquire buildings and equipment.

In other words: businesses have assets and so they can not, even if they want to, immediately turn these into cash at the end of each period. Often, these businesses owe money to suppliers and to tax authorities, and the proprietors do not withdraw all their original capital and profits at the end of each period. In other words businesses also have liabilities.

Origin

It was the Flemish mathematician Simon Stevin who persuaded merchants to make it a rule to summarize accounts at the end of every year in a chapter entitled *Coopmansbouckhouding op de Italiaensche wyse* (Dutch: "Commercial Book-keeping in the Italian Way") of his *Wisconstigheg hedachtenissen* (Dutch: "Mathematical memoirs", Leiden, 1605–08).

Although the balance sheet he required every enterprise to prepare every year was based on entries of the ledger, it was prepared separately from the major books of account. The oldest semi-public balance sheet recorded was that of the East India Company dated 30 April 1671, which was submitted to the company's General Meeting on in 30 August 1671. The publication and audit of the balance sheet was still a rarity in England until the passing of the Bank Charter Act 1844.

Types

A balance sheet summarizes an organization or individual's assets, equity and liabilities at a specific point in time. Individuals and small businesses tend to have simple balance sheets. Larger businesses tend to have more complex balance sheets, and these are presented in the organization's annual report. Large businesses also may prepare balance sheets for segments of their businesses. A balance sheet is often presented alongside one for a different point in time (typically the previous year) for comparison.

Personal Balance Sheet

A personal balance sheet lists current assets such as cash in checking accounts and savings accounts, long-term assets such as common stock and real estate, current liabilities such as loan debt and mortgage debt due, or overdue, long-term liabilities such as mortgage and other loan debt. Securities and real estate values are listed at market value rather than at historical cost or cost basis.

Personal net worth is the difference between an individual's total assets and total liabilities.

US Small Business Balance Sheet

Table: *Sample Small Business Balance Sheet*

Assets		***Liabilities and Owners' Equity***	
Cash	$6,600	Liabilities	
Accounts Receivable	$6,200	Notes Payable	$30,000
		Accounts Payable	
		Total liabilities	$30,000
Tools and equipment	$25,000	Owners' equity	
		Capital Stock	$7,000
		Retained Earnings	$800
		Total owners' equity	$7,800
Total	$37,800	*Total*	$37,800

A really small business balance sheet lists current assets such as cash, accounts receivable, and inventory, fixed assets such as land, buildings, and equipment, intangible assets such as patents, and liabilities such as accounts payable, accrued expenses, and long-term debt. Contingent liabilities such as warranties are noted in the footnotes to the balance sheet. The small business's equity is the difference between total assets and total liabilities.

Public Business Entities Balance Sheet Structure

Guidelines for balance sheets of public business entities are given by the International Accounting Standards Committee and numerous country-specific organizations. Balance sheet account names and usage depend on the organization's country and the type of organization. Government organizations do not generally follow standards established for individuals or businesses.

If applicable to the business, summary values for the following items should be included on the balance sheet:

Assets

Current assets;

1. Cash and cash equivalents
2. Inventories
3. Accounts receivable
4. Prepaid expenses for future services that will be used within a year.

Fixed assets;

1. Property, plant and equipment
2. Investment property, such as real estate held for investment purposes
3. Intangible assets
4. Financial assets (excluding investments accounted for using the equity method, accounts receivables, and cash and cash equivalents)
5. Investments accounted for using the equity method
6. Biological assets, which are living plants or animals. Bearer biological assets are plants or animals which bear agricultural produce for harvest, such as apple trees grown to produce apples and sheep raised to produce wool.

Liabilities;

1. Accounts payable
2. Provisions for warranties or court decisions
3. Financial liabilities (excluding provisions and accounts payable), such as promissory notes and corporate bonds
4. Liabilities and assets for current tax
5. Deferred tax liabilities and deferred tax assets
6. Minority interest in equity
7. Issued capital and reserves attributable to equity holders of the Parent company
8. Unearned revenue for services paid for by customers but not yet provided.

Equity

The net assets shown by the balance sheet equals the third part of the balance sheet, which is known as the shareholders' equity. Formally, shareholders' equity is part of the company's liabilities: they are funds "owing" to shareholders (after payment of all other liabilities); usually, however, "liabilities" is used in the more restrictive sense of liabilities excluding shareholders' equity.

The balance of assets and liabilities (including shareholders' equity) is not a coincidence. Records of the values of each account in the balance sheet are maintained using a system of accounting known as double-entry bookkeeping. In this sense, shareholders' equity by construction must equal assets minus liabilities, and are a residual.

1. Numbers of shares authorized, issued and fully paid, and issued but not fully paid
2. Par value of shares
3. Reconciliation of shares outstanding at the beginning and the end of the period
4. Description of rights, preferences, and restrictions of shares
5. Treasury shares, including shares held by subsidiaries and associates
6. Shares reserved for issuance under options and contracts
7. A description of the nature and purpose of each reserve within owners' equity.

Sample Balance Sheet Structure

The following balance sheet structure is just an example. It does not show all possible kinds of assets, equity and liabilities, but it shows the most usual ones. Because it shows goodwill, it could be a consolidated balance sheet. Monetary values are not shown, summary (total) rows are missing as well.

Income Statement

Income statement, also referred as *profit and loss statement (P&L), earnings statement, operating statement* or *statement of operations*, is a company's financial statement that indicates how the revenue (money received from the sale of products and services before expenses are taken out, also known as the "top line") is transformed into the net income (the result after all revenues and expenses have been accounted for, also known as the "bottom line").

It displays the revenues recognized for a specific period, and the cost and expenses charged against these revenues, including write-offs (e.g., depreciation and amortization of various assets) and taxes. The purpose of the income statement is to show managers and investors whether the company made or lost money during the period being reported. The important thing to remember about an income statement is that it represents a period of time. This contrasts with the balance sheet, which represents a single moment in time. Charitable organizations that are required to publish financial statements do not produce an income statement.

Instead, they produce a similar statement that reflects funding sources compared against program expenses, administrative costs, and other operating commitments. This statement is commonly referred to as the statement of activities. Revenues and expenses are further categorized in the statement of activities by the donor restrictions on the funds received and expended. The income statement can be prepared in one of two methods. The Single Step income statement takes a simpler approach, totaling revenues and subtracting expenses to find the bottom line. The more complex Multi-Step income statement (as the name implies) takes several steps to find the bottom line, starting with the gross profit.

It then calculates operating expenses and, when deducted from the gross profit, yields income from operations. Adding to income from operations is the difference of other revenues and other expenses. When combined with income from operations, this yields income before taxes. The final step is to deduct taxes, which finally produces the net income for the period measured.

Usefulness and Limitations of Income Statement

Income statements should help investors and creditors determine the past financial performance of the enterprise, predict future performance, and assess the capability of generating future cash flows through report of the income and expenses. However, information of an income statement has several limitations:

- Items that might be relevant but cannot be reliably measured are not reported (*e.g.* brand recognition and loyalty).
- Some numbers depend on accounting methods used (*e.g.* using FIFO or LIFO accounting to measure inventory level).
- Some numbers depend on judgments and estimates (*e.g.* depreciation expense depends on estimated useful life and salvage value).

Items on Income Statement

Operating Section

- Revenue-Cash inflows or other enhancements of assets of an entity during a period from delivering or producing goods, rendering services, or other activities that constitute the entity's ongoing major operations. It is usually presented as sales minus sales discounts, returns, and allowances.
- Expenses-Cash outflows or other using-up of assets or incurrence of liabilities during a period from delivering or producing goods, rendering services, or carrying out other activities that constitute the entity's ongoing major operations.

- o General and administrative expenses (G & A)-represent expenses to manage the business (officer salaries, legal and professional fees, utilities, insurance, depreciation of office building and equipment, office rents, office supplies)
- o Selling expenses-represent expenses needed to sell products (*e.g.*, sales salaries, commissions and travel expenses, advertising, freight, shipping, depreciation of sales store buildings and equipment)
- o Selling General and Administrative expenses (SG&A or SGA)-consist of the combined payroll costs (salaries, commissions, and travel expenses of executives, sales people and employees), and advertising expenses a company incurs. SGA is usually understood as a major portion of non-production related costs, opposing production related costs such as raw material and (direct) labour
- o R & D expenses-represent expenses included in research and development
- o Depreciation-is the charge for a specific period (*i.e.* year, accounting period) with respect to fixed assets that have been capitalised on the balance sheet.

Non-operating Section

- Other revenues or gains-revenues and gains from other than primary business activities (e.g. rent, patents). It also includes unusual gains and losses that are either unusual or infrequent, but not both (e.g. sale of securities or fixed assets)
- Other expenses or losses-expenses or losses not related to primary business operations.

Irregular Items

They are reported separately because this way users can better predict future cash flows-irregular items most likely will not recur. These are reported net of taxes.

- Discontinued operations is the most common type of irregular items. Shifting business location, stopping production temporarily, or changes due to technological improvement do not qualify as discontinued operations.
- Extraordinary items are both unusual (abnormal) and infrequent, for example, unexpected natural disaster, expropriation, prohibitions under new regulations. Note: natural disaster

might not qualify depending on location (e.g. frost damage would not qualify in Canada but would in the tropics).

- Changes in accounting principle is, for example, deciding to depreciate an investment property that has previously not been depreciated. However, changes in estimates (e.g. estimated useful life of a fixed asset) do not qualify.

Bottom Line

"Bottom line" is the net income that is calculated after subtracting the expenses from revenue. Since this forms the last line of the income statement, it is informally called "bottom line." It is important to investors as it represents the profit for the year attributable to the shareholders.

Cash Flow Statement

In financial accounting, a cash flow statement, also known as *statement of cash flows* or *funds flow statement*, is a financial statement that shows how changes in balance sheet accounts and income affect cash and cash equivalents, and breaks the analysis down to operating, investing, and financing activities. Essentially, the cash flow statement is concerned with the flow of cash in and cash out of the business. The statement captures both the current operating results and the accompanying changes in the balance sheet.

As an analytical tool, the statement of cash flows is useful in determining the short-term viability of a company, particularly its ability to pay bills. International Accounting Standard 7 (IAS 7), is the International Accounting Standard that deals with cash flow statements.

People and groups interested in cash flow statements include:

- Accounting personnel, who need to know whether the organization will be able to cover payroll and other immediate expenses
- Potential lenders or creditors, who want a clear picture of a company's ability to repay
- Potential investors, who need to judge whether the company is financially sound
- Potential employees or contractors, who need to know whether the company will be able to afford compensation
- Shareholders of the business.

Purpose

The cash flow statement was previously known as the flow of funds statement. The cash flow statement reflects a firm's liquidity. The balance sheet is a snapshot of a firm's financial resources and obligations at a single point in time, and the income statement summarizes a firm's financial transactions over an interval of time. These two financial statements reflect the accrual basis accounting used by firms to match revenues with the expenses associated with generating those revenues. The cash flow statement includes only inflows and outflows of cash and cash equivalents; it excludes transactions that do not directly affect cash receipts and payments.

These noncash transactions include depreciation or write-offs on bad debts or credit losses to name a few. The cash flow statement is a cash basis report on three types of financial activities: operating activities, investing activities, and financing activities. Noncash activities are usually reported in footnotes.

The cash flow statement is intended to

1. provide information on a firm's liquidity and solvency and its ability to change cash flows in future circumstances
2. provide additional information for evaluating changes in assets, liabilities and equity
3. improve the comparability of different firms' operating performance by eliminating the effects of different accounting methods
4. indicate the amount, timing and probability of future cash flows.

The cash flow statement has been adopted as a standard financial statement because it eliminates allocations, which might be derived from different accounting methods, such as various timeframes for depreciating fixed assets.

History and Variations

Cash basis financial statements were common before accrual basis financial statements. The "flow of funds" statements of the past were cash flow statements. In 1863, the Dowlais Iron Company had receovered from a business slump, but had no cash to invest for a new blast furnace, despite having made a profit. To explain why there were no funds to invest, the manager made a new financial statement that was called a *comparison balance sheet*, which showed that the company was holding too much inventory. This new financial statement was the genesis of Cash Flow Statement that is used today.

In the United States in 1971, the Financial Accounting Standards Board (FASB) defined rules that made it mandatory under Generally Accepted Accounting Principles (US GAAP) to report sources and uses of funds, but the definition of "funds" was not clear." Net working capital" might be cash or might be the difference between current assets and current liabilities. From the late 1970 to the mid-1980s, the FASB discussed the usefulness of predicting future cash flows.

In 1987, FASB Statement No. 95 (FAS 95) mandated that firms provide cash flow statements. In 1992, the International Accounting Standards Board issued International Accounting Standard 7 (IAS 7), *Cash Flow Statements*, which became effective in 1994, mandating that firms provide cash flow statements. US GAAP and IAS 7 rules for cash flow statements are similar. Differences include:

- IAS 7 requires that the cash flow statement include changes in both cash and cash equivalents. US GAAP permits using cash alone or cash and cash equivalents.
- IAS 7 permits bank borrowings (overdraft) in certain countries to be included in cash equivalents rather than being considered a part of financing activities.
- IAS 7 allows interest paid to be included in operating activities or financing activities. US GAAP requires that interest paid be included in operating activities.
- US GAAP (FAS 95) requires that when the direct method is used to present the operating activities of the cash flow statement, a supplemental schedule must also present a cash flow statement using the indirect method. The IASC strongly recommends the direct method but allows either method. The IASC considers the indirect method less clear to users of financial statements. Cash flow statements are most commonly prepared using the indirect method, which is not especially useful in projecting future cash flows.

Cash Flow Activities

The cash flow statement is partitioned into three segments, namely: cash flow resulting from operating activities, cash flow resulting from investing activities, and cash flow resulting from financing activities. The money coming into the business is called cash inflow, and money going out from the business is called cash outflow.

Operating Activities

Operating activities include the production, sales and delivery of the company's product as well as collecting payment from its customers. This could include purchasing raw materials, building inventory, advertising, and shipping the product.

Under IAS 7, operating cash flows include:

- Receipts from the sale of goods or services
- Receipts for the sale of loans, debt or equity instruments in a trading portfolio
- Interest received on loans
- Dividends received on equity securities
- Payments to suppliers for goods and services
- Payments to employees or on behalf of employees
- Interest payments (alternatively, this can be reported under financing activities in IAS 7, and US GAAP).

Items which are added back to [or subtracted from, as appropriate] the net income figure (which is found on the Income Statement) to arrive at cash flows from operations generally include:

- Depreciation (loss of tangible asset value over time)
- Deferred tax
- Amortization (loss of intangible asset value over time)
- Any gains or losses associated with the sale of a non-current asset, because associated cash flows do not belong in the operating section. (unrealized gains/losses are also added back from the income statement).

Investing Activities

Examples of Investing activities are

- Purchase of an asset (assets can be land, building, equipment, marketable securities, etc.)
- Loans made to suppliers or customers
- Payments related to mergers and acquisitions.

Financing Activities

Financing activities include the inflow of cash from investors such as banks and shareholders, as well as the outflow of cash to shareholders as dividends as the company generates income. Other activities which impact the long-term liabilities and equity of the company are also listed in the financing activities section of the cash flow statement.

Under IAS 7;

- Proceeds from issuing short-term or long-term debt
- Payments of dividends
- Payments for repurchase of company shares
- Repayment of debt principal, including capital leases
- For non-profit organizations, receipts of donor-restricted cash that is limited to long-term purposes.

Items under the financing activities section include:

- Dividends paid
- Sale or repurchase of the company's stock
- Net borrowings
- Payment of dividend tax.

Disclosure of Noncash Activities

Under IAS 7, noncash investing and financing activities are disclosed in footnotes to the financial statements. Under US General Accepted Accounting Principles (GAAP), noncash activities may be disclosed in a footnote or within the cash flow statement itself. Noncash financing activities may include

- Leasing to purchase an asset
- Converting debt to equity
- Exchanging noncash assets or liabilities for other noncash assets or liabilities
- Issuing shares in exchange for assets.

Indirect Method

The indirect method uses net-income as a starting point, makes adjustments for all transactions for non-cash items, then adjusts for all cash-based transactions. An increase in an asset account is subtracted from net income, and an increase in a liability account is added back to net income. This method converts accrual-basis net income (or loss) into cash flow by using a series of additions and deductions.

Direct Method

The direct method for creating a cash flow statement reports major classes of gross cash receipts and payments. Under IAS 7, dividends received may be reported under operating activities or under investing activities. If taxes paid are directly linked to operating activities, they are reported under operating activities; if the taxes are directly linked to investing activities or financing activities, they are reported under investing or financing activities.

Sample cash flow statement using the direct method :

***Table:** Cash flows from (used in) operating activities*

Cash receipts from customers	27,500
Cash paid to suppliers and employees	(20,000)
Cash generated from operations (sum)	7,500
Interest paid	(2,000)
Income taxes paid	(4,000)
Net cash flows from operating activities	1,500

***Table:** Cash flows from (used in) investing activities*

Proceeds from the sale of equipment	7,500
Dividends received	3,000
Net cash flows from investing activities	10,500
Cash flows from (used in) financing	
activities Dividends paid	(2,500)
Net cash flows used in financing activities	(2,500).
Net increase in cash and cash equivalents	9,500
Cash and cash equivalents, beginning of year	1,000
Cash and cash equivalents, end of year	$10,500

Rules

The following rules are used to make adjustments for changes in current assets and liabilities, operating items not providing or using cash and nonoperating items.

- Likami
- Increase in non-cash current asset are subtracted from net income
- Increase in current liabilities are added to net income
- Decrease in current liabilities are subtracted from net income
- Expenses with no cash outflows are added back to net income (depreciation and/or amortization expense are the only operating items that have no effect on cash flows in the period)
- Revenues with no cash inflows are subtracted from net income

- Non operating losses are added back to net income
- Non operating gains are subtracted from net income.

Example: cash flow of Citigroup:

Table: *Citigroup Cash Flow Statement (all numbers in millions of US$)*

Period ending	*12/31/2007*	*12/31/2006*	*12/31/2005*
Net income	21,538	24,589	17,046
Operating activities, cash flows provided by or used in:			
Depreciation and amortization	2,790	2,592	2,747
Adjustments to net income	4,617	621	2,910
Decrease (increase) in accounts receivable	12,503	17,236	—
Increase (decrease) in liabilities (A/P, taxes payable)	131,622	19,822	37,856
Decrease (increase) in inventories	—	—	—
Increase (decrease) in other operating activities	(173,057)	(33,061)	(62,963)
Net cash flow from operating activities	13	31,799	(2,404)
Investing activities, cash flows provided by or used in:			
Capital expenditures	(4,035)	(3,724)	(3,011)
Investments	(201,777)	(71,710)	(75,649)
Other cash flows from investing activities	1,606	17,009	(571)
Net cash flows from investing activities	(204,206)	(58,425)	(79,231)
Financing activities, cash flows provided by or used in:			
Dividends paid	(9,826)	(9,188)	(8,375)
Sale (repurchase) of stock	(5,327)	(12,090)	133
Increase (decrease) in debt	101,122	26,651	21,204
Other cash flows from financing activities	120,461	27,910	70,349
Net cash flows from financing activities	206,430	33,283	83,311
Effect of exchange rate changes	645	(1,840)	731
Net increase (decrease) in cash and cash equivalents	2,882	4,817	2,407

Equity (Finance)

In accounting and finance, equity is the residual claim or interest of the most junior class of investors in assets, after all liabilities are paid. If valuations placed on assets do not exceed liabilities, negative equity exists. In an accounting context, Shareholders' equity (or stockholders' equity, shareholders' funds, shareholders' capital or similar terms) represents the remaining interest in assets of a company, spread among individual shareholders of common or preferred stock. At the start of a business, owners put some funding into the business to finance assets. This creates liability on the business in the shape of capital as the business is a separate entity from its owners. Businesses can be considered to be, for accounting purposes, sums of liabilities and assets; this is the accounting equation. After liabilities have been accounted for, the positive remainder is deemed the owner's interest in the business.

This definition is helpful to understand the liquidation process in case of bankruptcy. At first, all the secured creditors are paid against proceeds from assets. Afterward, a series of creditors, ranked in priority sequence, have the next claim/right on the residual proceeds. Ownership equity is the last or residual claim against assets, paid only after all other creditors are paid. In such cases where even creditors could not get enough money to pay their bills, and nothing is left over to reimburse owners' equity. Thus owners' equity is reduced to zero. Ownership equity is also known as risk capital, liable capital and equity.

Equity Investments

Equity investments generally refers to the buying and holding of shares of stock on a stock market by individuals and firms in anticipation of income from dividends and capital gain as the value of the stock rises. It also sometimes refers to the acquisition of equity (ownership) participation in a private (unlisted) company or a startup (a company being created or newly created). When the investment is in infant companies, it is referred to as venture capital investing and is generally understood to be higher risk than investment in listed going-concern situations.

The equities held by private individuals are often held via mutual funds or other forms of pooled investment vehicle, many of which have quoted prices that are listed in financial newspapers or magazines; the mutual funds are typically managed by prominent fund management firms (e.g. Schroders, Fidelity Investments or the Vanguard Group).

Such holdings allow individual investors to obtain the diversification of the fund(s) and to obtain the skill of the professional fund managers in charge of the fund(s). An alternative, usually employed by large private investors and pension funds, is to hold shares directly; in the institutional environment many clients who own portfolios have what are called segregated funds as opposed to, or in addition to, the pooled e.g. mutual fund alternative.

A calculation can be made to assess whether an equity is over or underpriced compared with a long-term government bond. This is called the Yield Gap or Yield Ratio. It is the ratio of the dividend yield of an equity and that of the long-term bond. In financial accounting, it is the owners' interest on the assets of the enterprise after deducting all its liabilities. It appears on the balance sheet/Statement of Financial Position, one of the four primary financial statements. Ownership equity includes both tangible and intangible items (such as brand names and reputation/goodwill).

Accounts listed under ownership equity include (example):

- Preferred stock
- Share capital, common stock
- Capital surplus
- Stock options
- Retained earnings
- Treasury stock
- Reserve (accounting).

Book Value

The book value of equity will change in the case of the following events:

- Changes in the firm's assets relative to its liabilities. For example, a profitable firm receives more cash for its products than the cost at which it produced these goods, and so in the act of making a profit it is increasing its assets.
- Depreciation. Equity will decrease, for example, when machinery depreciates, which is registered as a decline in the value of the asset, and on the liabilities side of the firm's balance sheet as a decrease in shareholders' equity.

- Issue of new equity in which the firm obtains new capital increases the total shareholders' equity.
- Share repurchases, in which a firm gives back money to its investors, reducing on the asset side its financial assets, and on the liability side the shareholders' equity. For practical purposes (except for its tax consequences), share repurchasing is similar to a dividend payment, as both consist of the firm giving money back to investors. Rather than giving money to all shareholders immediately in the form of a dividend payment, a share repurchase reduces the number of shares (increases the size of each share) in future income and distributions.
- Dividends paid out to preferred stock owners are considered an expense to be subtracted from net income (from the point of view of the common share owners).
- Other reasons. Assets and liabilities can change without any effect being measured in the Income Statement under certain circumstances; for example, changes in accounting rules may be applied retroactively. Sometimes assets bought and held in other countries get translated back into the reporting currency at different exchange rates, resulting in a changed value.

Shareholders' Equity

When the owners are shareholders, the interest can be called shareholders' equity; the accounting remains the same, and it is ownership equity spread out among shareholders. If all shareholders are in one and the same class, they share equally in ownership equity from all perspectives. However, shareholders may allow different priority ranking among themselves by the use of share classes, and options. This complicates both analysis for stock valuation, and accounting. The individual investor is interested not only in the total changes to equity, but also in the increase/decrease in the value of his own personal share of the equity. This reconciliation of equity should be done both in total and on a per share basis.

- Equity (beg. of year)
- + net income inter net money you gained
- " dividends how much money you gained or lost so far
- +/" gain/loss from changes to the number of shares outstanding.more or less
- = Equity (end of year) if you get more money during the year or less or not anything.

Market Value of Shares

In the stock market, market price per share does not correspond to the equity per share calculated in the accounting statements. Stock valuations, often much higher, are based on other considerations related to the business' operating cashflow, profits and future prospects; some factors are derived from the accounting statements. Thus, there is little or no correlation between the equity seen in financial statements and the stock valuation of the business.

Real Estate Equity

Individuals can also use market valuations to calculate equity in real estate. An owner refers to his or her equity in a property as the difference between the market price of a property and the liability attached to the property (mortgage or home equity loan).

Statement of Retained Earnings

The Statement of Retained Earnings (also known as Equity Statement, Statement of Owner's Equity for a single proprietorship, Statement of Partner's Equity for partnership, and Statement of Retained Earnings and Stockholders' Equity for corporation) is one of the basic financial statements as per Generally Accepted Accounting Principles, and it explains the changes in a company's retained earnings over the reporting period.

It breaks down changes affecting the account, such as profits or losses from operations, dividends paid, and any other items charged or credited to retained earnings. A retained earnings statement is required by Generally Accepted Accounting Principles (GAAP) whenever comparative balance sheets and income statements are presented. It may appear in the balance sheet, in a combined income statement and changes in retained earnings statement, or as a separate schedule.

Therefore, the statement of retained earnings uses information from the income statement and provides information to the balance sheet. Retained earnings are part of the balance sheet (another basic financial statement) under "stockholders equity," and is mostly affected by net income earned during a period of time by the company less any dividends paid to the company's owners/stockholders. The retained earnings account on the balance sheet is said to represent an "accumulation of earnings" since net profits and losses are added/ subtracted from the account from period to period.

The general equation can be expressed as following:

Ending Retained Earnings = Beginning Retained Earnings- Dividends Paid + Net Income.

Generally Accepted Auditing Standards

Generally Accepted Auditing Standards, or GAAS are sets of standards against which the quality of audits may be judged. Several organizations have developed such sets of principles, which vary by territory.

US GAAS

US GAAS are ten auditing standards, developed by the American Institute of Certified Public Accountants, consisting of general standards, standards of field work, and standards of reporting, along with interpretations. They were developed by the AICPA in 1947 and have undergone minor changes since then.

The US GAAS are as follows:

General Standards

1. The auditor must have adequate technical training and proficiency to perform the audit.
2. The auditor must maintain independence in mental attitude in all matters related to the audit.
3. The auditor must use due professional care during the performance of the audit and the preparation of the report.

ISAs

International Standards on Auditing are developed by the International Auditing and Assurance Standards Board of the International Federation of Accountants. Derivatives of ISAs are used in the audit of several other juristictions, including the United Kingdom.

Internal Audit

Internal auditing is a profession and activity involved in helping organizations achieve their stated objectives. It does this by using a systematic methodology for analysing business processes, procedures and activities with the goal of highlighting organizational problems and recommending solutions. Professionals called internal auditors are employed by organizations to perform the internal auditing activity.

The scope of internal auditing within an organization is broad and may involve topics such as the efficacy of operations, the reliability of financial reporting, deterring and investigating fraud, safeguarding assets, and compliance with laws and regulations. Internal auditing frequently involves measuring compliance with the entity's policies and procedures. However, Internal auditors are not responsible for the execution of company activities; they advise management and the Board of Directors (or similar oversight body) regarding how to better execute their responsibilities. As a result of their broad scope of involvement, internal auditors may have a variety of higher educational and professional backgrounds.

Publicly-traded corporations typically have an internal auditing department, led by a Chief Audit Executive ("CAE") who generally reports to the Audit Committee of the Board of Directors, with administrative reporting to the Chief Executive Officer. The profession is unregulated, though there are a number of international standard setting bodies, an example of which is the Institute of Internal Auditors ("IIA"). The IIA has established Standards for the Professional Practice of Internal Auditing and has over 150,000 members representing 165 countries, including approximately 65,000 Certified Internal Auditors.

History of Internal Auditing

The Internal Auditing profession evolved steadily with the progress of management science after World War II. It is conceptually similar in many ways to financial auditing by public accounting firms, quality assurance and banking compliance activities. Much of the theory underlying internal auditing is derived from management consulting and public accounting professions. With the implementation in the United States of the Sarbanes-Oxley Act of 2002, the profession's growth accelerated, as many internal auditors possess the skills required to help companies meet the requirements of the law.

Organizational Independence

To perform their role effectively, internal auditors require organizational independence from management, to enable unrestricted evaluation of management activities and personnel. Although internal auditors are part of company management and paid by the company, the primary customer of internal audit activity is the entity charged with oversight of management's activities. This is typically the Audit Committee, a subcommittee of the Board of Directors. To provide independence, most Chief Audit Executives report to the Chairperson of the Audit Committee and can only be replaced with the concurrence of that individual.

Role in Internal Control

Internal auditing activity is primarily directed at improving internal control. Under the COSO Framework, internal control is broadly defined as a process, effected by an entity's board of directors, management, and other personnel, designed to provide reasonable assurance regarding the achievement of objectives in the following internal control categories:

- Effectiveness and efficiency of operations.
- Reliability of financial reporting.
- Compliance with laws and regulations.

Management is responsible for internal control. Managers establish policies and processes to help the organization achieve specific objectives in each of these categories. Internal auditors perform audits to evaluate whether the policies and processes are designed and operating effectively and provide recommendations for improvement.

In the United States, internal auditors may assist management with compliance with the Sarbanes-Oxley Act (SOX).

Role in Risk Management

Internal auditing professional standards require the function to monitor and evaluate the effectiveness of the organization's Risk management processes. Risk management relates to how an organization sets objectives, then identifies, analyses, and responds to those risks that could potentially impact its ability to realize its objectives. Under the COSO enterprise risk management (ERM) Framework, risks fall under strategic, operational, financial reporting, and legal/regulatory categories. Management performs risk assessment activities as part of the ordinary course of business in each of these categories. Examples include: strategic planning, marketing planning, capital planning, budgeting, hedging, incentive payout structure, and credit/lending practices. Sarbanes-Oxley regulations also require extensive risk assessment of financial reporting processes.

Corporate legal counsel often prepares comprehensive assessments of the current and potential litigation a company faces. Internal auditors may evaluate each of these activities, or focus on the processes used by management to report and monitor the risks identified. For example, internal auditors can advise management regarding the reporting of forward-looking operating measures to the Board, to help identify emerging risks.

In larger organizations, major strategic initiatives are implemented to achieve objectives and drive changes. As a member of senior management, the Chief Audit Executive (CAE) may participate in status updates on these major initiatives.

This places the CAE in the position to report on many of the major risks the organization faces to the Audit Committee, or ensure management's reporting is effective for that purpose. Internal auditors may help companies establish and maintain Enterprise Risk Management processes. Internal auditors also play an important role in helping companies execute a SOX 404 top-down risk assessment. In these latter two areas, internal auditors typically are part of the project team in an advisory role.

Role in Corporate Governance

Internal auditing activity as it relates to corporate governance is generally informal, accomplished primarily through participation in meetings and discussions with members of the Board of Directors. Corporate governance is a combination of processes and organizational structures implemented by the Board of Directors to inform, direct, manage, and monitor the organization's resources, strategies and policies towards the achievement of the organizations objectives. The internal auditor is often considered one of the "four pillars" of corporate governance, the other pillars being the Board of Directors, management, and the external auditor.

A primary focus area of internal auditing as it relates to corporate governance is helping the Audit Committee of the Board of Directors (or equivalent) perform its responsibilities effectively. This may include reporting critical internal control problems, informing the Committee privately on the capabilities of key managers, suggesting questions or topics for the Audit Committee's meeting agendas, and coordinating carefully with the external auditor and management to ensure the Committee receives effective information.

Nature of the Internal Audit Activity

Based on a risk assessment of the organization, internal auditors, management and oversight Boards determine where to focus internal auditing efforts. Internal auditing activity is generally conducted as one or more discrete projects. A typical internal audit project involves the following steps:

1. Establish and communicate the scope and objectives for the audit to appropriate management.

2. Develop an understanding of the business area under review. This includes objectives, measurements, and key transaction types. This involves review of documents and interviews. Flowcharts and narratives may be created if necessary.
3. Describe the key risks facing the business activities within the scope of the audit.
4. Identify control procedures used to ensure each key risk and transaction type is properly controlled and monitored.
5. Develop and execute a risk-based sampling and testing approach to determine whether the most important controls are operating as intended.
6. Report problems identified and negotiate action plans with management to address the problems.
7. Follow-up on reported findings at appropriate intervals. Internal audit departments maintain a follow-up database for this purpose.

Project length varies based on the complexity of the activity being audited and Internal Audit resources available. Many of the above steps are iterative and may not all occur in the sequence indicated. By analysing and recommending business improvements in critical areas, auditors help the organization meet its objectives. In addition to assessing business processes, specialists called Information Technology (IT) Auditors review information technology controls.

Developing the Plan of Engagements

Internal auditing standards require the development of a plan of audit engagements (projects) based on a risk assessment, updated at least annually. The input of senior management and the Board is typically included in this process. Many departments update their plan of engagements throughout the year as risks or organizational priorities change. This effort helps ensure the audit activity is aligned with the organization's objectives, by answering two key questions: First, what goals are the organization trying to accomplish in the upcoming period? Second, how can the Internal Audit Department assist the organization in achieving these goals?

Internal auditors often conduct a series of interviews of senior management to identify potential engagements. Changes in people, processes, or systems often generate audit project ideas. Various documents are reviewed, such as strategic plans, financial reports, consulting studies, etc.

Further, the results of prior audits and resolution of open issues are considered. For example, even if a business area is important, prior audit work and the nature and status of open issues may render further audit effort unnecessary. If the organization has a formal enterprise risk management (ERM) program, the risks identified therein help limit the amount of separate risk assessment performed by Internal Audit. The preliminary plan of engagements is documented and prioritized. Audit resources and expertise are then considered and a final plan is presented to senior management and the Audit Committee. The presentations vary based on the needs of the stakeholders and may include the following:

- Summary of key goals, risks and corresponding major audits, to illustrate alignment;
- Analyses of audit effort along a variety of dimensions (e.g., by business segment, COSO objective category, IT, Sarbanes-Oxley, vs. prior year, etc.) along with commentary regarding changes;
- Brief description of critical projects identified;
- Projects requested but not planned for execution due to prioritization and resources;
- Required co-sourcing effort, typically where outside expertise is required or during peak periods;
- Coordination with other risk functions, such as legal, compliance or insurance, to ensure coverage of key organizational risks;
- Update on audit staffing levels, experience and certification; and
- Appendix materials, such as planning approach, assumptions (e.g., days per auditor and staffing level) and brief descriptions of all planned audits and related prioritization.

Best Practices in Internal Auditing

Measuring the Internal Audit Function

The measurement of the internal audit function can involve a balanced scorecard approach. Internal audit functions are primarily evaluated based on the quality of counsel and information provided to the Audit Committee and top management. However, this is primarily qualitative and therefore difficult to measure.

"Customer surveys" sent to key managers after each audit project or report can be used to measure performance, with an annual survey to the Audit Committee. Scoring on dimensions such as professionalism, quality of counsel, timeliness of work product, utility of meetings, and quality of status updates are typical with such surveys. Understanding the expectations of senior management and the audit committee represent important steps in developing a performance measurement process, as well as how such measures help align the audit function with organizational priorities. Quantitative measures can also be used to measure the function's level of execution and qualifications of its personnel. Key measures include:

Plan completion: This is a measure of the degree to which the annual plan of engagements is completed, measured at a point in time. This may be measured using the number of projects completed, weighted by the planned size of each project, with estimates for projects in-progress. Measured throughout the year, it is compared against the percentage of the year elapsed.

Report issuance: This is a measure of the time elapsed from completion of testing to issuance of the final audit report, including management's action plans. This can be measured in average days or percentage of reports issued within a certain standard, such as 30 days. Establishing expectations for the timing of management's response to report recommendations is critical. In addition, the scope and degree of change involved in the report's action plans are key variables. For example, a report for a single retail store requiring only the store manager's action might take 3–5 days to issue. However, a report consolidating findings from 20 retail stores, with action plans with national implications determined by top management, may take 30–60 days in complex organizations.

Issue closure: Reported audit findings are often called "issues" or "deficiencies." Professional standards require audit functions to track reported findings to resolution, which effectively requires the maintenance of an issues follow-up database. The number of days that reported issues remain open, or open after their agreed-upon closure date, are key measures. In addition, reporting database statistics such as the number of issues open (unresolved), closed (resolved), and issues opened/closed during a given period are useful statistics.

Staff qualifications: This can be measured through the percentage of staff with professional certifications, graduate degrees, and overall years of experience.

Staff utilization rate: This is measured as the percentage of time spent on projects, as opposed to administrative time such as training or vacation. Many internal audit departments track time by audit project. This is typically captured in a database or spreadsheet.

Staffing level: The number of positions filled relative to the authorized staffing level. Due to the challenge of finding qualified staff, departments may have rotational programs to bring in management to complete tours in the function or be "guest" auditors. Audit departments also "co-source," meaning they obtain contract auditors from service providers.

Developing and Retaining Staff

Developing and retaining quality professionals is a key concern in the profession. Key methods for developing and retaining internal audit staff personnel include:

- Providing challenging, varied assignments
- Ensuring quality supervision
- Ensuring staff participates in projects from start to finish, to learn all phases of the audit process
- Providing opportunities to lead (in-charge) projects, starting with more structured projects such as Sarbanes-Oxley work
- Participating on departmental improvement task forces, such as preparation for quality assurance review
- Participating in the recruiting and interviewing process for new hires
- Rotating through various audit teams (in larger departments) or audits of various businesses
- Providing both outside training (e.g., seminars) and in-house training (e.g., company systems) for two weeks/year
- Participation in annual risk assessment activities, whether asking key questions or just taking notes.

Reporting of Critical Findings

The Chief Audit Executive (CAE) typically reports the most critical issues to the Audit Committee quarterly, along with management's progress towards resolving them. Critical issues typically have a reasonable likelihood of causing substantial financial or reputational damage to the company. For particularly complex issues, the responsible manager may participate in the discussion. Such reporting is critical to ensure the function is respected, that the proper "tone at the top" exists in the organization, and to expedite resolution of such issues. It is a matter of considerable judgment to select appropriate issues for the Audit Committee's attention and to describe them in the proper context.

10

Cost Accounting Standards

Cost Accounting Standards (popularly known as CAS) are a set of 19 standards and rules promulgated by the United States Government for use in determining costs on negotiated procurements. CAS differs from the Federal Acquisition Regulation (FAR) in that FAR applies to substantially all contractors, whereas CAS applies primarily to the larger ones.

System of Integrated Environmental and Economic Accounting

System of Integrated Environmental and Economic Accounting (SEEA) is a framework to compile statistics linking environmental statistics to economic statistics. SEEA is described as a satellite system to the United Nations System of National Accounts (SNA). This means that the definitions, guidelines and practical approaches of the SNA are applied to the SEEA. This system enables environmental statistics to be compared to economic statistics as the system boundaries are the same after some processing of the input statistics. By analysing statistics on the economy and the environment at the same time it is possible to show different patterns of sustainability for production and consumption. It can also show the economic consequences of maintaining a certain environmental standard.

Scope

The SEEA is a satellite system of the SNA that consists of several sets of accounts. In broad terms, the area can be described as enabling any user of statistics to compare environmental issues to general economics, knowing that the comparisons are based on the same entities, for example, pollution levels caused by a producing industry can be linked to the specific economics of that industry.

The different areas of SEEA can be briefly described as follows:

Environmental Economic Statistics

Economic variables that are already included in the national accounts but are of obvious environmental interest, such as investments and expenditure in the area of environmental protection, environment-related taxes and subsidies, and environmental classification of activities and the employment associated with them, etc. In principle, environmental taxes and environmental protection expenditures can be regarded as two sides of the same coin. Both entail costs involved in production processes that are related to the exploitation of the environment in different ways. On the one hand, environmental protection expenditures record spending on measures aimed at improving the environment, while on the other hand, taxes record the costs set by a government for the exploitation of the environment. Thus, in the total cost of production, the environmental taxes paid can be added to expenditure on environmental protection.

Enron Corporation

Enron Corporation was an American energy, commodities, and services company based in Houston, Texas. Before its bankruptcy on December 2, 2001, Enron employed approximately 22,000 staff and was one of the world's leading electricity, natural gas, communications, and pulp and paper companies, with claimed revenues of nearly $101 billion in 2000. *Fortune* named Enron "America's Most Innovative Company" for six consecutive years. At the end of 2001, it was revealed that its reported financial condition was sustained substantially by institutionalised, systematic, and creatively planned accounting fraud, known as the "Enron scandal". Enron has since become a popular symbol of willful corporate fraud and corruption. The scandal also brought into question the accounting practices and activities of many corporations throughout the United States and was a factor in the creation of the Sarbanes–Oxley Act of 2002. The scandal also affected the wider business world by causing the dissolution of the Arthur Andersen accounting firm.

Enron filed for bankruptcy protection in the Southern District of New York in late 2001 and selected Weil, Gotshal & Manges as its bankruptcy counsel. It emerged from bankruptcy in November 2004, pursuant to a court-approved plan of reorganisation, after one of the biggest and most complex bankruptcy cases in U.S. history. A new board of directors changed the name of Enron to Enron Creditors

Recovery Corp., and focused on reorganising and liquidating certain operations and assets of the prebankruptcy Enron. On September 7, 2006, Enron sold Prisma Energy International Inc., its last remaining business, to Ashmore Energy International Ltd. (now AEI).

Misleading Financial Accounts

In 1990, Enron Finance CEO Jeff Skilling hired Andrew Fastow, who was well acquainted with the burgeoning deregulated energy market Skilling wanted to exploit. In 1993, Fastow set to work establishing numerous limited liability special purpose entities (common business practice); however, it also allowed Enron to place liability so that it would not appear in its accounts, allowing it to maintain a robust and generally growing stock price and thus keeping its critical investment grade credit ratings.

Enron was originally involved in transmitting and distributing electricity and natural gas throughout the United States. The company developed, built, and operated power plants and pipelines while dealing with rules of law and other infrastructures worldwide. Enron owned a large network of natural gas pipelines, which stretched ocean to ocean and border to border including Northern Natural Gas, Florida Gas Transmission, Transwestern Pipeline company and a partnership in Northern Border Pipeline from Canada.

The states of California, New Hampshire and Rhode Island had already passed power deregulation laws by July 1996, the time of Enron's proposal to acquire Portland General Electric. In 1998, Enron moved into the water sector, creating the Azurix Corporation, which it part-floated on the New York Stock Exchange in June 1999. Azurix failed to break into the water utility market, and one of its major concessions, in Buenos Aires, was a large-scale money-loser. After the move to Houston, many analysts criticized the Enron management as swimming in debt. The Enron management pursued aggressive retribution against its critics, setting the pattern for dealing with accountants, lawyers, and the financial media.

Enron grew wealthy due largely to marketing, promoting power, and its high stock price. Enron was named "America's Most Innovative Company" by *Fortune* for six consecutive years, from 1996 to 2001. It was on the *Fortune*'s "100 Best Companies to Work for in America" list in 2000, and had offices that were stunning in their opulence. Enron was hailed by many, including labour and the workforce, as an overall great company, praised for its large long-term pensions, benefits for its workers and extremely effective management until its exposure in corporate fraud. The first analyst to publicly disclose Enron's financial flaws was Daniel Scotto, who in August 2001 issued a report entitled "All Stressed up and no place to go", which encouraged investors to sell Enron stocks and bonds at any and all costs.

As was later discovered, many of Enron's recorded assets and profits were inflated or even wholly fraudulent and nonexistent. Debts and losses were put into entities formed "offshore" that were not included in the firm's financial statements, and other sophisticated and arcane financial transactions between Enron and related companies were used to take unprofitable entities off the company's books.

Its most valuable asset and the largest source of honest income, the 1930s era Northern Natural Gas, was eventually purchased back by a group of Omaha investors, who moved its headquarters back to Omaha, and is now a unit of Warren Buffett's MidAmerican Energy Holdings Corp. NNG was put up as collateral for a $2.5 billion capital infusion by Dynegy Corporation when Dynegy was planning to buy Enron. When Dynegy looked closely at Enron's books, they backed out of the deal and fired their CEO, Chuck Watson. The new chairman and head CEO, the late Daniel Dienstbier, had been president of NNG and an Enron executive at one time and was forced out of Enron by Ken Lay. Dienstbier was an acquaintance of Warren Buffett. NNG continues to be profitable today.

Project Accounting

Project accounting (sometimes referred to as job cost accounting) is the practice of creating financial reports specifically designed to track the financial progress of projects, which can then be used by managers to aid project management. Standard accounting is primarily aimed at monitoring financial progress of organisational elements (geographical or functional departments, divisions and the enterprise as a whole) over defined time periods (typically weeks, months, quarters and years).

Projects differ in that they frequently cross organisational boundaries, may last for anything from a few days or weeks to a number of years, during which time budgets may also be revised many times. They may also be one of a number of projects that make up a larger overall project or program.

Consequently, in a project management environment costs (both direct and overhead) and revenues are also allocated to projects, which may be subdivided into a work breakdown structure, and grouped together into project hierarchies. Project accounting permits reporting at any such level that has been defined, and often allows comparison with historical as well as current budgets.

Project accounting is commonly use at government contractors, where the ability to account for costs by contract (and sometimes contract line item, or CLIN) is usually a requirement for interim payments.

Percentage-of-completion is frequently independently assessed by a project manager. Funding advances and actual-to-budget cost variances are calculated using the project budget adjusted to percent-of-completion.

Where labour costs are a significant portion of overall project cost, it is usually necessary for employees to fill out a timesheet in order to generate the data to allocate project costs.

The capital budget processes of corporations and governments are chiefly concerned with major investment projects that typically have upfront costs and longer term benefits. Investment go / no-go decisions are largely based on net present value assessments. Project accounting of the costs and benefits can provide crucially important feedback on the quality of these important decisions.

An interesting specialised form of project accounting is production accounting, which tracks the costs of individual movie and television episode film production costs. A movie studio will employ production accounting to track the costs of its many separate projects.

Accounting

Accounting is one of several academic events sanctioned by the University Interscholastic League. The contest began in the 1986-87 scholastic year.

Accounting is designed to test students' understanding of general accounting principles and practices used in the business environment.

Eligibility

Students in Grade 9 through Grade 12 are eligible to enter this event. All grades compete in one division.

The test covers elementary principles and practices of accounting for sole proprietorships, partnerships, and corporations, and may include bookkeeping terminology, the worksheet with adjustments, income statement, balance sheet, trial balance, account classification, journalising, posting, bank reconciliation, payroll, and other items related to the basic accounting cycle.

Each school may send up to four students; however, in districts with more than eight schools the district executive committee can limit participation to three students per school. In order for a school to participate in team competition, the school must send at least three students.

Rules and Scoring

The test consists of 80-100 questions, which must be completed in one hour. A time signal is given at 55 minutes warning students that only five minutes remain; at the end of the hour the students must immediately stop writing. The questions may be answered in any order; there is no penalty for skipping questions.

Students are allowed to use scratch paper and highlighter pens during the contest. Calculators are also allowed during the contest, provided the following criteria are met:

- The calculators must be basic "four-function" models, though simple functions such as percent, square root, and simple memory are allowed. Higher-level business, financial, statistical, graphing, and scientific calculators are not permitted.
- The calculators must be hand-held, operate silently, not be equipped with a tape output, and be able to operate without requiring external power (rechargeable batteries are permitted but they must be charged prior to competition).
- All memory must be cleared prior to the contest.

Exact answers are required on all questions.

Five points are awarded for each correct answer, no points are deducted for wrong or unanswered problems. In addition, starred questions answered correctly receive one bonus point for each star (e.g., a two-star question answered correctly is worth 7 points, 5 base points for the correct answer plus one point for each star).

Determining the Winner

The top three individuals and the top team (determined based on the scores of the top three individuals) will advance to the next round.

In addition, within each region, the highest-scoring second place team from all district competitions advances as the "wild card" to regional competition (provided the team has four members), and within the state, the highest-scoring second place team from all regional competitions advances as the wild card to the state competition.

Members of advancing teams who did not place individually remain eligible to compete for individual awards at higher levels.

There is no tiebreaker in individual competition; all tied individuals will advance.

For team competition, the score of the fourth-place individual is used as the tiebreaker. If a team has only three members it is not eligible to participate in the tiebreaker. If the fourth-place score still results in a tie, the individual tiebreaker rules will not apply, and all remaining tied teams will advance. At the state level ties for first place are not broken.

For district meet academic championship and district meet sweepstakes awards, points are awarded to the school as follows:

- Individual places: 1st—15, 2nd—12, 3rd—10, 4th—8, 5th—6, and 6th—4.
- Team places: 1st—10 and 2nd—5.
- The maximum number of points a school can earn in Accounting is 37.

Sterling Management Systems

Sterling Management Systems offers practice management seminars and training to Accounting, Medical and Dental and other private practice professionals. Founded in 1983 in the back office of a dental practice in Vacaville, Ca., it is currently located in a 20,000 square foot (1,900 m) office in Glendale, CA. It has been named in 1988 and 1989 by INC Magazine as among the 500 fastest growing companies in the US.

According to the company's website it has delivered practice management seminars to over 160,000 professionals, and courses to more than 70,000 clients and staff.

For practice owners and key executives Sterling's services involve formal training delivered at their facilities in Glendale, CA. For staff, training is typically delivered at weekend workshops held by Sterling for that purpose throughout the year in key cities around the country.

Hubbard Management Technology

Sterling offers training and implementation support programs based on the management techniques developed by L. Ron Hubbard, author and founder of the Church of Scientology. These services are provided under a license from WISE, the World Institute of Scientology Enterprises, an international membership organisation which licenses the use of Hubbard's copyrighted management materials and oversees their use in applications in the business community at large.

Controversy

According to *New Religions: A Guide*, Sterling Management is a subsidiary of the Church of Scientology. According to the books *Perspectives on the New Age* and *The New Age Movement and the Biblical Worldview*, the Church of Scientology oversees the operations of both WISE, and Sterling Management.

Both of these facts are apparently contradicted by the company's status as a private corporation and its inclusion on the INC 500, which is limited to verified private corporations, and by the company's web site, which states that it is a private corporation owned by Kevin Wilson, that it is not a subsidiary but a licensee of the Hubbard Management materials.

Wilson's *New Religious Movements* and Heela's *The New Age Movement* describe Sterling Management Systems as an "*est*-like movement", referring to Werner Erhard's Erhard Seminars Training. Sterling Management Systems has been criticized for its "high-pressure sales tactics".

WISE, SMS and the Church of Scientology

WISE consulting companies like SMS may introduce their client to the religious aspects of Scientology and refer clients to the church for training and/or other religious services. Estimates vary as to the number of people introduced to Scientology in this manner, officials of the WISE consulting company *Singer Consultants* estimate that 20% of their clients end up taking courses in Scientology while Pat Lusey, co-founder of another WISE consulting group, *Uptrends*, has stated that 50% of the clients of WISE consulting groups end up in Scientology..

No such estimates are available for SMS. The company states on their site that they are licensed to deliver the secular management technologies of L. Ron Hubbard only, that it has "happened where clients have asked for assistance in personal matters that lie beyond the scope of Sterling's work. At that point, if asked by a client, we let them know that, if they want, we can introduce them to a Scientology practitioner who can tell them more."

Social Accounting

Social accounting (also known as social and environmental accounting, corporate social reporting, corporate social responsibility reporting, non-financial reporting, or sustainability accounting) is the process of communicating the social and environmental effects of organisations' economic actions to particular interest groups within society and to society at large. Social accounting is commonly used in the context of business, or corporate social responsibility (CSR), although any organisation, including NGOs, charities, and government agencies may engage in social accounting.

Social accounting emphasises the notion of corporate accountability. D. Crowther defines social accounting in this sense as "an approach to reporting a firm's activities which stresses the need for the identification of socially relevant behaviour, the determination of those to whom the company is accountable for its social performance and the development of appropriate measures and reporting techniques."

Social accounting is often used as an umbrella term to describe a broad field of research and practice. The use of more narrow terms to express a specific interest is thus not uncommon. Environmental accounting may e.g. specifically refer to the research or practice of accounting for an organisation's impact on the natural environment. Sustainability accounting is often used to express the measuring and the quantitative analysis of social and economic sustainability.

Accountability

Social accounting for accountability purposes is designed to support and facilitate the pursuit of society's objectives. These objectives can be manifold but can typically be described in terms of social and environmental desirability and sustainability.

In order to make informed choices on these objectives, the flow of information in society in general, and in accounting in particular, needs to cater for democratic decision-making. In democratic systems, Gray argues, there must then be flows of information in which those controlling the resources provide accounts to society of their use of those resources: a system of corporate accountability.

Society is seen to profit from implementing a social and environmental approach to accounting in a number of ways, e.g.:

- Honouring stakeholders' rights of information;
- Balancing corporate power with corporate responsibility;
- Increasing transparency of corporate activity;
- Identifying social and environmental costs of economic success.

Management Control

Social accounting for the purpose of management control is designed to support and facilitate the achievement of an organisation's own objectives.

Because social accounting is concerned with substantial self-reporting on a systemic level, individual reports are often referred to as social audits.

Organisations are seen to benefit from implementing social accounting practices in a number of ways, e.g.:

- Increased information for decision-making;
- More accurate product or service costing;
- Enhanced image management and Public Relations;
- Identification of social responsibilities;
- Identification of market development opportunities;
- Maintaining legitimacy.

According to BITC the "process of reporting on responsible businesses performance to stakeholders" (i.e. social accounting) helps integrate such practices into business practices, as well as identifying future risks and opportunities.

The management control view thus focuses on the individual organisation.

Critics of this approach point out that the benign nature of companies is assumed. Here, responsibility, and accountability, is largely left in the hands of the organisation concerned.

Environmental Accounting

Environmental accounting, which is a subset of social accounting, focuses on the cost structure and environmental performance of a company. It principally describes the preparation, presentation, and communication of information related to an organisation's interaction with the natural environment. Although environmental accounting is most commonly undertaken as voluntary self-reporting by companies, third-party reports by government agencies, NGOs and other bodies posit to pressure for environmental accountability.

Accounting for impacts on the environment may occur within a company's financial statements, relating to liabilities, commitments and contingencies for the remediation of contaminated lands or other financial concerns arising from pollution. Such reporting essentially expresses financial issues arising from environmental legislation. More typically, environmental accounting describes the reporting of quantitative and detailed environmental data within the non-financial sections of the annual report or in separate (including online) environmental reports. Such reports may account for pollution emissions, resources used, or wildlife habitat damaged or reestablished.

In their reports, large companies commonly place primary emphasis on eco-efficiency, referring to the reduction of resource and energy use and waste production per unit of product or service. A complete picture which accounts for all inputs, outputs and wastes of the organisation, must not necessarily emerge. Whilst companies can often demonstrate great success in eco-efficiency, their ecological footprint, that is an estimate of total environmental impact, may move independently following changes in output.

Legislation for compulsory environmental reporting exists in some form e.g. in Denmark, Netherlands, Australia and Korea. The United Nations has been highly involved in the adoption of environmental accounting practices, most notably in the United Nations Division for Sustainable Development publication Environmental Management Accounting Procedures and Principles (2002).

Applications

Social accounting is a widespread practice in a number of large organisations in the United Kingdom. Royal Dutch Shell, BP, British Telecom, The Co-operative Bank, The Body Shop, and United Utilities all publish independently audited social and sustainability accounts. In many instances the reports are produced in (partial or full) compliance with the sustainability reporting guidelines set by the Global Reporting Initiative (GRI).

Traidcraft plc, the fair trade organisation, claims to be the first public limited company to publish audited social accounts in the UK, starting in 1993. The website of the Centre for Social and Environmental Accounting Research contains a collection of exemplary reporting practices and social audits.

Multidisciplinary Professional Services Networks

Multidisciplinary professional services networks are organisations formed by law, accounting and other professional services firms to offer clients new multidisciplinary approaches solving increasingly complex issues. They are a type of professional services network which operates to provide services to their members. They operate in the same way as accounting firm networks and associations and law firm networks. They do not practice a profession such as law or accounting but provide services to members so they can serve clients needs. There are 10 multidisciplinary networks. The largest are: MSI Global, Morison International, Geneva Group, International Practice Group and WSG - World Services Group. These networks have more than 100 member firms in as many as 90 countries in hundreds of offices. The members employ thousands of professionals.

Hollywood Accounting

Hollywood accounting (also known as Hollywood Bookkeeping) refers to the opaque accounting methods used by the film, video and television industry not only in Hollywood, CA, USA to budget and record profits for film projects. Expenditures can be inflated to reduce or eliminate the profit of the project thereby reducing the amount which the corporation must pay in royalties or other profit-sharing agreements based on the net profit.

Creative Accountants

Hollywood accounting gets its name from its prevalence in the entertainment industry — that is, in the movie studios of Hollywood. Those affected can range from the writers to the actors.John D. MacDonald's novel *Free Fall in Crimson* (1981) references Hollywood accounting in its dialogue:

> *"Darling! This is the Industry! The really creative people are the accountants. A big studio got over half the profit, after setting breakeven at about three times the cost, taking twenty-five percent of income as an overhead charge, and taking thirty percent of income as a distribution charge, plus rental fees, and prime interest on what they advanced."*

How it Works

Hollywood accounting can take several forms. In one form, a subsidiary is formed to perform a given activity and the parent entity will extract money out of the subsidiary not in terms of profits but in the form of charges for certain "services". The specific schemes can range from the simple and obvious to the extremely complex.

Three main factors in Hollywood accounting reduce the reported profit of a movie, and all have to do with the calculation of overhead:

- Production overhead – Studios, on average, calculate production overhead by using a figure around 15% of total production costs.
- Distribution overhead – Film distributors typically keep 30% of what they receive from movie theaters ("gross rentals").
- Marketing overhead – To determine this number, studios usually choose about 10% of all advertising costs.

All of the above means of calculating overhead are highly controversial, even within the accounting profession. Namely, these percentages are assigned without much regard to how, in reality, these estimates relate to actual overhead costs. In short, this method does not, by any rational standard, attempt to adequately trace overhead costs.

Due to Hollywood accounting, it has been estimated that only about 5% of movies officially show a net profit, and the "losers" include such blockbuster films as *Rain Man*, *Forrest Gump*, *Who Framed Roger Rabbit*, and *Batman*, which all took in huge amounts in box office and video sales.

Because of this, net points are sometimes referred to as "monkey points," a term attributed to Eddie Murphy, who is said to have also stated that only a fool would accept net points in his or her contract.

All of this shows why so many big-name actors insist on "gross points" (a percentage of some definition of gross revenue) rather than net profit participation. This practice reduces the likelihood of a project showing a profit, as a production company will claim a portion of the reported box-office revenue was diverted directly to gross point participants.

Production Accounting

Production accounting is a filmmaking term, used especially in Hollywood, referring to the project accounting of the cost of a film project. As with construction accounting, salient issues are the accurate allocation of workers' time to specific projects (usually requiring each worker to fill out a weekly timesheet), and the correct assessment of indirect costs such as employee benefits.

Specialised software to support production accounting has been developed.

The purpose of Lean Accounting is to support the lean enterprise as a business strategy. It seeks to move from traditional accounting methods to a system that measures and motivates excellent business practices in the lean enterprise.

Financial Reports for Lean Operations

Value Stream Costing

Cost and profitability reporting is achieved using Value Stream Costing, a simple summary direct costing of the value streams. The value stream costs are typically collected weekly and there is little or no allocation of "overheads." This provides financial information that can be clearly understood by everybody in the value stream which in turn leads to good decisions, motivation to lean improvement across the entire value stream, and clear accountability for cost and profitability. Weekly reporting also provides excellent control and management of costs because they can be reviewed by the value stream manager while the information is still current.

Plain Language Financial Statements

Lean accounting provides financial reports that are readily understandable to anyone in the company. The income statements are in "plain language" and the information is presented in a way that is no more complicated than a household budget. Plain language income statements are easy to use because they do not include misleading and confusing data relating to standard costs and hosts of incomprehensible variance figures. When used in meetings, plain language financial statements change the question from "What does this mean?" to "What should we do?".

Box Score Reporting

Box Scores are used widely within lean accounting. The standard format of the box score shows a 3-dimensional view of value stream performance; operational performance measurements, financial performance, and how the value stream capacity is being used. The capacity information shows how much of the capacity within the value stream is used productively, how much is used to do non-productive activities, and how much value stream capacity is available for use. The box score shows the value stream performance on a single sheet of paper and using a simple and accessible format.

The box score shown on the right shows weekly value stream performance. Other box scores are used for decision-making, for assessing the financial impact of lean improvement, for selecting or prioritising such issues as capital acquisitions using the 3P approach, and other reporting and decision-making requirements. Companies using lean accounting often have a standard box score format and require that all decisions relating to a value stream be presented using the standard box scores. This leads to operational and financial information being consistent and well understood when it is used.

Making Decisions Without the Use of Product or Process Costs

Decision-Making using Box Scores and Value Stream Cost Information

Routine decision-making – including quotes, profitability, make/buy, sourcing, product rationalisation, and so forth – is achieved using simple yet powerful information that is readily available from the box score. There is no need to use a standard cost again for these important decisions. The Box Score shows an example of this method for decision-making related to sourcing of a new product.

Most companies using lean accounting create standard templates for the various kinds of daily routine decisions. These will include assessing the profitability of a sales order or request for quote, make-buy decisions for products or components, the impact of improvement projects, and so forth. These templates often access box score information from the lean accounting information within the company's systems. The availability of capacity is often a crucial issue when making these kinds of short-term decisions.

The box score show in this example demonstrates a short term decision and assume that the company's capacity and costs are largely fixed. There are two other kinds of decisions used regularly in lean companies; medium term decisions and strategic decisions. Box Scores are also used for medium term decisions but there is no assumption of fixed capacity and costs.

The template shows how the capacity and resources need to be changed to fulfill the decision. These decisions are linked in the SOFP (Sales, Operations, and Financial Planning) process that typically looks out 12–18 months. The Box Score is also used for strategic decisions such as the introduction of new products, and the templates feed into the company's Strategy Deployment (Hoshin Kanri) and Target Costing processes.

The Box Score method is flexible to meet the needs of different kinds of decisions, yet using the same underlying approach that we do not try to calculate a fully absorbed product cost. Instead the impact of these decisions on the value stream as a whole is used to assess the suitability of each of our choices. This leads to better understanding and better decisions, when used with standard decision-making processes.

Product or Service Costing

Under most circumstances it is not necessary to calculate product or service costs. Traditional manufacturing companies usually calculate a fully absorbed product cost using complex methods for the allocation of overhead costs, and they use these product costs for decision-making, inventory valuation, and performance measurements in the form of variance analysis and such metrics as individual efficiency. Similar methods are used in service organisations to estimate the cost of each service they provide.

Companies employing lean accounting methods recognise that standard costs and other methods for fully absorbed product or service costing lead to poor decisions and motivate anti-lean behaviour. These companies also find that there is no need to calculate a product cost because all the uses of product costs within traditional companies can be addressed in lean accounting using simpler and better methods. Decision-making, inventory valuation, performance measurements, and other uses of fully absorbed product costs are all achieved using other lean accounting methods. If a product cost is required – for reporting international transfer pricing, for example – then these can be calculated using simpler and more lean-focused methods like Features & Characteristics costing.

External Reporting

Closing the Books

The primary collection of revenue and costs is done using Value Stream Costing, and (typically) weekly value stream income statements are used by the value stream managers to control costs and work to reduce costs. A typical lean organisation will have several revenue earning or *order fulfillment* value streams, one or two *new product development* value streams, and then a small group of people and departments that *support* the value streams but are not in the value streams. These external support people include, for example, a plant or division manager, HR, Information systems, and so forth. The costs of these support people is relatively small in comparison to the value streams. External reporting is achieved by taking the monthly value stream income statements and the financial statement for the support people and adding them together to provide the consolidated financial report for the company or division as a whole. This month-end close provides financial reports for the company that can be used for all external reporting.

There is usually a requirement for some "below the line" adjustments to bring the income state in line with *generally accepted accounting principles* (GAAP). These adjustments include any change of inventory value between now and last month, group and corporate overhead allocations, and other miscellaneous adjustments like exchange rate gains and losses. The "bottom line" of the adjusted statement will of course be the same as the traditional statements. There is no formal change of accounting method and the bottom line will therefore be the same.

Inventory Valuation

An important aspect of financial control is the evaluation of inventory. Lean manufacturing always leads to substantial inventory reductions. When inventories are low and under good control (using pull systems, single-piece flow, supplier partnerships, etc.), the valuation of inventory becomes much less complex. Lean Accounting contains a number of methods for valuing inventory that are simple, accurate, and often visual. Several of these methods do not require any computer-based inventory tracking at all.

Compliance to Regulatory Requirements

A question that always comes up when discussing lean accounting is whether these methods comply with regulatory accounting requirements and GAAP (generally accepted accounting principles). Lean accounting fully complies with all statutory and generally accepted accounting requirements in the United States and Europe, including the unique requirements of German, Swiss, and Italian regulation. Lean accounting also complies with the increasingly popular International Accounting Standards (IAS) that is seeking to create a single worldwide approach. When moving from traditional accounting methods to lean accounting there is no "change of accounting" because the external reporting outcome of lean accounting uses the same accrual based actual costing required by GAAP and statutory regulations. There is an argument that lean accounting lends itself better to statutory regulations because they require reporting at actual cost. Lean accounting uses actual costs throughout, whereas traditional accounting uses standard costs that must then be adjusted to actual costing for external reporting

Further Simplifying the Accounting Processes

Transaction Elimination

Traditional companies use complex, transaction-based information systems like MRPII or Enterprise Systems (ERP) to maintain financial and operational control of their processes. Lean organisations bring their process under good control using lean methods, visual control, low inventories, short lead times, and – most importantly – identifying and resolve the root causes of the problems that create the lack of control. Once these root causes have been addressed and the process brought under control, it is no longer necessary to use these complex and wasteful transactional systems, and they can be gradually eliminated.

In manufacturing companies the transaction-heavy documents tend to be production work orders and inventory tracking on the computer. Over time, as lean methods eliminate the need for these documents in favour of visual management, these documents can be eliminated and the thousands of wasteful transaction can be eliminated. One large North American aircraft manufacturer eliminated three trillion transactions in one year using this approach. The "ideal" for a manufacturing company is to have only two types of transactions within the production processes; the receipt of raw materials and the shipment of finished product. These two transactions are legally required owing to change of ownership. Everything else within the production process can be addressed better, quicker, easier, and less wastefully using visual, lean methods.

Other kinds of service companies like banks, healthcare, insurance and others, have similarly transaction-heavy processes that can be radically simplified through the use of lean methods of control. Almost every company can largely eliminate their purchasing and accounts payable processes together with the wasteful and complicated three-way matching through using lean methods.

Accounting controls have always been important, and it is essential that Lean Accounting enhance these controls, and does not weaken them. It is important to bring the company's auditors into the Lean Accounting process at the earliest stages. A primary tool to ensure that Lean Accounting changes are made prudently is the *Transaction*

Elimination Matrix. Using the transaction elimination matrix we can determine what lean methods must be in place to enable us to eliminate traditional, transaction-based processes without jeopardizing financial (or operational) control. These decisions are made ahead of time and become a part of the overall lean transformation; in some cases driving the lean changes and improvements.

Focusing on Customer Value

Target Costing

Target costing is the tool for understanding how the company creates value for the customer and what must be done to create more value. Target Costing is used when new products are being designed and/or when the value stream team needs to understand the changes required to increase the value for the customers. The outcome of this highly cross-functional and cooperative process is a series of initiatives to create more value for the customer and to bring the product costs into line with the company's need for short and long term financial stability. These improvement initiatives encompass sales and marketing, product design, operations, logistics, and administrative processes within the company.

Value-based Pricing

The first of the five principles of lean thinking is *value to the customer*. The prices of products and services are set according to the value created for the customers. Lean accounting includes methods for calculating the amount of value created by a company's products and services, and form that knowledge to establish prices. This approach is in stark contrast to many traditional companies that calculate their prices using the cost-plus method. The cost-plus method establishes prices by calculating a fully absorbed product cost and then adding on an acceptable profit margin. This cost-plus methods leads to serious errors in pricing because it creates a false linkage between price and cost. The price of a product is unrelated to the cost of manufacturing and supplying that product. The price of a product or services is entirely determined by the amount of value created by the product in the eyes of the customers. Lean accounting methods enable value-based pricing.

11

Full Cost Accounting

Full cost accounting (FCA) generally refers to the process of collecting and presenting information - about environmental, social, and economic costs and benefits/advantages (collectively known as the "triple bottom line") - for each proposed alternative when a decision is necessary. It is a conventional method of cost accounting that traces direct costs and allocates indirect costs. A synonym, true cost accounting (TCA) is also often used. Experts consider both terms problematic as definitions of "true" and "full" are inherently subjective.

Since costs and advantages are usually considered in terms of environmental, economic and social impacts, full or true cost efforts are collectively called the "triple bottom line". A large number of standards now exist in this area including Ecological Footprint, eco-labels, and the United Nations International Council for Local Environmental Initiatives approach to triple bottom line using the Ecobudget metric. The International Organisation for Standardisation (ISO) has several accredited standards useful in FCA or TCA including for greenhouse gases, the ISO 26000 series for corporate social responsibility coming in 2010, and the ISO 19011 standard for audits including all these.

Because of this evolution of terminology in public sector use especially, the term full-cost accounting is now more commonly used in management accounting, e.g. infrastructure management and finance. Use of the terms FCA or TCA usually indicate relatively conservative extensions of current management practices, and incremental improvements to GAAP to deal with waste output or resource input.

These have the advantage of avoiding the more contentious questions of social cost.

Concepts

Full cost accounting embodies several key concepts that distinguish it from standard accounting techniques. The following list highlights the basic tenets of FCA.

1. Accounting for costs rather than outlays
2. Accounting for hidden costs and externalities
3. Accounting for overhead and indirect costs
4. Accounting for past and future outlays
5. Accounting for costs according to lifecycle of the product.

Costs Rather than Outlays

Expenditure of cash to acquire or use a resource. A cost is the cash value of the resource as it is used. For example, an outlay is made when a vehicle is purchased, but the cost of the vehicle is incurred over its active life (e.g., 10 years).

The cost of the vehicle must be allocated over a period of time because every year of its use contributes to the depreciation of the vehicle's value.

Overhead and Indirect Costs

FCA accounts for all overhead and indirect costs, including those that are shared with other public agencies. Overhead and indirect costs might include legal services, administrative support, data processing, billing, and purchasing.

Environmental costs as indirect costs include the full range of costs throughout the life-cycle of a product (Life cycle assessment), some of which even do not show up in the firm's bottom line. It also contains fixed overhead, fixed administration expense etc.

Past and Future Outlays

Past and future cash outlays often do not appear on annual budgets under cash accounting systems. Past (or upfront) costs are initial investments necessary to implement services such as the acquisition of vehicles, equipment, or facilities.

Future (or back-end) outlays are costs incurred to complete operations such as facility closure and postclosure care, equipment retirement, and post-employment health and retirement benefits.

Examples of Full-cost Accounting

Waste Management

For example, the State of Florida uses the term full cost accounting for its solid waste management. In this instance, FCA is a systematic approach for identifying, summing, and reporting the actual costs of solid waste management. It takes into account past and future outlays, overhead (oversight and support services) costs, and operating costs.

Integrated solid waste management systems consist of a variety of municipal solid waste (MSW) activities and paths. Activities are the building blocks of the system, which may include waste collection, operation of transfer stations, transport to waste management facilities, waste processing and disposal, and sale of byproducts. Paths are the directions that MSW follows in the course of integrated solid waste management (i.e., the point of generation through processing and ultimate disposition) and include recycling, composting, waste-to-energy, and landfill disposal.

The cost of some activities is shared between paths. Understanding the costs of MSW activities is often necessary for compiling the costs of the entire solid waste system, and helps municipalities evaluate whether to provide a service itself or contract out for it. However, in considering changes that affect how much MSW ends up being recycled, composted, converted to energy, or landfilled, the analyst should focus the costs of the different paths. Understanding the full costs of each MSW path is an essential first step in discussing whether to shift the flows of MSW one way another.

The Evolution of LCA to ECA

Process LCA

Process LCA is the most popular method, currently, for conducting life-cycle assessment, and is often referred to as the SETAC-EPA method because of the role played by SETAC and EPA in this method's development. The inputs and outputs of multiple stages of a product's life are investigated in turn, and the results are aggregated into single metrics of impact such as eutrophication, toxicity, and greenhouse gas emissions. Three tools exist on the market to assist researchers in conducting process LCA (such as GaBi, Ecoinvent, and Umberto). These tools contain data from previous researchers on the environmental impact of materials and processes that are then strung together by the user to form a system.

Economic Input-Output LCA

Input-Output LCA utilises economic input-output tables and industry-level environmental data to construct a database of environmental impacts per dollar sold by an industry.

The boundary problem of process LCA is solved in this method because the economic input-output table captures the interrelations of all economic sectors; however, aggregated industrial categories limit the specificity of the results. Input–output analysis is a very powerful tool for the upfront screening of corporate carbon footprints, for informing streamlined supply-chain GHG accounting and for setting priorities for more detailed analyses.

Hybrid LCA

Many methods for hybrid life-cycle assessments have been discussed, which aim to combine the infinite boundary of EIO-LCA with the specificity of Process LCA.

Enterprise Carbon Accounting (ECA)

At its core, ECA is essentially a hybrid life-cycle assessment; however, rather than the traditional bottom-up approach of life-cycle assessment, ECA links financial data directly to LCA data to produce a snapshot of the companies' operations. Rather than probing at areas thought to be problematic, ECA quickly identifies problem areas in the supply chain so that rapid action can be taken. This fundamental shift in thinking enables decision makers to rapidly address critical areas within the enterprise and supply chain.

Socialised Supply Chain

Socialised supply chain accounting is the term generally applied to Enterprise Carbon Accounting Solutions that provide a collaborative mechanism for supply chain participants to engage, expose and determine supply chain emissions through the process of shared knowledge. The term "Socialised Supply Chain" was coined by the CEO of Nootrol, Mark Kearns to describe a platform where supply chain participants exposed Process LCA and embedded emissions.

Bad Debt

A bad debt is an amount that is written off by the business as a loss to the business and classified as an expense because the debt owed to the business is unable to be collected, and all reasonable efforts have been exhausted to collect the amount owed. This usually occurs when the debtor has declared bankruptcy or the cost of pursuing further action in an attempt to collect the debt exceeds the debt itself.

The debt is immediately written off by crediting the debtor's account and therefore eliminating any balance remaining in that account. A bad debt represents money lost by a business which is why it is regarded as an expense.

Doubtful Debt

Doubtful debts are those debts which a business or individual is unlikely to be able to collect. The reasons for potential non payment can include disputes over supply, delivery, and conditions of goods or the appearance of financial stresswithin a customer's operations. When such a dispute occurs it is prudent s add this debt or portion thereof to the doubtful debt reserve. This is done to avoid over-stating the assets of the business as trade debtors is reported net of Doubtful debt. When there is no longer any doubt that a debt is uncollectable the debt becomes bad. An example of a debt becoming uncollectable would be:- once final payments have been made from the liquidation of a customer's limited liability company, no further action can be taken.

Doubtful Debt Reserve

Also known as *bad debt reserve*, this is a contra account listed within current asset section of the balance sheet. Doubtful debt reserve will hold a sum of money to allow a reduction in the accounts receivable ledger due to non-collection of debts. This can also be referred to as the allowance for bad debts. Once a doubtful debt becomes uncollectable, the amount will be written off.

US Accounting Practice

Allowance for bad debts are amounts expected to be uncollected, but still with possibilities of being collected (when there is no other possibility for them to be collected, they are considered as uncollectible accounts). For example, if gross receivables are $100,000 and the amount that is expected to remain uncollected is $5,000, net current asset section of balance sheet will be:

Gross accounts receivable	$100,000
Less: Allowance for bad debts	$5,000
Net receivables	$95,000

In financial accounting and finance, bad debt is the portion of receivables that can no longer be collected, typically from accounts receivable or loans. Bad debt in accounting is considered an expense.

There are two methods to account for bad debt:

1. Direct write off method (Non-GAAP) - a receivable which is not considered collectible is charged directly to the income statement.
2. Allowance method (GAAP) - an estimate is made at the end of each fiscal year of the amount of bad debt. This is then accumulated in a provision which is then used to reduce specific receivable accounts as and when necessary.

Because of the matching principle of accounting, revenues and expenses should be recorded in the period in which they are incurred. When a sale is made on account, revenue is recorded along with account receivable. Because there is an inherent risk that clients might default on payment, accounts receivable have to be recorded at net realizable value. The portion of the account receivable that is estimated to be not collectible is set aside in a contra-asset account called allowance for doubtful Accounts. At the end of each accounting cycle, adjusting entries are made to charge uncollectible receivable as expense. The actual amount of uncollectible receivable is written off as an expense from Allowance for doubtful accounts.

Taxability

Some types of bad debts expense, whether business or nonbusiness related, are considered deductible. Section 166 of the Internal Revenue Code provides the qualifications which must be met in order to meet deductibility status.

Criteria for Deduction

To be considered as deductible, debts:

- must be a bona fide debt, and
- worthless within the taxable year.

A debt is defined as a debt which arises from a debtor-creditor relationship based upon a valid and enforceable obligation to pay a determinable sum of money. The debt in question must also be considered worthless. This distinction is further broken down into the level of collectibles. One must determine whether the qualifying debt is completely or partially worthless. A partially worthless status means a portion of the debt may be recovered in future periods. Numerous factors are taken into consideration including the debtor's insolvency status, health conditions, credit standing, etc.

Section 166

Section 166 does limit the amount of deduction allowed. There must be an amount of tax capital, or basis, in question to be recovered. In other words, is there an adjusted basis for determining a gain or loss for the debt in question. An additional factor in applying the criteria is the classification of the debt (nonbusiness or business). A business bad debt is defined as a debt created or acquired in connection with a trade or business of the taxpayer. Whereas, a nonbusiness debt is defined as a debt that is not created or acquired in connection with a trade or business of the taxpayer. The classification is quite significant in terms of the deductibility. A nonbusiness bad debt must be completely worthless in order to be deducted. However, a business bad debt is deductible whether it is partially or completely worthless.

AME Accounting Software

AME Accounting Software is a business accounting software application developed by AME Software Products, Inc. AME Accounting Software includes Payroll, General Ledger, Accounts Receivable, Accounts Payable, 1099 Vendor Management, MICR check printing, and Direct Deposit. The software is mostly used by small and medium size businesses, as well as accounting practices that process payroll and do bookkeeping for other businesses.

The General Ledger software implements a double-entry bookkeeping system, and all modules are able to post entries to General Ledger. The General Ledger software features comprehensive reports, that include Income Statement, Balance Sheet, Cash Flow Statement, Trial Balance Worksheet. The Payroll software calculates federal and state taxes, prints W2, 1099, and payroll checks, and is capable of producing reports for 50 states.

AME Accounting Software was initially developed for DOS. In 1998 AME released payroll software for Windows. The current version, AME 2.0 released in 2004, includes all features that are required for running a small business or an accounting practice. The user interface is simple and intuitively understandable.

As noted in 2008 June/July issue of CPA Technology Advisor Magazine: "AME offers a good payroll module and core financial functions that are sufficient for smaller entities, especially for businesses with limited technical expertise. It is attractively priced and covers the basic needs of a small company." AME stands for Accounting Made Easy.

California Board of Accountancy

The California Board of Accountancy (CBA), created by statute in 1901, is a semi-autonomous State of California agency under the California Department of Consumer Affairs whose purpose is to protect consumers by ensuring only qualified licensees practice public accountancy in accordance with established professional standards in California.

The CBA currently regulates over 5,000 firms and nearly 81,000 Certified Public Accountant (CPA) licensees, the largest group of licensed accounting professionals in the nation. The agency is unique in California in its authority to license and discipline not only individuals but also firms including partnerships and corporations. Its mandate is to regulate the accounting profession for the protection of the public by establishing and maintaining standards of qualification and conduct within the profession. It fulfills this mandate primarily through its authority to license.

History

The California Board of Accountancy (CBA) was established in 1901 in San Francisco. All the records were destroyed in the 1906 San Francisco earthquake and fire, including all the documents of the first 65 licensees. The secretary-treasurer of the CBA was able to reconstruct the records by corresponding with each of the licensees.

In 1929, the CBA became part of the Department of Professional and Vocational Standards. In 1971 it was moved to the California Department of Consumer Affairs and subsequently moved to Sacramento.

Functions

The CBA protects California consumers by performing several functions. It starts by ensuring candidates are qualified to take the Uniform Certified Public Accountant Examination (CPA Exam). Once a candidate has passed the CPA Exam, completed any additional educational requirements, and fulfilled certain experience requirements, the CBA will issue a CPA license. The CBA renews that license every two years provided the licensee has met specified continuing educational requirements. The CBA also registers CPA partnerships and corporations. The CBA ensures licensee compliance with the law through its Enforcement Division. It receives and investigates complaints and takes enforcement action against licensees for violation of CBA statutes and regulations.

The above functions are carried out by various units and divisions within the CBA.

- The Examination Unit ensures that only candidates who meet certain qualifications are able to take the Uniform CPA Examination.
- The Initial Licensing Unit ensures that only those who have passed the Uniform CPA Examination and meet the appropriate experience requirements are issued licenses to practice public accountancy in California.
- The Renewal and Continuing Competency Unit ensures that only licensees who have met specific continuing education requirements are allowed to continue practicing public accountancy in California.
- The Practice Privilege Unit ensures that the CBA is aware of out-of-state licensees who are practicing public accountancy in California.
- The Enforcement Division ensures that practicing licensees in California are held to the highest standards, both professional and ethical.

Peer Review

On January 1, 2010, a new law, AB 138 (Chapter 312 of 2009), took effect in California requiring all accounting firms providing accounting and auditing services to undergo a mandatory peer review. A peer review is a study of a firm's accounting and auditing work, performed by an unaffiliated CPA following professional standards. Tax practice is not required to be monitored by peer review. The CBA's peer review program is designed to equip firms to deliver high quality accounting and auditing services to consumers and assist in designing quality control systems to ensure that work products meet professional standards; provide firms an opportunity to learn new or better ways to improve services; and give consumers an extra measure of assurance by knowing the CPA firm they hire has successfully completed a peer review and meets the profession's standards. Firms that fail their peer review are required to report that fact to the CBA.

Board

The 15 member board is composed of seven CPA licensees and eight public members. The Governor appoints four of the public members and all seven of the licensees. The Senate Rules Committee and the Speaker of the Assembly each appoint two public members.

In appointing the seven licensees, the Governor must appoint at least two licensee members who represent small accounting firms. Each member of the CBA is appointed to a four year term and may only serve two consecutive terms.

The CBA is currently made up of the following membership:

- Sarah (Sally) Anderson, CPA, President
- Marshal Oldman, Esq., Vice President
- Leslie J. LaManna, CPA, Secretary/Treasurer
- Diana L. Bell
- Alicia Berhow
- Michelle R. Brough, Esq.
- Donald A. Driftmier, CPA
- Herschel T. Elkins, Esq.
- Laurence (Larry) Kaplan
- Louise Kirkbride
- Kitak (K.T.) Leung, CPA
- Manuel Ramirez, CPA
- Michael M. Savoy, CPA
- David L. Swartz, CPA
- Lenora Taylor, Esq.

The CBA appointed Patti Bowers as its Executive Officer in October 2008.

Comprehensive Annual Financial Report

A Comprehensive Annual Financial Report (CAFR) is a set of government financial statements comprising the financial report of a state, municipal or other governmental entity that complies with the accounting requirements—generally accepted accounting principles (GAAP)—promulgated by the Financial Accounting Standards Board (FASB).

A CAFR is "compiled" by a state, municipal or other governmental accounting staff and "audited" by an external American Institute of Certified Public Accountants (AICPA) certified accounting firm utilising FASB requirements. It is composed of three sections: Introductory, Financial and Statistical. It combines the financial information of fund accounting and Enterprise Authorities accounting.

History

The National Committee on Municipal Accounting (NCMA) was formed in 1934 by the Government Financial Officers Association to create accounting standards. As a result of its work, the 'Principles of Municipal Accounting', the predecessor to the CAFR, was created. The successor to the NCMA, the National Council on Governmental Accounting (NCGA), issued 'Governmental Accounting, Auditing and Financial Reporting', which is the basis of the format for the current standard.

This document, known as the "Blue Book", and its successors documented the CAFR accounting structure and provided standardisation and example documents. By 1946, the various levels of government—federal, state, local and municipal—each began producing a CAFR to catalog an accurate picture of institutional funds, enterprise or financial holdings, assets and total investment incomes for those government and nongovernmental entities using the report. This measure is above and beyond the budget process and replaced what was regularly an "off-the-books" practice called the "general fixed-asset account group". General Purpose government "budget" reports did not reflect accounting of this financial data, only reporting on the budget or "rainy day" funds or pension fund investments. By the 1970s, the CAFR became the nationwide paradigm for local government accounting.

The resulting CAFR is presented to the GFOA, which conducts each year a review of applicant local government CAFRs and upon review awards their Certificate of Achievement Award for Excellence in Financial Reporting to those local governments that are in compliance with their CAFR accounting standards of preparation. Presently, accounting principles for government entities are set by transmittal letters issued to local governments by the GASB.

Differences between General Budgets and CAFR

The primary difference between a budget and a CAFR is that where the budget is a plan for the a fiscal period (often year) primarily showing where tax income is to be allocated, the CAFR contains the results of the period (year) with previous years accumulations. A CAFR shows the total of all financial accounting that a general purpose budget reports does not. The CAFR contains a section that provides a comparison of period budget and actual. Additionally, the CAFR gives a detailed showing of investment accounts by category reflecting balances over previous years.

A Government budget document is a blueprint for a "specific grouping" of government agencies' spending over the course of an annual financial period. General Purpose Budgets contain both the spending categories of specified units of government, such as school districts, social services, transportation, police, fire, and park services; along with estimates of revenues expected to occur during the year, such as investment return; overrides of money from the previous year, and tax payments. They are usually more limited to the expected costs of running the aforementioned government operations through tax income as opposed to describing the status of any government fixed assets and investment wealth.

A CAFR is a report of the complete overall financial results of both those "specific groupings" of government agencies that appear in the current fiscal year General Purpose Budget and all other agencies and departments. These can be autonomous, enterprise (for example government or city owned golf courses), recycling, water, sewer, and financial management - often these agencies were created with the inception of that local, state or government.

The CAFR provides information about all of these other government agencies that may have their own budgets and separate investment accounts but their financial holdings are *not* combined with the general purpose budget that the same government presents to the public. The CAFR, or as it is called in CANADA CanFR can be used along with a budget document to compare the organisations total financial standing to the annual general purpose budget. The CAFR is the complete showing of the financial investment and income records from all sources, that reflects what has developed over decades whereas a budget report is an inferior document to the CAFR being that it is primarily focused on what revenue is expected to be brought in and spent for just the year.

In contrast with the rules applying to governments, publicly traded companies such as IBM or Microsoft who are required by the U.S. Securities and Exchange Commission, SEC, to send what is called their Annual Financial Report (AFR) to every shareholder each year. Publicly funded non-profits(or Not-for-profit) quasi-government private associations have claimed that they are not subject to the public records laws & their reports are not subject to open records acts like the Kentucky Association of Cities (KACO for Counties). However, news stories covering the Kentucky Association of Counties whose spending came under scrutiny by the Lexington Herald-Leader exposed these types of entities as well as their surpluses and claimed spending excesses using money acquired from government fees for products like municipal insurance at premium rates which build surpluses beyond the needs of the entity.

Recent Developments

From at least 1998, a former Commodities Trading Adviser (CTA) who had been a active CTA for about fourteen years, Walter Bubien AKA Burien, and a federal auditor of thirty years, Gerald Klatt, have claimed upon showings seen and from referencing within the now 184,000 local government CAFRs, AFRs and other Federal audit reports, including Audit of the IRS, US Treasury Audit of Bank derivative holdings (tables 1, 2, 3 on pages 22, 23, 24 show that the top three banks were trading and holding over 150 trillion dollars worth of derivatives, apparently in primarily government accounts, US Treasury Audit of Bank Mortgage holdings, Federal Consolidated Financial Statements, CAFR for the Federal Reserve and List of State CAFRs.

While some have called these the "2nd set of books", Burien refers to the CAFR as "the book" with the budget being a section contained therein. Their assessments of government assets, holdings and investment supporting globalism, ownership by government investment "for profit" and government's international investments profits, significantly enhanced with the use of the now 600 trillion dollar international derivatives markets with government investments strategically placed for profit from free trade, war, commodity market, stock market, International investment movement and extreme price volatility is created by these massive moves by "institutional government funds" speculators scattered around the globe manipulating the market either deliberately or by volume.

Since 1998, with the CAFR being brought to the attention of the public by the efforts of Walter Burien and Gerald Klatt, the Government Accounting Standards Board (GASB), starting making significant reporting standards changes using transmittal letters.

Burien and Klatt claimed that such changes were calculated steps to hide from the general public's view massive domestic and international wealth, investment assets and authority "enterprise funds", all of which could be seen more visibly outlined in the combined financial columns of 1999 and previous CAFRs, which required a showing of gross totals. The modifications transitioned the accounting from a primary showing of gross totals to that of net totals. Burien and Klatt claim that because these changes are being made without inclusion in the formal standard, there has been virtually no media attention on these issues.

While a budget may indicate that a specific government or agency has financial trouble and debt as a result of excess spending within the select grouping of "general fund" accounts, the CAFR may indicate that overall the same government entity has many facets possessing large holdings and income considerably greater than what is shown in a budget report or the "general fund" alone.

- In 1994, Orange County California government lost about $1.5 Billion on investments in the derivatives market and claimed they needed to declare bankruptcy per their general purpose budget while holding approximately 11.3 billion in profitable holdings in their investment portfolios.
- The University of Kentucky's holdings of 85% of CHA Health insurance stock was documented in 2005 in the Lexington Herald Leader newspaper when CHA was sold to a rival firm as part of the UK president's effort to raise a billion dollars to fund becoming a "top 20" research university an ongoing effort.
- In 2010, Oregon Rep. Bruce Hanna during general session when the floor was discussing what to do about the state's 3.5 billion dollar budget shortfall (fire employees, cut back on services, close state parks), stood up with the cover page from the state CAFR in hand and stated that in less than a few minutes he found $3.5B to satisfy the state shortfall, there being no shortfall when comparing the state CAFR and the previous "selective" presentation of the State general purpose.

12

Practice of Law and Accountancy

In its most general sense, the practice of law involves giving legal advice to clients, drafting legal documents for clients, and representing clients in legal negotiations and court proceedings such as lawsuits, and is applied to the professional services of a lawyer or attorney at law, barrister, solicitor, or civil law notary. However, there is a substantial amount of overlap between the practice of law and various other professions where clients are represented by agents. These professions include real estate, banking, accounting, and insurance. Moreover, a growing number of legal document assistants (LDAs) are offering services which have traditionally been offered only by lawyers and their employee paralegals. Many documents may now be created by computer-assisted drafting libraries, where the clients are asked a series of questions posed by the software in order to construct the legal documents.

United States

In the United States, the practice of law is conditioned upon admission to practice of law, and specifically admission to the bar of a particular state or other territorial jurisdiction. The American Bar Association and the American Law Institute are among the organisations that are concerned with the interests of lawyers as a profession and the promulgation of uniform standards of professionalism and ethics, but regulation of the practice of law is left to the individual states, and their definitions vary.

Unauthorised Practice of Law

Conversely, the definition of "unauthorised practice of law" is variable, and is often conclusory and tautological, *i.e.*, it is the doing of a lawyer's or counsellor's work by a non-lawyer for money.There is some agreement that appearing in a legally-constituted court in a legal proceeding to represent clients (particularly for a fee) is considered to be unauthorised practice of law. But other variations are subject to interpretation and conflicting regulation, particularly as to the scope and breadth of the prohibition. *Black's Law Dictionary* succinctly defines "unauthorised practice of law. The practice of law by a person, typically a nonlawyer, who has not been licensed or admitted to practice law in a given jurisdiction. — Abbr. UPL."

The Restatement of the Law notes:

> *"The definitions and tests employed by courts to delineate unauthorised practice by non-lawyers have been vague or conclusory, while jurisdictions have differed significantly in describing what constitutes unauthorised practice in particular areas. The "COMMERCIAL" practice of law, pleading for hire, should not be confused with the common law right to practice law. The former being fully subject to the regulation of law as a commercial endeavour, and the later being the exercise of a common right beyond legislation. Sims v. Aherns, 271 SW 720 (1925) "The practice of law is an occupation of common right." "In the federal courts, the right of self-representation has been protected by statute since the beginnings of our Nation. Section 35 of the Judiciary Act of 1789, 1 Stat. 73, 92, enacted by the First Congress and signed by President Washington one day before the Sixth Amendment [422 U.S. 806, 813] was proposed, provided that "in all the courts of the United States, the parties may plead and manage their own causes personally or by the assistance of... counsel...." The right is currently codified in 28 U.S.C. 1654." "The colonists brought with them an appreciation of the virtues of self-reliance and a traditional distrust of lawyers. When the Colonies were first settled, "the lawyer was synonymous with the cringing Attorneys-General and Solicitors-General of the Crown and the arbitrary Justices of the King's Court, all bent on the conviction of those who opposed the King's prerogatives, and twisting the law to secure convictions." This prejudice gained strength in the Colonies where "distrust of lawyers became an institution." Several Colonies prohibited pleading for*

hire in the 17th century. The prejudice persisted into the 18th century as "the lower classes came to identify lawyers with the upper class." The years of Revolution and Confederation saw an upsurge of antilawyer sentiment, a "sudden revival, after the War of the Revolution, of the old dislike and distrust of lawyers as a class." In the heat of these sentiments the Constitution was forged." FARETTA v. CALIFORNIA, 422 U.S. 806 (1975) Even for our founders this extreme dislike of injustice was not new for it had always been so when any system was controlled and manipulated by any group. To remove a mans life, liberty or Happiness and call it law was very clearly detailed as being out of bounds. Thus was the Declaration of Law, (Independence), penned to forever put those issues beyond the reach of the government without Due Process of law. Under the common law, the practice of law is simply the full and equal protection of law coupled with securing all of the rights of the petitioner/defendant, by whomever takes up that task, to the exclusion of all others, even government!

"Certain activities, such as the representation of another person in litigation, are generally proscribed. Even in that area, many jurisdictions recognise exceptions for such matters as small-claims and landlord-tenant tribunals and certain proceedings in administrative agencies. Moreover, many jurisdictions have authorised law students and others not locally admitted to represent indigent persons or others as part of clinical legal education programs...."

The rest of the article goes on to describe out-of-court activities, particularly drafting of documents and giving advice, and whether that is considered to be unauthorised practice of law, which is more controversial.

"Unauthorised practice of law" (UPL) is an act sometimes prohibited by statute, regulation, or court rules.

The practice of law was not formally regulated in Arizona for a time. However, the Arizona Supreme Court found independent inherent authority to regulate the practice of law, *In re Creasy*, 198 Ariz. 539 (2000). See generally Jonathan Rose, "Unauthorised Practice of Law in Arizona: A Legal and Political Problem That Won't Go Away", 34 Ariz. St. L.J. 585. Arizona's statute criminalising unauthorised practice of law was allowed to lapse from a sunset law in 1985. Rose suggests that legislative proposals to recriminalise the unauthorised practice of law have heretofore failed because of anti-lawyer sentiment in Arizona politics. *Id.* at 593.

Moreover, Rose asserts that resentment lingers from an unpopular interpretation of the old statute in *State Bar v. Arizona Land Title & Trust Co.*, 90 Ariz. 76 (1961). This ruling sanctioned a title and realty company engaged in drafting contracts. Rose says, "Throughout the country, various jurisdictions have developed numerous tests for defining the practice of law. But none is broader nor more all-encompassing than that articulated in *Arizona Title.*" Rose at 588. For example, Texas law generally prohibits a person who is not an attorney from representing a client in a personal injury or property damage matter, and punishes a violation as a misdemeanor. Some states also criminalise the separate behaviour of falsely claiming to be lawyer (in Texas, for example, this is a felony).

Despite the state's interest in protecting the public and so-called "learned professions" from having unschooled persons practicing them, and the state's insistence on enforcing a monopoly, the existence of laws governing (or defining) "unauthorised practice of Law" does not, *ipso facto* mean that they will be enforced.

The American Bar Association proposed model rules regarding the unauthorised practice of law, which Judge Richard Posner characterised as an attempt to perpetuate a monopoly to the disadvantage of consumers. The judge observed that the legal profession is "a cartel of providers of services relating to society's laws" which cartel's focus is to restrict entry. "Modern economists call it 'rent seeking', but throughout recorded history, skilled crafts and professions have tried to raise their members' incomes by using the power of the state to limit entry." Criminal laws and enforcement of "Unauthorised Practice of Law (UPL)" statutes is the organised bar's preferred method. Thus, New Jersey has a law which makes it a "disorderly persons offence" to knowingly to engage in the unauthorised practice of law, and a "crime in the fourth degree" to commit UPL if one (a) creates a false impression that one is a lawyer; (b) derives a benefit from UPL, or (c) causes an injury by UPL.

Some states have defined the "practice of law" to include those who appear as a representative in arbitration or act as arbitrators in disputes. For example, there is a growing conflict between the multijurisdictional practice of law in arbitration proceedings in the financial service industry and state regulation of lawyers. With a few exceptions, the general rule is that an appearance at an arbitration does not constitute the practice of law.

Attorney Participation

In the United States, the rules of professional conduct generally prohibit an attorney from assisting a non-attorney from engaging in the unauthorised practice of law. An attorney therefore may not partner with or split fees with a non-attorney in the performance of any sort of legal work. Furthermore, an attorney may not employ a disbarred or suspended attorney in a legal practice where former clients of the disbarred or suspended attorney will be represented.

Walsh College of Accountancy and Business Administration

Walsh College of Accountancy and Business Administration is a private, non-profit business college based in Troy, Michigan, "offering a broad range of business and related technology degree programs, the college grants degrees at the bachelor's, master's, and doctoral levels that are responsive to student, employer, and community needs."

Founded in 1922, Walsh College offers upper-division undergraduate and graduate business and technology degrees and certificate programs at locations in Troy, Novi, Harper Woods, Clinton Township, and Port Huron, as well as online. "Walsh College is accredited by The Higher Learning Commission of the North Central Association of Colleges and Schools, the International Assembly for Collegiate Business Education (IACBE), and The Accreditation Council for Business Schools and Programs (ACBSP)."

History

The College began with the founding of the Walsh Institute of Accountancy and the introduction of the Pace Accounting Method, at the time an innovative way of teaching accounting. Mervyn B. Walsh, a certified public accountant, purchased a Pace & Pace franchise to offer the Pace Accounting Method exclusively in Detroit. He founded the Walsh Institute of Accountancy on July 7, 1922, and on September 18 of that year, 23 students were enrolled in the first Institute courses.

When Mervyn Walsh retired in 1965, the State of Michigan had adopted a new bachelor's degree requirement for candidates to sit for the Uniform Certified Public Accountant (CPA) Examination.

At this time, Michigan's community college system was developing and a pivotal decision was made to build upon, rather than compete with, the community colleges by becoming an upper-division college. On December 31, 1968, Walsh Institute became an upper-division college offering a business education to juniors and seniors who had finished two years of college.

The new Walsh College of Accountancy and Business Administration forged partnerships with Oakland and Macomb community colleges and in 1970 broke ground for a 10,000 square foot building in the Michigan City of Troy, near both colleges. Community college partnerships continued to flourish over the next two decades, and business leaders were invited to teach and develop curriculum.

The College offered its first bachelor degrees, a Bachelor of Accountancy and Bachelor of Business Administration, in 1970. The first graduate degree, the Master of Science in Taxation, was offered in 1974. The following year, the North Central Association of Colleges and Schools (NCA) accredited Walsh College. Over the next several years, Walsh introduced Master of Science degrees in Professional Accountancy (1980), Finance (1986), and Management (1989). During the 1990s, the College continued to enlarge its facilities, offer classes at other locations in metropolitan Detroit, and introduce new degrees and online technology. The Master of Science in Information Management and Communication (MSIMC) degree was introduced in 1996. In 1998, a western campus was built and opened in Novi, Michigan, and the Master of Business Administration (MBA) degree was introduced. The first online courses were offered in 1998.

In 2001, the NCA granted Walsh approval to offer full online degree programs and provided the College with a full ten-year extension on its accreditation. The first fully online degree, the Master of Science in Information Assurance, was offered in 2005. Walsh information assurance curriculum maps to industry standards and National Security Agency and the Department of Homeland Security specifications. Since 2003, these agencies have renewed the College's designation as a U.S. Centre of Academic Excellence for Information Assurance Education.

In 2006, the NCA gave the College approval to offer its first doctoral degree, the Doctor of Management (DM) in Executive Leadership. In the fall of 2007, the first student cohort entered the program.

The College also received national recognition in April 2010 for a major grant to promote entrepreneurship among students and alumni. The Blackstone Charitable Foundation of New York announced that it had selected Walsh College and Detroit's Wayne State University to share a $2 million grant to initiate Blackstone LaunchPad.

Facts

Walsh College is:

- Southeast Michigan's only freestanding, upper-division all-business college.
- One of Michigan's largest graduate business schools.
- A provider of high-quality programs in accounting, finance, information technology and assurance, management and leadership, marketing, and taxation.
- One of the area's first colleges to cater primarily to working adults. More than 90 percent of Walsh on-ground courses are offered in the evenings and on weekends.
- Attended by undergraduate students whose average age is 30 and by graduate students whose average age is 34.
- One of the first institutions to establish transfer articulation agreements with area community colleges.
- Eighty-seven percent of Walsh undergraduates transfer from a community college, completing a bachelor's degree in an efficient and cost-effective way. Walsh requires a minimum of 60 semester credit hours (30 of which must be in liberal arts) from all entering undergraduate students.
- Meeting market demand by offering approximately 42 percent of all course credit hours online.
- Accredited by the Accreditation Council for Business Schools and Programs (ACBSP) and the International Assembly for Collegiate Business Education (IACBE).
- Investing its intellectual capital back into the local community: 84 percent of its 22,000 alumni work or own businesses in southeast Michigan.
- Reaching out to Michigan's workers in transition by offering free "Take Charge" skill-building workshops. Since January 2009, more than 2,000 people attended 95 free workshops and classes.
- Well-respected by employers. During the 2009-10 academic year, 900 companies recruited at Walsh College. Students and

alumni could access more than 1,800 job opportunities posted through Career Services.

- Committed to green design and building practices. In June 2010, the U.S. Green Building Council certified the Troy campus Jeffery W. Barry Centre to the LEED Gold Level. The building is named for the late Jeffery W. Barry, the third president of Walsh College (1970-1991).
- Capturing several advertising industry awards for its "Live. Breathe. Business." campaign.
- Named a Crain's Detroit Business "Cool Place to Work" for each of the years the award was given.
- Using Facebook, LinkedIn, and Twitter to connect with students and its community as part of its mission to model the global business environment.

Campus Locations

The college currently has 2 main campuses and offers classes at three other university centre locations, plus online.. The main campus is located in Troy, MI. This campus has undergone an expansion which was open for the Winter 2008 semester. The second campus is located in Novi, MI. Classes are also offered in Clinton Township, Michigan at the University Centre at Macomb Community College, in Harper Woods, Michigan at the University Square location of Wayne County Community College District, and in Port Huron at the University Centre at St. Clair County Community College.

Walsh College is accredited by The Higher Learning Commission of the North Central Association of Colleges and Schools, the International Assembly for Collegiate Business Education (IACBE), and The Accreditation Council for Business Schools and Programs.

Academic Profile

Average Class Size	21
Full-time Faculty	21
Adjunct Faculty Teaching Each Semester	113 Average
52 week semesters (not quarters)	4
Undergraduate Degrees	3
Graduate Degrees	9 (includes doctoral degree)
For-Credit Certificate Programs	11
Non-Credit Certificate Programs	1

Undergraduate Degrees

- Bachelor of Accountancy (B. Acct.)
- Bachelor of Business Administration (B.B.A.)
- Bachelor of Science in Business Information Systems (BSBIS)

Graduate Degrees

- Master of Science in Taxation (MST)
- Master of Science in Accountancy (MAC)
- Master of Science in Finance (MSF)
- Master of Business Administration (MBA)
- Master of Science in Information Systems (MSIS)
- Master of Science in Information Assurance (MSIA)
- Doctor of Management (DM) in Executive Leadership
- Dual Master of Business Administration/Master of Science in Finance (Dual MBA/MSF)
- Master of Management (MM).

Accounting Networks and Associations

Accounting networks and associations are professional services networks whose principal purpose is to provide members resources to assist the clients around the world.

The networks and associations operate independently of the independent members. The largest accounting networks are known as the Big Four (audit firms). There are currently 30 recognised networks and associations.

History of Accounting Networks and Associations

Foundations

Accounting networks were created to meet a specific need. "The accounting profession in the U.S. was built upon a state-established monopoly for audits of financial statements."Accounting networks arose out of the necessity for public American companies to have audited financial statements for the Securities Exchange Commission (SEC). For over 70 years, the SEC has continually sought for greater coordination and consistent quality in audits everywhere in the world. Networks were the logical model to address these requirements. They expanded outside of the United States since financial results had to be audited wherever a company conducted business. In the US, the

Public Company Accounting Oversight Board's (PCAOB) regulations provide for inspection of non-United States firms. Without a network with common standards and internal means of communications, conducting the required audits would not be possible.

There were other profession-based factors which favoured the growth of accounting networks. As a result of competition for the audit work, consolidation was inevitable. These include the fact that a network can establish a brand. A brand establishes the credibility of the network and allows the individual members to charge more. Creating a brand is very difficult when all of the members of a network are providing essentially the same services.

Being a network member establishes that the firm is part of a large group. Additionally, the larger the firm, the more likely it will be invited to render auditing engagements. A large organised network allows for spreading the costs to price competitively. Ultimately, size is the only real means of differentiation that is readily available on accounting firms to assure clients that they can do international work.

Networks also reflect the clients' needs for seamless worldwide services because they are more efficient and cost-effective., From the perspective of the accounting firm, a global regulated organisation with consistently applied standards significantly reduced the risk. However, increasing the size of the networks can enhance legal liability risks and quality control issues that have not been resolved.

With these factors in play, some networks continued to grow; others remained in a stasis position. Individual members of networks began to offer other services related to accounting. These services included forensic accounting, business appraisals, employee benefits planning, strategic planning, and almost anything associated with financial parts of the client's business. The network's structure easily accommodated these services and their geographical expansion.

As the Big 8 consolidated to become Big 6, the Big 5 and then the Big 4, new networks naturally developed to emulate them. BDO and Grant Thornton were the earliest followers. Networks were then developed to serve mid-market companies and private businesses. New networks also sprang up as an extension of a single accounting firm in the same way the Big 8 were formed. New structures were created to further extend the networks.

The largest accounting networks adopted trade names that each member used. The names of the original firms that became part of the networks were lost and replaced with trade names. For example,

Price Waterhouse Coopers became PWC. The perception was created that these networks were more than networks, but single entities rather than completely independent firms. This was never the case. The result was that the Big 8 concept was established which separated the eight firms from all other accounting firms.

Another factor in the development of networks in accounting was the American Institute of Certified Public Accountants(AICPA)'s prohibition of advertising. While the largest firms indirectly advertised their services, the small firms complied with the rules and believed advertising to be unprofessional. Additionally, midsize firms were de facto restricted from advertising simply because of limited budgets. They could not create a brand that was able to compete with the one established by the Big 8. The advertising restriction was lifted in the 1970s by the Federal Trade Commission.

Multidisciplinary Expansion

In the 1990s, the large accounting firms reached another ceiling in the services they made available to their clients. Having reached their natural limit on growth with more than 90% of auditing for public companies, the Big 6 branched out to become multidisciplinary in legal, technology, and employment services. Since the essential infrastructure was in place, it was thought to be relatively simple to incorporate other services into the existing network. As a network, it was natural to create independent entities in these other professions which themselves could be part of the network. The method and structures varied from firm to firm. When the Big 6 began its expansion to the legal profession, it was met with fierce opposition from law firms and bar associations. Commissions, panels and committees were established by legal and accounting firms to argue their positions. Government agencies were enlisted. For more than five (5) years the debate escalated. This movement ended abruptly with the fall of Arthur Anderson as a result of its association with Enron. Sarbanes Oxley followed, which effectively ended this trend.

Today there are 44 accounting networks whose members' cumulative revenues range from $25 million to $26.2 billion. The top 30 networks have cumulative revenues of $142 billion dollars. The primary sources of revenue are from audit, tax and financial consultancy services.

Vicarious Liability

Accounting networks are now facing a new challenge that go to the heart of the image that the firms wish to project to clients. The perception has been that the Big 4, Grant Thornton and BDO are single entities that perform services around the world for clients of this single entity. As a result of court cases this has introduced significant vicarious liability issues requiring the networks to distance themselves from the perception of being a single entity. The Parmalat case is the best illustration of the issues. While the firms have lost a number of cases, the facts and circumstance, or procedural elements have reduced their actual liability.

Networks versus Associations

The vicarious liability issues carry over into operations. Regulations in the EU have been imposed that require the "networks" to define whether they are "associations" of independent firm or are more integrated networks operationally and financially. Additional standards have been passed by IFAC, an independent associations of accountants, on distinguishing networks from associations. The objectives of each are to provide the clients a level of understanding about the degree of integration with each other. A number accounting firms have also organised a "networks of networks" called the Forum of Firms under the auspices of IFAC to protect and advance their interests.

Conflicts of Interest

Self-definition as a network or associations may determine if there is a conflict of interest. If the group is perceived as a network, it may be foreclosed from representation of clients because they cannot represent a competitor. Association members would not be foreclosed from representation because the firms are perceived as independent by clients.

Big 4 Dominance of Public Company Audits

Accounting scandals have again focused on the fact that the Big 4 has a near monopoly on audits of public companies. Networks are demanding regulations on auditing to require that auditors rotate and include the smaller networks in this rotation. The demands also request that mid-market firms be able to participate to break up the monopoly of the Big 4.

School of Accountancy

The School of Accountancy (SOA) at Brigham Young University is a department within the Marriott School of Management. The school offers one bachelor's degree and one master's degree.

Degrees and Programs

The School of Accountancy offers two degrees. The Bachelor of Science in Accountancy requires that students complete a core curriculum during their junior year that comprises 24 credit hours of accounting classes over the course of the fall and winter semesters. Students work in a team of five or six for the entire year and stay in the classroom for a three hour block while professors rotate in and out.

The Master of Accountancy (MAcc) graduate degree has two emphases, a tax emphasis or a professional (auditing) emphasis. Within either emphasis, students can apply to enter the Ph.D. Prep Track, which focuses on preparing students to apply for and enter a Ph.D. program upon graduating from BYU.

Many undegraduate students at the SOA opt in to a dual-degree BSAcc/MAcc, which takes five years to complete.

Conferences and Endeavours

Since 2004, the SOA has hosted an annual Accounting Research Symposium. The purpose of the symposium is "to unite BYU alumni and friends in our efforts to foster relevant and consequential accounting research." One of the explicit purposes of the symposium is to bring back students who have graduated from the Ph.D. Prep Track to network and receive feedback on research ideas.

Under the direction of Norm Nemrow and with the assistance of BYU's Centre for Instructional Design, the SOA has also developed the "Value-Added Teaching Model", a CD-based program used to teach accounting that employs vector-based technology from Macromedia Flash. The reduction in lectures due to the CD supplement has proven effective in doubling student's interest in accounting as a major, and over 90 percent of students prefer the CD based approach over a traditional textbook/lecture approach.

BYU accounting faculty members and students, in conjunction with a Utah State University faculty member, developed a new set of accounting research rankings. The rankings are based on the authors' research and separately rank accounting institutions and accounting Ph.D. programs. The rankings build on prior research by (1) breaking accounting rankings into separate topical area and methodological rankings, (2) giving institutions research credit only for publications of faculty currently employed at the institution, and (3) providing rankings for three time windows.

Faculty

- W. Steve Albrecht served as President of the American Accounting Association (1997–1998) and as the first president of the Association of Certified Fraud Examiners.,
- Douglas F. Prawitt served as a Board member on the Auditing Standards Board (2006–2008)
- Lee H. Radebaugh served as Editor of Journal of International Accounting Research (2004–2007) and as president of the World Trade Association of Utah (1994–1995).
- Scott L. Summers served as president of the Information Systems Section of the American Accounting Association (2006–2007)
- Dave N. Stewart served as president of the American Taxation Association (2003–2004)
- Kevin D. Stocks served as president of the Federation of Schools of Accountancy (2000).

Alumni

The School of Accountancy has been highly successful at placing students upon graduating. In 2007, 97% of MAcc students had a job at the time of graduation and 100% of the MAcc students had a job within 3 months after graduation.In 2007, 89% of undergraduates had a job at the time of graduation and 97% had a job within 3 months after graduation. All four of the Big Four accounting firms as well as many national and regional firms recruit graduates. The Ph.D. Prep Track has been successful in placing into doctoral programs 100 percent of its graduates who have submitted applications. Ph.D. Prep Track alumni are invited back to BYU to participate in the School of Accountancy's annual *Accounting Research Symposium*.

BYU alumni include many corporate executives, partners in CPA firms, and entrepreneurs.

Theory of Constraints

The theory of constraints (TOC) adopts the common idiom "A chain is no stronger than its weakest link" as a new management paradigm. This means that processes, organisations, etc., are vulnerable because the weakest person or part can always damage or break them or at least adversely affect the outcome.

The analytic approach with TOC comes from the contention that any manageable system is limited in achieving more of its goals by a very small number of constraints, and that there is always at least one constraint. Hence the TOC process seeks to identify the constraint and restructure the rest of the organisation around it, through the use of five focusing steps.

Key Assumption

The underlying premise of theory of constraints is that organisations can be measured and controlled by variations on three measures: throughput, operational expense, and inventory. Throughput is the rate at which the system generates money through sales. Inventory is all the money that the system has invested in purchasing things which it intends to sell. Operational expense is all the money the system spends in order to turn inventory into throughput.

The goal itself is to make money. All other benefits are derived, in one way or another, from that single primary goal.

The Five Focusing Steps

Theory of constraints is based on the premise that the rate of goal achievement is limited by at least one constraining process. Only by increasing flow through the constraint can overall throughput be increased.

Assuming the goal of the organisation has been articulated (e.g., "Make money now and in the future") the steps are:

1. Identify the constraint (the resource or policy that prevents the organisation from obtaining more of the goal)
2. Decide how to exploit the constraint (get the most capacity out of the constrained process)
3. Subordinate all other processes to above decision (align the whole system or organisation to support the decision made above)
4. Elevate the constraint (make other major changes needed to break the constraint)
5. If, as a result of these steps, the constraint has moved, return to Step 1. Don't let inertia become the constraint.

The five focusing steps aim to ensure ongoing improvement efforts are centred around the organisation's constraints. In the TOC literature, this is referred to as the *process of ongoing improvement* (POOGI).

These focusing steps are the key steps to developing the specific applications mentioned below.

Constraints

A constraint is anything that prevents the system from achieving more of its goal. There are many ways that constraints can show up, but a core principle within TOC is that there are not tens or hundreds of constraints. There is at least one and at most a few in any given system. Constraints can be internal or external to the system. An internal constraint is in evidence when the market demands more from the system than it can deliver. If this is the case, then the focus of the organisation should be on discovering that constraint and following the five focusing steps to open it up (and potentially remove it). An external constraint exists when the system can produce more than the market will bear. If this is the case, then the organisation should focus on mechanisms to create more demand for its products or services.

Types of (internal) constraints:

- Equipment: The way equipment is currently used limits the ability of the system to produce more salable goods/services.
- People: Lack of skilled people limits the system. Mental models held by people can cause behaviour that becomes a constraint.
- Policy: A written or unwritten policy prevents the system from making more.

The concept of the constraint in Theory of Constraints differs from the constraint that shows up in mathematical optimisation. In TOC, the constraint is used as a focusing mechanism for management of the system. In optimisation, the constraint is written into the mathematical expressions to limit the scope of the solution (X can be no greater than 5).

Please note: organisations have many problems with equipment, people, policies, etc. (A breakdown is just that – a breakdown – and is not a constraint in the true sense of the TOC concept) The constraint is the thing that is preventing the organisation from getting more throughput (typically, revenue through sales).

Buffers

Buffers are used throughout the theory of constraints. They often result as part of the exploit and subordinate steps of the five focusing steps. Buffers are placed before the governing constraint, thus ensuring that the constraint is never starved. Buffers are also placed behind the constraint to prevent downstream failure to block the constraint's output. Buffers used in this way protect the constraint from variations in the rest of the system and should allow for normal variation of processing time and the occasional upset (Murphy) before and behind the constraint.

Buffers can be a bank of physical objects before a work centre, waiting to be processed by that work centre. Buffers ultimately buy you time, as in the time before work reaches the constraint and are often verbalised as time buffers. There should always be enough (but not excessive) work in the time queue before the constraint and adequate offloading space behind the constraint.

Buffers are *not* the small queue of work that sits before every work centre in a Kanban system although it is similar if you regard the assembly line as the governing constraint. A prerequisite in the theory is that with one constraint in the system, all other parts of the system must have sufficient capacity to keep up with the work at the constraint and to catch up if time was lost.

In a balanced line, as espoused by Kanban, when one work centre goes down for a period longer than the buffer allows, then the entire system must wait until that work centre is restored. In a TOC system, the only situation where work is in danger, is if the constraint is unable to process (either due to malfunction, sickness or a "hole" in the buffer – if something goes wrong that the time buffer can not protect).

Buffer management therefore represents a crucial attribute of the theory of constraints. There are many ways to do it, but the most often used is a visual system of designating the buffer in three colours: green (okay), yellow (caution) and red (action required). Creating this kind of visibility enables the system as a whole to align and thus subordinate to the need of the constraint in a holistic manner. This can also be done daily in a central operations room that is accessible to everybody.

Operations

Within manufacturing operations and operations management, the solution seeks to pull materials through the system, rather than push them into the system. The primary methodology use is drum-buffer-rope (DBR) and a variation called simplified drum-buffer-rope (S-DBR).

Drum-buffer-rope is a manufacturing execution methodology, named for its three components. The *drum* is the physical constraint of the plant: the work centre or machine or operation that limits the ability of the entire system to produce more. The rest of the plant follows the beat of the drum. They make sure the drum has work and that anything the drum has processed does not get wasted. The *buffer* protects the drum, so that it always has work flowing to it. Buffers in DBR have time as their unit of measure, rather than quantity of material. This makes the priority system operate strictly based on the time an order is expected to be at the drum.

Traditional DBR usually calls for buffers at several points in the system: the constraint, synchronisation points and at shipping. S-DBR has a buffer at shipping and manages the flow of work across the drum through a load planning mechanism.

The *rope* is the work release mechanism for the plant. Orders are released to the shop floor at one "buffer time" before they are due. In other words, if the buffer is 5 days, the order is released 5 days before it is due at the constraint. Putting work into the system earlier than this buffer time is likely to generate too-high work-in-process and slow down the entire system.

Project Management

Critical Chain Project Management (CCPM) is utilised in this area. CCPM is based on the idea that all projects look like A-plants: all activities converge to a final deliverable. As such, to protect the project, there must be internal buffers to protect synchronisation points and a final project buffer to protect the overall project.

Marketing and Sales

While originally focused on manufacturing and logistics, TOC has expanded lately into sales management and marketing. Its role is explicitly acknowledged in the field of sales process engineering. For effective sales management one can apply Drum Buffer Rope to the sales process similar to the way it is applied to operations.

This technique is appropriate when your constraint is in the sales process itself or you just want an effective sales management technique and includes the topics of funnel management and conversion rates.

Claimed Suboptimality of Drum-buffer-rope

While TOC has been compared favourably to linear programming techniques, D. Trietsch from University of Auckland argues that DBR methodology is inferior to competing methodologies. Linhares, from the Getulio Vargas Foundation, has shown that the TOC approach to establishing an optimal product mix is unlikely to yield optimum results, as it would imply that P=NP.

Unacknowledged Debt

Duncan (as cited by Steyn) says that TOC borrows heavily from systems dynamics developed by Forrester in the 1950s and from statistical process control which dates back to World War II. And Noreen Smith and Mackey, in their independent report on TOC, point out that several key concepts in TOC "have been topics in management accounting textbooks for decades."

People claim Goldratt's books fail to acknowledge that TOC borrows from more than 40 years of previous management science research and practice, particularly from PERT/CPM and JIT. A rebuttal to these criticisms is offered in Goldratt's "What is the *Theory of Constraints* and How Should it be Implemented?", and in his audio program, "Beyond The Goal".

In these, Goldratt discusses the history of disciplinary sciences, compares the strengths and weaknesses of the various disciplines, and acknowledges the sources of information and inspiration for the thinking processes and critical chain methodologies. Articles published in the now-defunct Journal of *Theory of Constraints* referenced foundational materials. Goldratt published an article and gave talks with the title "Standing on the Shoulders of Giants" in which he gives credit for many of the core ideas of Theory of Constraints.

Goldratt has sought many times to show the correlation between various improvement methods. However, many Goldratt adherents often denigrate other methodologies as inferior to TOC.

Credit Business Associate

The Credit Business Associate (CBA) is a professional designation for a credit manager. This designation was created by the National Association of Credit Management, a nonprofit organisation based in Columbia, MD (USA) that promotes standards for the business-to-business credit profession, serving as an advocate in addition to providing education and services.

The CBA is an academic-based designation that signifies mastery of three business credit-related disciplines: basic financial accounting, business credit principles and introductory financial statement analysis. The coursework needed to qualify for this designation can be obtained through colleges, local NACM Affiliate programs, self-study or nationally-sponsored programs. There are two plans from which to choose to achieve this designation, Plan A or Plan B.

CPA Australia

CPA Australia is one of three professional accounting bodies in Australia, the others being the Institute of Public Accountants and the Institute of Chartered Accountants of Australia.

CPA Australia is one of the largest global accounting bodies, having members through Asia Pacific as well as its home base.

Membership

CPA Program consists of 14 education segments and a fully integrated practical experience requirement. The educational component of CPA Program has two parts: the foundation level and the professional level.

To be a CPA, candidates must hold a degree or a postgraduate award recognised by CPA Australia, have demonstrated competence in CPA Australia's prescribed foundation level knowledge and with in a six-year period have successfully completed CPA Australia's professional level examinations and the Practical Experience Requirement.

The foundation level represents the first eight exams (segments) of CPA Program, and each designed to assess technical knowledge gained through work experience or study to ensure candidates are ready to undertake the professional level of CPA Program. The completion of an accredited or recognised degree, such as an accounting degree, will often meet all the requirements of the Foundation level and allow candidates to commence at the professional level.

The professional level is made up of six post-graduate education segments and builds on this strong foundation with higher level analysis, judgment, decision making and reporting and focuses on areas that ensure a CPA is valued by any employer - ethics, governance, leadership and strategy.

The three year practical experience requirement, part of the professional level of CPA Program, has been designed in response to the needs of different stakeholders including employers, industry and graduates. The practical experience requirement develops candidates technical, business, personal effectiveness and leadership skills.

Candidates entry point into CPA Program will be determined by an individual assessment of prior education and experience. The completion of an accredited or recognised degree, such as an accounting degree, will often meet all the requirements of the foundation level and allow you to commence at the professional level.

Compulsory CPD applies to all ASA, CPA and FCPA members, including retired members who provide public accounting services, in any year (whether or not this is for reward). Upon renewing membership each year members are required to declare their ongoing compliance with the CPA Australia constitution, by laws and minimum continuing professional development (CPD) requirements. Fulfilment of 120 Continuing Professional Development (CPD) hours per triennium (3-year period) with a minimum of 20 CPD hours in each year is required for continued membership. Members must monitor their own CPD hours and CPA Australia also conducts random audits of members to confirm that they are meeting the CPD requirements.

Full members of CPA Australia use the designatory letters CPA, (CPA (Aust.) in Hong Kong). Senior members may become Fellows and use the letters FCPA, (FCPA (Aust.) in Hong Kong).

CPA Australia has approximately 132,000 members (CPA/FCPA/ASA). An increasing proportion of these members are from other countries or Australians located overseas.

Bibliography

Arya, A. K. : *Advanced Financial Accounting*, Aadi Publications, Delhi, 2011.

Bazilevskii, Y. Y.: *The Theory of Mathematical Machines*, Pergamon Press, Macmillan Co., New York, 1963.

Belkaoui, A.R.: *Accounting Theory*, London, Academic Press Ltd, 1992.

Black, Geoff : *Applied Financial Accounting and Reporting*, Oxford University Press, Delhi, 2007.

Bruner, J.: *Toward a Theory of Accountancy*, Cambridge, Harvard University Press, 1966.

Commons, J. R., *Institutional Economics-Its Place in Political Economy*, The University of Wisconsin Press, Madison, Wisconsin, 1934.

Damasio, AR.: *Descarte's Error: Emotion, Reason and the Human Brain*, New York, 1994.

Edward J.: *The Gathering Crisis in Federal Deposit Insurance*. The MIT Press. Cambridge, 1985.

Friedman, M.: *Capitalism and Freedom*, Chicago:University of Chicago Press, 1982.

Ghosh, T.P. : *Accounting and Finance for Managers*, Taxmann, Delhi, 2007.

Gupta, Nirmal and Chhavi Sharma: *Cost Accounting : Theory and Practice*, Ane Books, Delhi, 2009.

Harrigan, K. R.: *Strategies for Declining Businesses*. Lexington, MA: Heath, 1980

Hayek, F. A. *Individualism and Economic Order*, The University of Chicago Press, Chicago, 1948.

Howard, P.: *Business Finance*, Roseville, 1990

John A. Tuccillo: *Taxation and Regulation of the Savings and Loan Industry*, Lexington, MLA: Heath Co., 1976.

John M.: *How The Stock Market Works,* Prentice Hall Press. New York Institute of Finance, 1988.

Karthikeyan, M. : *Accounting Information Systems*, Avinash, Delhi, 2010.

Link, Albert N.: *Evaluating Economic Damages, A Handbook for Attorneys*, Westport, CT, Quorum Books, 1992.

March, J. G.: *A Behavioural Theory of the Firm*, Englewood-Cliffs, Prentice Hall, 1963.

Mueller, G. G.: *International Accounting*, New York, Prentice-Hall International Inc, 1992.

Nelson, Judy A.: *Feminism, Objectivity and Economics,* London and New York, Routledge, 1996.

Peter L.: *Against The Gods – The Remarkable Story of Risk.* John Wiley and Sons. New York, NY, 1996.

Pramanik, Alok Kumar : *Accounting Standards and Convergence Scenario*, Deep and Deep Publications, Delhi, 2011.

Rana, Girish : *Practical Cost Accounting : Modern Methods and Techniques*, ABD, Delhi, 2006.

Roth, A. E.: *The Handbook of Experimental Economics*, Princeton, Princeton University Press, 1995.

Santos, A.C.: *The Social Epistemology of Experimental Economics,* London, Routledge 2009.

Schotter, A.: *The Foundations of Positive and Normative Economics*, New York, Oxford University Press, 2008.

Scott, D.R.: *The Cultural Significance of Accounts,* New York, Henry Holt, 1931.

Sharan, Bhairav : *Corporate and Managerial Accounting*, Rajat Pub, Delhi, 2008.

Sharma, Shafali: *Book of Accounting Terms*, Vista International, Delhi, 2007.

Shyam Lal : *A Textbook of Hotel Accounting*, Cyber Tech, Delhi, 2011.

Smith, V. L.: *Papers in Experimental Economics*, Cambridge, Cambridge University Press, 1991.

Stewart C. Meyers: *Principles of Corporate Finance,* Irwin, McGraw-Hill, 2000.

Sugan C : *Accounting Reforms*, RBSA Pub, Delhi, 2006.

Throsby, David, *Economics and Culture*, Cambridge University Press, 2001.

Towse, Ruth: *A Handbook of Cultural Economics*, Edward Elgar, 2003.

Vataliya, K S : *Accounting Information Systems : Theory and Applications*, Paradise Pub, Delhi, 2007.

West, Thomas L.: and Jeffrey D. Jones: *Handbook of Business Valuation,* New York: Wiley, 1992.

Weston, J.F. : *Financial Theory and Corporate Policy*. Addison-Wesley, 1988.

Index

❑❑❑